A WAY FORWARD:
Building *a* Globally Competitive South

Global Research Institute

THE UNIVERSITY OF NORTH CAROLINA AT CHAPEL HILL
DANIEL P. GITTERMAN AND PETER A. COCLANIS, EDITORS

CONTENTS

FOREWORD
6 William B. Harrison Jr.
Chair, External Advisory Board,
Global Research Institute

7 **ACKNOWLEDGMENTS**

INTRODUCTION
8 *Lessons from the Past and A Way Forward*
Peter A. Coclanis
University of North Carolina at Chapel Hill

Daniel P. Gitterman
University of North Carolina at Chapel Hill

10 Defining the South

1. THE SOUTH AND 20TH-CENTURY ECONOMIC HISTORY
12 *Southern Economic Commentary in Historical Perspective*
David L. Carlton
Vanderbilt University

Peter A. Coclanis
University of North Carolina at Chapel Hill

17 *The Rural South and the Burden of the Past*
Peter A. Coclanis
University of North Carolina at Chapel Hill

Louis M. Kyriakoudes
University of Southern Mississippi

26 *African American Economic Progress and the Post–Civil Rights South*
Gavin Wright
Stanford University

31 *The Knowledge Economy and the Crisis of Economic Development Policy in South Carolina, 1986–2011*
Lacy Ford
University of South Carolina

2. 25 YEARS LATER: REVISITING *HALFWAY HOME* AND *SHADOWS IN THE SUNBELT* 1986-2011
35 *Revisiting the 1986 Commission on the Future of the South's Halfway Home and a Long Way to Go*
Jesse L. White Jr.
University of North Carolina at Chapel Hill

37 *The Southern "Consensus" on Education and Economic Development*
Daniel P. Gitterman
University of North Carolina at Chapel Hill

3. PROVIDING A NATIONALLY COMPETITIVE EDUCATION FOR ALL STUDENTS
46 *Southern Education Progress: Half Past Halfway, but Still a Ways to Go*
Trip Stallings
North Carolina State University

54 *Treading Water: K–12 Educational Attainment in the South and North Carolina*
Lance D. Fusarelli
North Carolina State University

57 *Assessing Progress: Almost Home?*
Daniel P. Gitterman
University of North Carolina at Chapel Hill

Brittany L. Reid
University of North Carolina at Chapel Hill

4. PREPARING A FLEXIBLE, GLOBALLY COMPETITIVE WORKFORCE
67 *Toward a "Globally Competitive" Southern Workforce*
Patrick J. Conway
University of North Carolina at Chapel Hill

Daniel P. Gitterman
University of North Carolina at Chapel Hill

73 *The American South in the Global Economy*
Thomas Kemeny
University of North Carolina at Chapel Hill

5. PUBLIC UNIVERSITIES IN A NEW ECONOMIC ERA

79
Our Southern Universities as Engines of Innovation
Holden Thorp
University of North Carolina at Chapel Hill

Buck Goldstein
University of North Carolina at Chapel Hill

83
The Relevant University
Randy Woodson
North Carolina State University

89
North Carolina Community Colleges and a New Economic Landscape
Scott Ralls
North Carolina Community College System

92
The Unique Role of Southern Historically Black Colleges and Universities in Economic Development
Charles Nelms
North Carolina Central University

6. INCREASING THE ECONOMIC DEVELOPMENT ROLE OF HIGHER EDUCATION

96
Shadows and Light on the Way Home: The University of North Carolina's Role in Higher Education and Economic Development
Leslie Boney
University of North Carolina General Administration

100
State Investment in Higher Education: Rethinking the Impact on Economic Growth
Jay Schalin
The John William Pope Center for Higher Education Policy

105
University and Community: What Is the Role for Economic Development?
Jesse L. White Jr.
University of North Carolina at Chapel Hill

7. INCREASING THE SOUTH'S CAPACITY TO INNOVATE AND IMPLEMENT NEW ECONOMIC DEVELOPMENT STRATEGIES

109
Southern Industrialization Revisited: Industrial Recruitment as a Strategic Tool for Local Economic Development
Nichola Lowe
University of North Carolina at Chapel Hill

115
Southern Regional Innovation Strategies
Maryann Feldman
University of North Carolina at Chapel Hill

Stuart Rosenfeld
Regional Technology Strategies

120
North Carolina's Board of Science and Technology: A Model for Guiding Technology-Based Economic Development in the South
John Hardin
North Carolina Board of Science and Technology and University of North Carolina at Chapel Hill

Maryann Feldman
University of North Carolina at Chapel Hill

124
Infrastructure and Rural Economic Development: The Case of a Rural Broadband Initiative
Joe Freddoso
MCNC

128 Infrastructure, Southern Style

8. URBAN, RURAL, AND GREEN

131
The New Metro American South
Ferrel Guillory
University of North Carolina at Chapel Hill

135
Closing the Urban-Rural Gap: The Future of North Carolina and the South
Michael L. Walden
North Carolina State University

140
The Future of the Green South
Jerry Weitz
East Carolina University

9. WORK, THE SAFETY NET, AND FAITH

148 *Creating "Good Jobs" in North Carolina and the South*
Arne L. Kalleberg
University of North Carolina at Chapel Hill

Jennifer E. Swanberg
University of Kentucky

152 *Will the Government Strengthen at-Risk Families?*
Amanda Sheely
University of North Carolina at Chapel Hill

Annie Jenkins
University of North Carolina at Chapel Hill

156 *Faith-Based Nonprofits and the Social Safety Net in the South*
Maureen Berner
University of North Carolina at Chapel Hill

Sharon Paynter
East Carolina University

10. A CHANGING SOUTHERN DEMOGRAPHY

159 *Disruptive Demographics and the American South*
James H. Johnson Jr.
University of North Carolina at Chapel Hill

165 *Generation Z and North Carolina's Future*
Patrick Cronin
North Carolina State University

168 *The Old in the New Economy: Challenges and Opportunities for the South and North Carolina*
John C. Scott
University of North Carolina at Chapel Hill

173 *Adapting to a Plural Culture and the Future of the South*
Hannah Gill
University of North Carolina at Chapel Hill

Deborah Weissman
University of North Carolina at Chapel Hill

11. SOUTHERN POLITICS AND POLICY: THEN, NOW, AND TOMORROW

179 *On Terry Sanford's Legacy for Southern Progressives Today*
Mac McCorkle
Duke University

185 *Southern Poverty, Southern Politics*
Gene Nichol
University of North Carolina at Chapel Hill

188 *Getting Past Our Civil War Hangover and Moving toward Real Southern Progress*
Andy Brack
Center for a Better South

12. VISIONS FOR THE FUTURE OF THE SOUTH

193 *Southern-Style Creativity: New Methods for Tackling Nagging Challenges in the Next 25 Years*
Anita Brown-Graham
North Carolina State University

199 *Strategic Philanthropy and the State of the South*
David Dodson
MDC

204 *Globalization and Urbanization: The Changing Context of Competition*
Ted Abernathy
Southern Growth Policies Board

CONCLUSION

209 *The Future of the South and A Way Forward*
Daniel P. Gitterman
University of North Carolina at Chapel Hill

Peter A. Coclanis
University of North Carolina at Chapel Hill

Halfway Home and a Long Way to Go

THE CHOICE IS ONE OF ACTION OR INACTION, OF MOVING FORWARD FROM THIS CROSSROADS ON OUR CONTINUING JOURNEY HOME OR OF FREEZING IN OUR TRACKS WITH LITTLE PROSPECT OF EVER COMPLETING THE JOURNEY

*Halfway Home and a Long Way to Go: The Report of the
1986 Commission on the Future of the South*
Southern Growth Policies Board
November 1986

Shadows in the Sunbelt

STATES IN THE SOUTH MUST TEND TO OUR ROOTS, OR IN THE END, RISK OUR VALUES.

*Shadows in the Sunbelt: Developing the Rural South
in an Era of Economic Change*
A Report of the MDC Panel on Rural Economic Development
MDC
May 1986

FOREWORD

A quarter of a century ago, two important and widely accessible reports relating to the future of the U.S. South were released: *Halfway Home and a Long Way to Go*, issued by the Southern Growth Policies Board's 1986 Commission on the Future of the South, and *Shadows in the Sunbelt*, issued by MDC's Panel on Rural Economic Development. Both reports lauded the region's recent economic accomplishments but focused on the remaining problems and challenges. *Halfway Home* called attention to a broad range of economic development issues, while *Shadows in the Sunbelt* homed in on the rural sector, wherein growth and development, so rapid in the postwar decades, were beginning to wane. Taken together, these two reports, each the work of a Triangle-area nonprofit research organization, captured very well the state of the southern region in the mid-1980s. The recommendations received a great deal of attention in policy circles and remain influential to this day.

With this background in mind, principals at the University of North Carolina at Chapel Hill's newly established Global Research Institute (GRI) thought 2011 — the 25th anniversary of the reports — a good time to reexamine their findings and recommendations, to assess the progress the southern economy has made since 1986, and to suggest some ways to forge ahead in a new global era. Accordingly, the GRI assembled a first-rate team of contributors — academic leaders, scholars, and practitioners — to write short analytical essays on various aspects of the current southern economy and public policy. The GRI has no partisan orientation, and the individual authors differ in ideology and perspective. What unites them is clear thinking on important policy questions and an abiding interest in promoting economic progress — and *A Way Forward* — in the region they (and I) call home.

William B. Harrison Jr., '66
Former CEO and Board Chairman of JPMorgan Chase & Co.
Chair, External Advisory Board
Global Research Institute
University of North Carolina at Chapel Hill

ACKNOWLEDGMENTS

First of all, we would like to express our appreciation to the contributors to *A Way Forward*, who wrote accessible and policy-relevant essays in a short amount of time — and received only "psychic income" for so doing. Calvin Trillin is responsible for a famous quip about writers' compensation at *The Nation* ("the high two figures"). We didn't even offer that. We also would like to take this opportunity to thank William B. Harrison Jr., the chair of the Global Research Institute's External Advisory Board, for his advice, counsel, and uncommon generosity, and the FedEx Corporation for its loyal support. We are grateful for the thoughtful essays from Ted Abernathy, Southern Growth Policies Board, and David Dodson, MDC Inc., representing two organizations that have made major contributions to the policy dialogue in the South. Holden Thorp, Ronald Strauss, Nancy Davis, Daniel Lebold, and Katie Bowler helped to guide this project home, Ellen Goldlust-Gingrich provided expert editorial help, and graphic designer Lauren Norwood performed her magic in producing *A Way Forward*. We wish to thank Terry Tamari, coordinator at the Global Research Institute, without whose wisdom, judgment, organizational skills, and good humor this collection of essays undoubtedly would have derailed. Our special thanks to participants in the Carolina Seminar on the Future of the South, supported by the Massey-Weatherspoon Fund, who laid the foundation for this work.

Daniel P. Gitterman
Peter A. Coclanis

Chapel Hill, North Carolina
November 2011

INTRODUCTION:
Lessons *from the* Past and *A* Way Forward

PETER A. COCLANIS AND DANIEL P. GITTERMAN

In the landmark 1949 study, *Southern Politics in State and Nation*, distinguished social scientist V. O. Key Jr. wrote that "the prevailing mood in North Carolina is not hard to sense: it is energetic and ambitious. The citizens are determined and confident; they are on the move." After taking a few swipes at the rest of the South, Key went on to say that North Carolina "enjoys a reputation for progressive outlook and action in many phases of life, especially industrial development, education, and race relations."

One can certainly challenge aspects of Key's characterization of North Carolina—and, indeed, his depiction of the rest of the South—but even today, more than sixty years after the fact, he appears to have been on to something about the Old North State. Widely known in the nineteenth century as the Rip Van Winkle State because of its economic inertia, North Carolina woke up economically in the first half of the twentieth century and as a result had become one of the most dynamic states in the region by the time Key wrote. It also had acquired a reputation as the South's leading generator of ideas pertaining to regional economic and social development, education, and poverty eradication, a reputation based in part on the work of men and women associated with the University of North Carolina at Chapel Hill.

A lot has changed about both North Carolina and the South more broadly in the last half century. Both our state and the region as a whole experienced rapid economic growth in the second half of the twentieth century, and living standards for the vast majority of the population in the South improved dramatically. The region's economic performance was particularly impressive between roughly 1950 and the mid-1980s, when the South converged rapidly on national norms in terms of per capita income and other measures. Moreover, by the mid-1980s, sufficient time had elapsed so that the South's postwar economic record could be placed in a broader and more balanced historical context, a task that seemed particularly important because signs of economic distress had begun to surface in both the state and the region as a whole. And, once again, much of the best analysis emanated from North Carolina, this time from two Triangle-based research organizations, the Southern Growth Policies Board (SGPB) and MDC. Both of these organizations had close ties to UNC and to Chapel Hill, and their 1986 reports—the SGPB's *Halfway Home and a Long Way to Go* and MDC's *Shadows in the Sunbelt*—are considered two of the best assessments of the achievements and limitations of the so-called Sunbelt boom.

The 25 years since the issuance of these reports have been marked by profound economic changes from which neither North Carolina nor the South has been spared. Some of these changes in the broader global economy have proven enormously beneficial, while others have led to dislocations and still others to economic devastation and social despair. Given the magnitude of change, 2011 seemed to principals at UNC-Chapel Hill's newly established Global Research Institute (GRI), a think tank devoted to applied research on pressing policy questions, a good time to take another look at these famous reports, to assess how the recommendations contained therein held up over time, to offer fresh analyses of the economic challenges facing both North Carolina and the South, and to lay out some new ideas about how to forge ahead.

A lot has changed about both North Carolina and the South more broadly in the last half century.

The GRI therefore undertook (and underwrote) a collaborative research project, commissioning an impressive group of academic leaders, scholars, and policy professionals from North Carolina and elsewhere to contribute short analytical essays on key questions and themes relating to the region's economic and social development. One important result is *A Way Forward: Building a Globally Competitive South*, which contains thought-provoking essays on topics ranging from education to entrepreneurship, from changing demographics to fraying safety nets, and from the rise of Research Triangle Park to the crisis in the rural economy. The GRI's primary goal is to make a forceful and valuable contribution to the debate on the economic future of North Carolina and the South. Secondarily, we also wish to announce our arrival on the policy scene, to reaffirm UNC-Chapel Hill's commitment to addressing the problems of the state and region, and to demonstrate again that North Carolina is energetic and ambitious and that its citizens are determined and confident — and on the move. ➡

DEFINING *the* SOUTH

PETER A. COCLANIS

This report is about the economy of North Carolina and that of the U.S. South. We all have a pretty good idea of where North Carolina is, but "locating" the U.S. South is a bit trickier. For example, the U.S. Bureau of the Census includes 16 states and the District of Columbia in the three census subregions of which the South is comprised: The South Atlantic (Delaware, Florida, Georgia, Maryland, North Carolina, South Carolina, Texas, and Virginia), East South Central (Kentucky, Tennessee, Alabama, and Mississippi), and West South Central (Arkansas, Louisiana, Oklahoma, and Texas). This definition is quite broad, including, as it does, the states of Delaware, West Virginia, and Oklahoma, as well as Washington, D.C. For some purposes, the definition is quite helpful, but for others, a narrower definition is preferable. In this regard, many scholars and policy analysts view the South as consisting of the eleven states of the Confederacy: Alabama, Arkansas, Florida, Georgia, Louisiana, Mississippi, North Carolina, South Carolina, Tennessee, Texas, and Virginia. MDC often defines the South as these eleven states plus Kentucky and West Virginia. In 1986 the Southern Growth Policies Board defined the South in yet another way—that is, as a region of twelve states and one commonwealth (Puerto Rico), but the SGPB definition has shifted over time, depending on membership in the organization. Several common definitions of the South are depicted in the adjacent maps. The authors of the essays included in this report do not all agree on the definition of the South and therefore readers will at times find them talking about slightly different Souths. None of the authors, however, has adopted UNC-Chapel Hill sociologist John Shelton Reed's classic cultural definition of the South: the area populated by people "who eat grits, listen to country music, follow stockcar racing, support corporal punishment in the schools, hunt possum, go to Baptist churches, and prefer bourbon to scotch (if they drink at all)." In pondering these questions, maybe at the end of the day we should just look for inspiration to the great (southern) jazz trumpeter Louis Armstrong, who, when asked about the definition of jazz, famously responded,

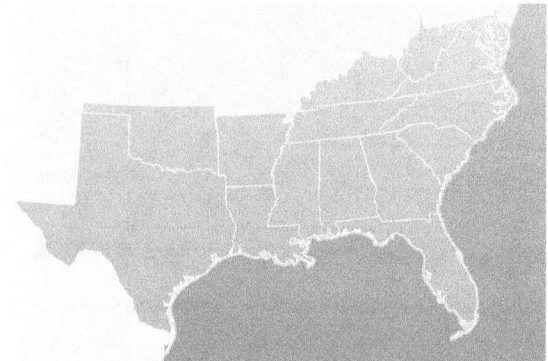
U.S. Bureau of the Census (2011)

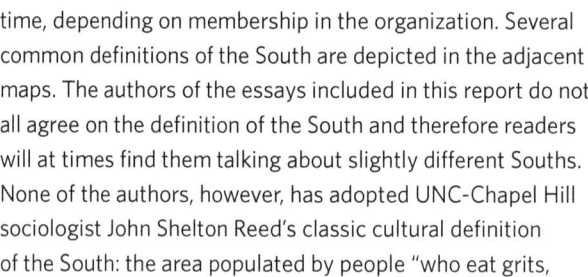
MDC (2011)

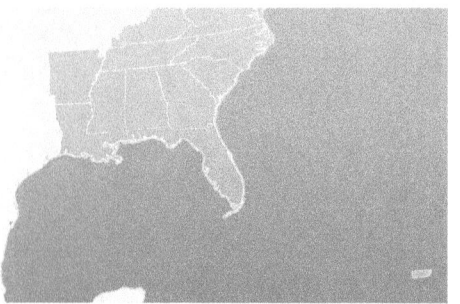
Southern Growth Policies Board (1986)

"If you gotta ask, you'll never know."

THE SOUTH AND 20TH-CENTURY ECONOMIC HISTORY

Southern Economic Commentary *in* Historical Perspective

DAVID L. CARLTON AND PETER A. COCLANIS

Why do people think the economic problems of the American South merit special treatment? It can be argued that they no longer do, that there is no longer anything especially peculiar about the Southern economy. Yet the South has long seen itself and been seen as a distinctive region within the American polity and for that reason has nurtured a long tradition of self-reflection, including economic self-reflection. That tradition has been bolstered by the fact that for most if not all of its existence as a self-conscious region, the South really has been peculiar in its institutions, especially with its chronic relative poverty and underdevelopment. In this regard, contributions such as the Southern Growth Policies Board's *Halfway Home and a Long Way to Go* and MDC's *Shadows in the Sunbelt* are heirs to a long tradition of economic commentary.

ORIGINS: THE NINETEENTH CENTURY

The enduring themes of that commentary originated in antebellum times and addressed an increasingly perplexing problem for the region: Why were the slave states, which at the beginning of the republic were the wealthiest of the states, falling behind the free states by many measures of economic prowess? Northern critics of slavery such as Frederick Law Olmsted and North Carolina exile Hinton Rowan Helper thought they knew the answer: The slave system itself was a blight, stunting urban and industrial development, stifling the opportunities of the white nonslaveholding majority, and denying slaves the economic promise of American life. Slavery's defenders for the most part vigorously countered those charges by pointing to the enormous wealth generated by the slave plantation, but some proponents of slavery admitted the substance of much of this argument.

Internal critics of Southern developmental deficiencies generally blamed them on the region's overreliance on agriculture and its peripheral role in the Atlantic system of trade and finance—an early version of what would later be termed the colonial economy thesis. Thus, manufacturing advocates such as South Carolina's William Gregg pressed for industrial diversification as a means of more fully utilizing the region's resources and remedying its disadvantageous terms of trade with the industrializing world. Boosters based in the region's cities sought to exploit rising Southern nationalist sentiments to develop better internal transportation and wrest control of the South's external commerce from New York, Boston, London, and Liverpool. However, divided by urban rivalries, these boosters had difficulty developing a Southwide strategy, and more generally, their arguments had little effect on a region that by world standards was quite wealthy and whose political leaders were convinced that their control of King Cotton placed the world over their barrel.

The illusion of slaveholder power was dramatically shattered by the Civil War and Emancipation and the subsequent period of turmoil. Both wartime destruction and the social disorganization attendant on the end of slavery sent the region into an economic nosedive; whereas in 1860 the South could boast a per capita income (whole population) of roughly 85 percent of U.S. levels, by 1880, that figure had plummeted to 50 percent. More important, the region was unable to regain ground on the non-South for well over half a century; even as late as 1940, the per

> In a sense, the American South had always been global, having been deeply entwined in international product and factor markets since its foundation.

capita income of the Old Confederacy was only 60 percent of that of the United States as a whole, while the per capita income for the Deep South was only 50 percent of the nationwide amount. Thus, the fundamental problem of Southern economic exceptionalism was set: Why was the South the poor relative in the rich American family?

The earliest attempts to answer that question came from late-19th-century promoters of the New South. Primarily publishers and editors based in the South's cities and wedded to an agenda of urban boosterism, men such as Charlotte's D. A. Tompkins and Atlanta's Henry W. Grady urged Southerners to abandon cotton monoculture, replace northern goods with Southern manufactures, and above all welcome outside investment. However, the region moved in many ways counter to these prescriptions, as cotton and tobacco tightened their stranglehold on the land and industrialization skewed heavily toward low-wage and low-skill branches. More seriously, proponents of the New South had little to say about the impediments imposed on Southern agriculture by tenancy and perverse credit institutions, ignored Southern human capital deficiencies, and endorsed the emergent post-Emancipation Jim Crow regime.

An important step forward came around the end of the 19th century with the Progressive Era. Heirs in many ways of the New South promoters, Southern progressives, generally well-educated members of the urban middle class, supplemented New South prescriptions with calls for a greatly enlarged role for government. Recognizing that the region's status as a latecomer to the industrial world placed it at a disadvantage in competing with the dynamic, sophisticated economy of the Northeast-Midwest manufacturing belt, Southern progressives advocated using the state to nurture economic growth. Their strategies primarily involved improved internal transportation, especially through the development of an elaborate system of roads, and investments in human welfare and human capital through expansion of public health and education. They later broadened their public-infrastructure agenda to include electric power and comprehensive river-basin development (the Tennessee Valley Authority). Again, however, these reformers left untouched structural issues in Southern agriculture; questions of economic power were ignored, and if anything, these policies enhanced the discriminatory effect of Jim Crow on black Southerners. Nonetheless, the progressive legacy has endured, informing much of the economic development strategies of Southern states to the present day.

THE HEIGHT OF REGIONAL CONSCIOUSNESS: 1920-1950

What could be termed the "golden age" of Southern economic commentary came roughly between 1920 and 1950. By this time, an institutional research structure was falling into place as a consequence of the rise of philanthropic foundations and the first modern Southern universities, whether private (Duke, Vanderbilt) or public (land-grant colleges and state universities, especially the University of North Carolina). These institutions nurtured the beginnings of modern social science in the region, notably at Howard W. Odom's Institute for Research in Social Science at UNC, and disseminated their findings through publications such as those of the UNC Press. Odom and his associates sought to develop a comprehensive regional approach to Southern social problems, an approach to which a region discombobulated by the dislocations of the Great Depression was especially receptive. Outside the South, an increased awareness of the impact of Southern problems on national welfare led to sharper external criticism. Finally, the interwar period saw enhanced Southern regional awareness, spawning numerous regional organizations (the Southern Policy Association, the Southern Regional Council, the Southern Conference for

Human Welfare, the Southern Regional Education Board, the Southern Governors' Conference, and, for that matter, the Southern Historical Association and the Southern Economic Association). Some of these organizations still shape regional discourse today.

Far more than their predecessors, these "new regionalists" took dead aim at some fundamental structural deficiencies in the Southern economy. The institutional pathologies of the Southern countryside—tenancy and sharecropping, credit, monoculture, technological backwardness—were investigated in detail. So were the deficiencies of the newer Southern industrial order: low wages and skills, child labor, and enormous disparities of power between workers and managers. But the new consciousness of the region's exceptionalism also fed into an enhanced sectionalism. In 1932, Odum's associate, Rupert Vance, introduced the notion of the South as a "colonial economy," a peripheral region providing raw commodities and low-level goods to the more developed world while depending on outsiders for higher-order goods and services such as finance. This early form of "dependency theory" quickly took on a political edge, notably in the 1938 *Report on Economic Conditions of the South*, which intimated that the region was kept underdeveloped by outside control of its economy. Southern governors in particular took up that diagnosis and made it the basis for a sustained (and by the mid-1940s successful) assault on differential railroad freight rates between the South and the manufacturing belt.

For all its vitality, though, much of the analysis of the "long 1930s" turned out to be a dead end. Ironically, the assault on the pathologies of Southern agriculture came just as the postslavery order was collapsing, impelled by a combination of economic crisis and federal intervention; tenants were fleeing or being driven off the land, the old credit system was supplanted by new, better institutions, crop mixes were diversified, and mechanization reduced personnel requirements to a fraction of former needs. However politically popular, the "economic colonialism" argument attracted ridicule from economists and largely faded from postwar consciousness. Again like its predecessors, the economic commentary of the 1930s paid little attention to the deadening effect of white supremacy and Jim Crow institutions on regional development.

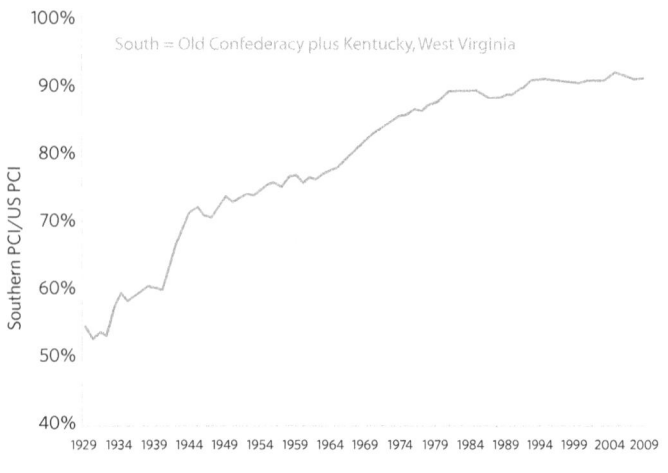

figure 1.1 PER CAPITA INCOME RELATIVES, 1929–2009: SOUTH AS PERCENT OF UNITED STATES

Source: Bureau of Economic Analysis, 1929–2009

THE GREAT CONVERGENCE: FROM WORLD WAR II TO 1973

The post–World War II years saw a dramatic socioeconomic revolution overtake the South. Masses of workers were cut loose from agricultural employment; while large numbers of people left the region and many others moved to the growing Southern cities, others remained underemployed in the countryside and small towns. In response, heirs to the old Southern progressives brought the state into the process of industrialization. Beginning with Mississippi's 1936 Balance Agriculture with Industry program, the South pioneered the modern use of government inducements to recruit outside manufacturing firms to the region. In the postwar era, industrial recruitment—"smokestack chasing" or "buffalo hunting"— became a core function of Southern state and local governments and was supplemented by increasingly elaborate worker-training programs. In the 1950s, manufacturing employment in the South for the first time exceeded agricultural employment. Service industries, especially in the expanding urban South, burgeoned as well. Finally, the fate of white supremacy at long last moved to the front of the Southern agenda; by the 1960s, civil rights activism and federal intervention had demolished Jim Crow and formal racial discrimination and dramatically expanded political access for black Southerners. Concurrently, the South broke out of its longtime relative poverty, reaching 85 percent of U.S. per capita income by 1973. By comparison, southern Italy, a region to which the American South has often been compared, remains at 60 percent of national income levels, roughly where the South was in 1940.

AFTER 1973: THE PARADOXES OF THE SUNBELT

With such far-reaching change sweeping over the Southern land, by the 1970s many observers could be forgiven for thinking that the South's traditional economic exceptionalism had reached an end. The concept of the South as an economically distinct region seemed outmoded and was increasingly supplanted in public discourse by an ersatz region called the Sunbelt that sprawled from the old eastern Cotton Belt all the way across the country to Los Angeles. In a new form of sectional warfare, a spate of writings in the 1970s attributed the Sunbelt's success to its ability to sap the old industrial core of its vitality through political manipulation. Boosters responded that the Sunbelt was benefiting from its internal dynamism and its relative lack of "institutional arteriosclerosis"—that is, the unions and overbuilt public institutions that adherents of this view believed weighed down the old industrial heartland.

> The notion of a distinctive Southern economy was founded on what Southern historian C. Vann Woodward famously described as "a long and quite un-American experience with poverty," a poverty that frustrated the aspirations of even the few affluent Southerners.

Yet beneath the self-congratulation was a persistent recognition that older Southern economic problems persisted and had been supplemented by new ones. These problems were not necessarily visible in the glittering new metropolises, many of which, like Charlotte or the Research Triangle, were carving out advanced roles in the national and global economy and essentially leaving the rest of the region behind. But economic stagnation persisted in the vast plantation belt reaching from eastern North Carolina across to the Lower Mississippi Valley and in the fastnesses of central Appalachia. Furthermore, even parts of the rural and small-town South that had done well in the post–World War II years found themselves facing a new, troubling phenomenon: deindustrialization.

Much of this trend resulted from technological innovation, which reduced manufacturing labor requirements and rendered obsolete many older facilities along with the communities they supported. Much of it could also be attributed to that complex of processes grouped under "globalization," as the traditional mature, footloose industries attracted to the South during the postwar era trotted beyond U.S. borders or succumbed to competition from the less-developed world. In a sense, the American South had always been global, having been deeply entwined in international product and factor markets since its foundation. The post-World War II national commitment to freer trade, however, enhanced globalization's visibility, since the South remained a somewhat underdeveloped region in a highly developed country. The South's heritage of relatively low wages and low-skill industries and its persistent gap in human capital development rendered it especially vulnerable to global trends.

These continuing problems became foci of economic commentary on the region in the 1980s. Here the lead was taken by two institutions based in the Research Triangle: the Southern Growth Policies Board, a cooperative venture of Southern state governors; and MDC, a private think tank. The Southern Growth Policy Board's *Halfway Home and a Long Way to Go* and MDC's *Shadows in the Sunbelt* acknowledged significant Southern progress but warned that large chunks of the South's people and places were being left behind. At the core of these analyses — and at the core of much recent analysis — was the region's continuing weakness in generating internal economic growth: its lack of appropriately skilled workers and its deficiencies in generating innovation, new enterprises, and new industry. The South still needed to break its dependence on attracting mature industries created elsewhere and develop a population and institutions capable of creating locally rooted industries and adjusting to the rapidly changing global economy. And, indeed, recent state economic development policies have to some degree involved just such development of internal capacity, especially through enhancement of human capital: improvements in primary and secondary education, expansion of preschool education and the community college system, and innovative approaches to helping workers manage job transitions.

However, since the release of these two epochal reports 25 years ago, there has been little further advancement of our understanding of the South's economic problems. In part, this stagnation can be attributed to what regionalists see as a disturbing trend: the continuing erosion of Southern regional consciousness at the highest policy levels. Regional bodies such as the Southern Growth Policy Board have lost influence as internal divisions regarding policy have sharpened and Southern states have become increasingly competitive with each other. Furthermore, a generation of criticism of the buffalo hunt approach to economic development has failed to make a serious dent in its political attractiveness. Indeed, it has become increasingly unclear that the critics' agenda is an improvement on the buffalo hunt: Does upgrading human capital really suffice to stem the erosion of much of the South's economic base? Finally, the possibility exists that the whole tradition of Southern regional economic analysis has reached exhaustion. The notion of a distinctive Southern economy was founded on what Southern historian C. Vann Woodward famously described as "a long and quite un-American experience with poverty," a poverty that frustrated the aspirations of even the few affluent Southerners. In this view, Southern economic problems had implications for the welfare of all Southerners. In the present South, where the techies of North Carolina's Research Triangle have little reason to make common cause with laid-off mill hands in Spindale or inner-city blacks in Durham, the concept of region seems to have little salience for public policy. Yet these disparate populations share a common polity, and their increasing divergence has potentially explosive social and political consequences. This volume seeks to revive that tradition and render it viable for the newest "New South" of the 21st century.

REFERENCES

Carlton, David L., and Peter A. Coclanis, eds., *Confronting Southern Poverty in the Great Depression: The Report on Economic Conditions of the South with Related Documents*. Boston: Bedford/St. Martins, 1996.

Carlton, David L., and Peter A. Coclanis. *The South, the Nation, and the World: Perspectives on Southern Economic Development*. Charlottesville: University of Virginia Press, 2003.

Cobb, James C. *The Selling of the South: The Southern Crusade for Industrial Development, 1936–1980*. Baton Rouge: Louisiana State University Press, 1982.

Danhof, Clarence H. "Four Decades of Thought on the South's Economic Problems." In *Essays in Southern Economic Development*, ed. Melvin L. Greenhut and W. Tate Whitman. Chapel Hill: University of North Carolina Press, 1964.

Gaston, Paul M. *The New South Creed: A Study in Southern Mythmaking*. New York: Knopf, 1970.

MDC. *Shadows in the Sunbelt: Developing the Rural South in an Era of Economic Change*. Chapel Hill: MDC, 1986.

Southern Growth Policies Board. *Halfway Home and a Long Way to Go: The Report of the 1986 Commission on the Future of the South*. Research Triangle Park, N.C.: Southern Growth Policies Board, 1986.

Wright, Gavin. *Old South, New South: Revolutions in the Southern Economy since the Civil War*. New York: Basic Books, 1986.

The Rural South *and the* Burden of the Past

PETER A. COCLANIS AND LOUIS M. KYRIAKOUDES

INTRODUCTION AND BACKGROUND

To say that the rural South is in deep crisis today will strike historically minded observers as troubling but hardly surprising. Playing off of one of the most overused quotations in the professional Southerners' tool kit, we might even say, pace William Faulkner, that a "rural crisis in the South is not new. It's not even news." Indeed, rural areas in the region have endured crises of one sort or another for 80 or 85 of the 146 years since the end of the Civil War. Between 1865 and about 1900, during the 1920s and 1930s, and from about 1980 until today, the rural South has experienced severe shocks to its social and economic structures that have changed the ways in which residents live and work. Although these crisis periods differed in important ways, we believe that all owed much to decisions made, processes begun, and institutions established deep in the region's past. Economists like to employ the concept of "path dependence" to convey this point, which basically translates into "history matters." In the case of the rural South, we believe that it matters a lot.

Just as slavery was "somehow" the cause of the Civil War, as Lincoln correctly put it in his Second Inaugural Address, the legacy of the peculiar institution is "somehow" related to many of the current problems in the rural South. "Somehow" has several meanings, but like Lincoln, we use it here to denote "one way or another" because the legacy of slavery for the rural South remains at once profound and pervasive even today.

Historians continue to debate whether the Southern economy was developing—becoming more sophisticated, diversifying, moving toward higher-value-added activities at a good clip, and so forth—in the decades before the Civil War. There is, however, broad agreement today that the economy of the region—based on the production, mainly for export, of a small range of staple agricultural commodities, largely by enslaved laborers—was growing rapidly. There is agreement as well that in relative terms the South—disaggregated from the United States as a whole—was one of the wealthiest regions in the world on the eve of the Civil War and that slavery was quite profitable to most individual slaveholders.

And the war came—Lincoln again—and with the war, the Old South was no more. Any assessment of the results of the war for the South immediately becomes complicated. Bluntly put, the war ended the moral abomination of slavery but in so doing wreaked havoc on the Southern economy. Some of the problems the Southern economy faced in the decades after the war were related to destruction and dislocations; others grew out of changes in demand for Southern agricultural commodities, particularly a significant slowdown in the growth rate of demand for cotton, which kept (real) prices far lower than the levels reached in the 1860s. The most serious problems, however, arose from the fact that emancipation destroyed the economic structure, and in its place emerged an economically inefficient and exploitive agricultural system built on sharecropping and tenancy. To be sure, rebuilding was not helped by the fact that (uncompensated) emancipation redefined almost 50 percent of the region's wealth into oblivion. Moreover, little was done to aid the adjustment process of the newly emancipated. As a result, what we find emerging in the rural South in the postwar period is the rapid transformation of a relatively modern and efficient agricultural regime, dominated by large units offering opportunities for scale economies, into an agricultural sector characterized by small, inefficient farms worked by undercapitalized tenants and sharecroppers, both black and white. These farmers lacked education and employed little technology. Moreover, because of perverse credit institutions and incentives, they were drawn increasingly into dependence on single-crop agriculture, particularly cotton or tobacco, the output from which was generally marketed by small-scale rural shopkeepers and "furnishing merchants" much less skillfully than had been the case under the factorage system in place prior to the war. Compounding these economic problems were high costs of agricultural credit and the social impediments to change arising from the emergence of the Jim Crow regime. Poverty and racial inequality made a terrible pair indeed.

In light of these changes, it is not at all surprising that the rural South was quickly rendered an economic backwater, there to remain for the next 75 years or so after the Civil War. Although the region began its modern industrialization in the late 19th century, the overall growth rate of the Southern economy was not rapid enough to prevent the region from sliding far behind the United States as a whole by almost every economic metric. If the rural Southern economy picked up a bit with the general rise in cotton prices before and during World War I, the collapse of prices in the 1920s brought Southern farmers back to earth, as it were. Simply put, the region's economy remained backward because agriculture was backward, because agriculture comprised so large a proportion of the Southern economy and farmers so large a percentage of the total Southern labor force; consequently, what happened in the farm sector reverberated throughout the region as a whole. Whereas per capita income in the region was about 85 percent of that of the United States as a whole at the time of the Civil War, income per capita in the South had fallen to 50 percent of the national average by 1880, remaining at that level 50 agonizing years later. And in a region characterized by massive poverty, ill health, and pinched lives, rural Southerners bore the heaviest burden.

THE 20TH-CENTURY RURAL SOUTH

And then came the Great Depression. During the 1930s, this burden broke the rural sector of the South beyond fixing—at least by traditional means. With farm prices falling below even the low prices of the 1920s and staying at such levels for years, the structural and institutional problems that had plagued the sector since the end of the Civil War overwhelmed the region's farmers, black and white alike. With prices depressed and farm credit increasingly unavailable, it became harder and harder for farm owners to hold onto, much less to improve, the stressed and fissured lands of the South, site of more than 60 percent of U.S. farmland "badly damaged by erosion." Tenants and croppers were increasingly let go, and farm laborers were rendered jobless. Living standards in the Southern countryside increasingly pressed the limits of subsistence and left rural communities in tatters when not completely ruined. If the South constituted "the Nation's No. 1 economic problem," as President Franklin D. Roosevelt put it in July 1938, the region's rural sector was Exhibit A.

For a variety of reasons, the economic crisis in the South during the 1930s captured widespread attention, resulting in some remedial action in the form of government farm programs, development projects such as the Tennessee Valley Authority, and public health initiatives. Such efforts met with only mixed success, and in 1940, Southern per capita income (rural and urban) still was only 60 percent of that of the nation as a whole. Per capita income was far lower in rural parts of the United States—income per capita in nonmetropolitan counties was 43 percent of the figure for metropolitan counties in 1929 and 46 percent in 1939—including in the heavily rural South.

With the coming of World War II and, more important, the beginnings of what is often called the second wave of Southern industrialization, the rural South at long last began to show signs of dynamism. During the war years, job opportunities at military bases and war-related manufacturing plants pulled people out of the rural sector, easing burgeoning Malthusian problems in many densely populated, low-productivity farming areas—Appalachia in particular. In addition, the recruitment to the rural South of branch plants, particularly low-skill, low-wage, light-assembly operations, provided many new jobs.

Scholars generally trace the origins of such recruitment strategies to 1936 with the establishment of Mississippi's Balance Agriculture with Industry program, whereby the state sanctioned the issuance and sale of municipal bonds to raise funds to help lure factories through subsidies. This scheme and others like it aroused opposition from various quarters virtually from the start. Most scholars, however, believe that such schemes played important roles in attracting footloose firms in search of lower costs—so-called runaway shops—to particular locales in the South. Many of the firms looking to relocate would have ended up in the South anyway because of the cost differentials vis-à-vis the North, but a sufficient subsidy—a tax abatement, a new road, a worker-training program, or free water or power—might mean an apparel plant or a light-assembly operation relocated to a particular county in Alabama rather than one in North Carolina.

Many of the companies moving to the South found rural areas to their liking. Real estate was cheap, labor—if not particularly skilled—was also cheap as well as abundant and nonunionized, and public officials were eager and accommodating. That labor was so cheap had much to do, of course, with the postwar transformation of Southern agriculture. The rebuilding of the region's agricultural sector after its collapse in the 1930s moved in tandem with and was in part predicated on its modernization, and more than anything else, modernization of Southern agriculture meant mechanization. Whereas northern agriculture was already quite mechanized by the late 19th century, until the 1920s and 1930s, the South's farm sector was almost completely dominated by muscles and mules. During the interwar years, farmers in the region began to mechanize preharvest activities (one of the reasons for job losses on Southern farms in the 1930s), but the crucial move to mechanize the harvest was a postwar phenomenon. As late as 1949, machines harvested only 7 percent of the South's cotton crop; the remainder was harvested as it had always been, by hand. In the subsequent two decades, however, mechanization of all facets of cotton production became complete. By 1969, the U.S. Census Bureau had even stopped collecting statistics on sharecropping, a form of land tenure that had faded into insignificance.

Whether the relative labor intensity of Southern agriculture owed more to the abundance in the region of cheap hands with few alternatives or to technological concerns—it was far more difficult in a technological sense to come up with an efficient machine to pick (cotton) than to reap (wheat)—what we find in the South is massive numbers of workers laboring in the agricultural sector. Fully 24 percent of working-age Southerners labored in agriculture in 1950, compared to 12 percent in the United States as a whole.

The situation changed dramatically in the 1950s and 1960s as the mechanical cotton picker and in North Carolina the bulk curing of tobacco led to drastic reductions in labor requirements on Southern farms. The need for year-round agricultural labor plummeted, a development that led in short order to massive out-migration of both whites and blacks either to Southern cities or to the North and West. The net outflow of population from the region was particularly strong among blacks—almost 4.2 million African Americans left the "Census South" between 1940 and 1970—but between 1940 and 1960, a net outflow of about 173,000 whites occurred from the region as well.

Not everyone displaced by the modernization of Southern agriculture quit the region or even the community where they had farmed. Because the remaining farms grew larger, more capital-intensive, more efficient, and whiter, jobs had to be found for those who stayed behind; otherwise, an economic and social cataclysm would result. After a good deal of planning, hard work, and strong politicking, this cataclysm was averted. As the agricultural sector was being modernized, new jobs were being created in spades in the rural South. Indeed, one of the key reasons for and achievements of the "Sunbelt boom" between the 1950s and the early 1980s was the movement of vast numbers of people out of agriculture (in full or in part) and into other economic sectors, particularly low-value-added manufacturing. And many of these manufacturing jobs were in rural areas or at least in areas characterized as "nonmetropolitan." Although the types of jobs erstwhile farmers took on, generally speaking, were not very skilled, labor productivity was, in the aggregate, greater in their new positions than in agriculture. As a result, overall efficiency was enhanced, contributing to rising incomes in the South and the convergence of the region on the nation as a whole in terms of income per capita.

This basic scenario played out all over the South, but we can use North Carolina as a case in point. In "nonmetropolitan" areas of the state in 1940, 38.4 percent of the labor force was employed in agriculture, and agriculture dwarfed the second-largest industry by employment—textiles, apparel, carpet, and knitting mills—which accounted for 16 percent of the total jobs in such areas. By 1960, agriculture's share of total employment in such areas had fallen to 15.8 percent, leaving it in second place behind textiles, apparel, and so on, whose share of total employment had risen to 17.9 percent of the total. Two decades later, agriculture accounted for only 5.6 percent of jobs in nonmetropolitan parts of the Old North State, while textiles and apparel accounted for 16.6 percent of the diversifying rural economy, more than twice as large a share as the second-largest industry, educational services. Together with the furniture and fixtures industry, whose share of total employment was growing in nonmetro regions, textiles and apparel accounted for well over 20 percent of all jobs.

Generally speaking, the types of nonfarm jobs becoming available in nonmetropolitan parts of North Carolina and other Southern states in the 1950s, 1960s, and 1970s—manufacturing jobs in textile/apparel plants, furniture factories, and sawmills; construction jobs; teaching positions, and low-level service work in health care and for the federal government—did not pay particularly well. But such jobs were far better than scratch farming, allowing people who did not wish to migrate to cities and suburbs of the South or to Chicago, New York, Los Angeles, or Detroit to remain rooted in their home communities and maybe even do a bit of part-time farming or tend vegetable gardens on the side.

And while, to most people, the rise of the Sunbelt invokes images of skyscrapers in Houston and Atlanta, suburban sprawl in Dallas and Charlotte, and the all-around ghastliness of Orlando, the small towns and unincorporated areas of the rural South—places far off the interstates—played their part, too. Indeed, the fact that per capita income in the region as a whole had climbed to 85 percent of the U.S. average by 1973 owed a good deal to this restructuring of the rural economy in the postwar period. This convergence clearly would not have taken place, particularly during the postwar boom, when other U.S. regions were growing smartly, unless rural and nonmetro parts of the South found ways to create income-generating jobs. Many of the companies and even industries responsible for such jobs were new to the South, and their presence resulted from successful recruitment efforts—or, more properly, campaigns—by private and public interests alike, for which considerable credit, even in hindsight, is due. Manufacturing filled the void created by the post–World War II collapse of agricultural jobs. Even today, a quarter of rural Southern workers labor in some form of manufacturing.

But most good or even decent things—including relatively successful economic development schemes—come to an end, and by the late 1970s or early 1980s, the South's rural manufacturing strategy was largely spent. This low-end strategy—whereby low-skill workers were paid low wages to produce low-cost manufactured goods—had eased the transition of millions of Southerners out of agriculture and bought time for the region to catch its collective breath. But by about 1980, technological change and hemispheric and increasingly global competition put stress on the strategy that for 30 years had worked so well. And despite the fact that the strategy's inherent limitations were recognized early on, that symptoms of the strategy's problems were identified and diagnosed almost as soon as they appeared, and that a variety of good ideas and well-thought-out remedial plans quickly surfaced, the rural South has basically flatlined ever since—in the era, that is to say, "after the factories," as the Southern Growth Policies Board put it in a trenchant report released in 1986.

To be sure, there have been some subsequent success stories: The emerging auto-industrial complexes

> Manufacturing filled the void created by the post–World War II collapse of agricultural jobs. Even today, a quarter of rural Southern workers labor in some form of manufacturing.

in rural parts of Alabama, Georgia, Mississippi, and Tennessee, in particular, have made the South a center of German, Japanese, and Korean automobile production. Other rural areas near large cities, near major tourist destinations, and near universities or military bases and installations have done well. Closer to home, the Global TransPark outside Kinston in eastern North Carolina is finally starting to show promise—or, given its focus on aerospace/aviation, perhaps we should say starting to spread its wings. But by and large, the economies in most parts of the rural South have crashed, stalled, or been in a holding pattern for the past 30 years. And in our view, here's where history comes in.

In short, the strengths and the limits of the postwar developmental strategy for the rural South are related to if not functions of the types of economic activities on which it generally was based. This strategy was based for the most part on "lows"—not the home improvement giant or even the supermarket chain—but low-skill, low-wage, low-cost, low-value-added manufacturing, often attracted or lured to given rural areas by subsidies, tax breaks, and giveaways. And the costs of all of these lows were high, and the rural South has being paying those costs ever since.

The irony if not tragedy of this development strategy is that barring abnegation of the region's entire history or the possibility of starting all over again, it was likely the best possible option. It is not easy to attract high-tech research facilities, advanced manufacturing partnerships, or the creative class to Aberdeen, Mississippi; Timmonsville, South Carolina; or in our own state to places such as Hamlet (home of the famous 1991 fire in a chicken-processing plant) or Tar Heel (home of the world's largest slaughtering house)—that is to say, to areas where the legacy of the past (slavery, Jim Crow, persistent economic and social inequalities, low levels of investment in human and social capital, and so forth) often loomed large. Not all parts of the rural South were affected in the same way, it is true: One cannot explain the economic stresses in a place like Clay County in eastern Kentucky or Graham County in the mountains of North Carolina through recourse to the same logic and empirics as would be the case for Madison Parish or East Carroll Parish in Louisiana. But there are reasons that many of the poorest parts of the rural South today are located in the areas that once comprised the heart of slavery and the plantation belt.

While low-end manufacturing was certainly the most obvious, probably the easiest, and arguably the most feasible option for many parts of the rural South as they transitioned out of agriculture, a new strategy has not been nearly as forthcoming. As powerful social processes and pressures—the introduction of advanced (labor-saving) technology, the large-scale relocation of plants to cheaper offshore production sites, and problems caused by currency fluctuation/manipulation come immediately to mind in this regard—bore down with greater urgency on the region, however, it became imperative that something or rather some things needed to be done to preserve the accomplishments of the postwar decades.

THE RURAL SOUTH AFTER *HALFWAY HOME* AND *SHADOWS IN THE SUNBELT*

In retrospect, the speed at which governmental officials, nongovernmental organizations, academics, journalists, and business and labor leaders responded to renewed crisis in the rural South is quite impressive. The two reports that sparked this project—the Southern Growth Policies Board's *Halfway Home and a Long Way to Go* and MDC's *Shadows in the Sunbelt*—appeared in 1986, with the latter report in particular focusing attention on the (proximate) causes of the crisis and making some careful recommendations regarding future development strategies for the region. In January 1987, the private, nonprofit North Carolina Rural Economic Development Center was established. The center, which was the "first organization in the country devoted exclusively to state rural advancement," hit the ground running and has been an invaluable (and indefatigable) resource for rural North Carolina ever since, serving as an advocate for the state's rural interests, a generator of innovative ideas regarding rural development, and a service and training provider for the state's rural populations. Similar centers subsequently have sprung up around the South—the Governor's Office of Rural Development in Louisiana, Maryland's Rural Development Council, the Southern Rural Development Center in Mississippi, the Texas Department of Rural Affairs, among others—though most are public and none is as comprehensive or influential as North Carolina's.

Which policies should be put into place in the rural South "after the factories"? Views differ, of course, but, generally speaking, most strategies have stressed broad environmental factors: Most notably, investment in human capital (including workforce training), infrastructure, and land/water resources); governmental policies to support entrepreneurship, innovation, rural investment, and small-business development; and in the agricultural sector continued modernization and movement toward either scale economies (hog and chicken "integrators," for example) or higher-value-added products, food/fibers of greater income elasticity, niche markets or specialty lines.

Despite agriculture's ever-shrinking presence in North Carolina—it now accounts for about 1 percent of the state's economy and just 2 percent of employment—the sector, having been modernized, has some real strengths. The state is the leading U.S. producer of flue-cured tobacco and sweet potatoes; number two in Christmas trees, hogs and pigs, trout, and turkeys; third in strawberries and processed cucumbers; fourth in fresh cucumbers and upland cotton; and fifth in burley tobacco, broiler catfish, peanuts, and greenhouse/nursery products. And as all of us in the Triangle area know, the organic/locavore segment of the industry is thriving in parts of North Carolina as well. Nevertheless, the state has only about 53,000 farmers, fewer than half of whom devote themselves full time to agriculture, and the average age of these operators is 57.3. Given farming's small size and limited labor demands, it is difficult to envision a future rural growth strategy in which agriculture plays the lead role.

The same probably holds true of strategies based primarily on recruiting outside firms into the rural South. For the most part, the newest thinking eschews "buffalo hunting," which is viewed as unlikely to succeed and as having high opportunity costs. Rather, in recognition of the diversity of the rural South, more organic, local development strategies based on a given part of the rural South's locale, specific circumstances, comparative advantages, and so forth, are being pushed. In other words, what is "good policy" for a rural community in the Alabama Black Belt or Arkansas Delta might not be appropriate for a rural community near the Rio Grande, within commuting distance of metropolitan Nashville, or near Camp Lejeune.

All of these insights seem sensible and valuable. And the best of the new thinking pays some attention as well to the legacy of the past or to what are referred to as "enduring issues" in *Choices for a New Century*, a 1999 report prepared by the North Carolina Rural Economic Development Center, and MDC's *Shadows in the Sunbelt Revisited*, issued in 2002. According

> Despite agriculture's ever-shrinking presence in North Carolina—it now accounts for about 1 percent of the state's economy and just 2 percent of employment—the sector, having been modernized, has some real strengths.

to the former, such issues "have to do with the consequences of inadequate education, poverty, infrastructure needs and lingering racial strains"— of history, in other words.

In our view, however, the determinative power of such "enduring issues" remains underplayed. In fact, the role of historical factors largely explains the intractability of the rural South's problems, the region's pattern of crisis, and much of its population's chronic difficulties. Much of what we identify as inherently urban problems—poverty, crime, drug abuse, chronic disease, and inadequate education—are just as prevalent and often more so in rural areas. Indeed, rural Southerners are not only poorer but also sicker. Rural North Carolina is a good example. On average, the state's 85 predominantly rural counties show higher rates of infant mortality, teen pregnancy, and deaths from heart disease, stroke, cancer, and diabetes. Beyond North Carolina, the rural South suffers from the same health problems. Smoking rates are highest in the South, contributing to higher cancer and heart disease mortality. An obesity-driven type II diabetes epidemic is sweeping the rural South, leading to a new coinage in Mississippi: "diabesity." Epidemiologists have deemed much of the rural South the "stroke belt," a broad region encompassing the rural South and stretching from eastern Virginia down the East Coast to northern Florida before turning west to the Mississippi Delta. In this broad region, stroke deaths are 1.3 to 2.0 times the national rate. These high levels of chronic disease have a measurable impact on the length and quality of life. A recent study of life expectancy trends shows that rural Southerners lag behind their urban counterparts as well as rural dwellers in other parts of the developed world. Rural Southerners simply do not live as long. Poor levels of health not only inflict suffering but also act as a drag on economic activity; sick employees are less productive and require larger health-care expenditures.

It should be noted as well that rural population patterns are making rural development strategies, particularly the old buffalo hunt strategy, more difficult. Once plentiful rural labor pools are now drying up. During most of the 20th century, the Southern countryside teemed with people eager for work. More than a century's worth of rural out-migration to cities along with declining birth rates has meant that large parts of the rural South now are home mostly to the very young and very old, reducing the pool of qualified workers. Employers have taken note. In 2000, Nissan located a major automobile manufacturing plant near the small county seat town of Canton, Mississippi, adding to the already substantial Southern automobile complex where one in four domestically manufactured vehicles is assembled. Even though the plant opened in the midst of a recession and the jobs offered a premium wage, Nissan faced challenges in recruiting qualified workers. Initial applications for work came in at less than one-third of the company's expectations. Two years later, when the Hyundai Motor Company considered locating an automotive assembly plant nearby, a Nissan official openly complained about the difficulty of finding qualified workers.

Thus, despite good thinking, supportive institutions, and many sensible policies, the crisis that began 30-odd years ago endures. There are still shadows in the rural South, which is still but halfway home. Our great fear is that the rural South may be succumbing to what development economists refer to as the middle-income trap, a situation of stagnation that sets in when a region reaches a certain rung on the development ladder. The mechanization of agriculture and the successful transition to low-skill, low-wage manufacturing helped the region to grow rapidly in the postwar era and to rise out of poverty. But it is a lot easier to get to the income level the rural South achieved by 1980 than to move higher up the ladder, particularly in a global economy wherein the region's previous cost advantages disappear. In an international context, Latin American countries such as Colombia, Argentina, Chile, and Venezuela and Southeast Asian countries such as Malaysia and Thailand have been running in place for years now. That the South's rapid postwar convergence on national norms in terms of income per capita peaked at 90 to 91 percent in the early 1990s and has subsequently remained in that vicinity also is suggestive in this regard—and very troubling.

THE FUTURE OF THE RURAL SOUTH

The rural South, a low-cost region in the U.S. context, is high-cost compared to many other parts of the world, including Thailand and Malaysia. Given the fact that the same production equipment and machinery is available pretty much everywhere and the fact that the skill level of the region's labor force (low) is not very different from levels in areas whose workers cost

much less, it is not hard to understand why the South's manufacturing prospects—old or new, rudimentary or advanced—are uncertain at best. Even one area of industry where the rural South has continued to hold its own—factory farming—is facing challenges from similar (but cheaper) operations in other parts of the world, increasingly in Southeast Asia and East Asia. Last year, one of the authors of this essay visited a state-of-the-art hog/chicken factory farm owned and operated by Cargill in Vietnam's Mekong Delta. Fierce competition has also arisen in recent years between catfish farms in rural Mississippi and catfish (Pangasius) farms in Thailand and Vietnam.

Economists and economic historians often debate whether development is more about places or people. There is a difference. Some places experience development by substituting one population for another—gentrifying urban areas, for example. Places in the rural South such as Hilton Head, South Carolina; St. Simons Island, Georgia; and parts of Watauga and Moore Counties in North Carolina have basically seen the removal of poor people and the arrival of the wealthy. Sometimes the best way for poor people in the rural South to improve their circumstances is in fact to relocate to areas with greater opportunities, whether in urban parts of the region or somewhere else, or at least to commute to jobs in such areas, though this brings about other types of problems in rural communities. (What happens to local businesses, the PTA, and the like?) It is true, of course, that places and people sometimes can develop in tandem. Development of this type is often slower and harder to bring about, but many observers believe it represents a richer and deeper form of development.

We envision the rural South—or, rather, the rural Souths—pursuing all of these strategies (and others) in the years ahead. Even in just one Southern state, North Carolina, we will need to see many different development strategies. As mentioned earlier, 85 of North Carolina's 100 counties are still classified as rural, and 3 of them (Hyde, Camden, and Tyrrell) have no medical doctors, with 5 others home to fewer than six doctors each. No two of North Carolina's counties are alike. Thus, it seems appropriate that some of these counties should focus on their linkages with growth nodes of one type or another: major cities, Fort Bragg, East Carolina University, Research Triangle Park, and so forth. Others might develop strategies based on tourism (beaches, mountains), recreational/retirement communities, logistics (Global TransPark, I-95 corridor, and so on), agribusiness, or, yes, manufacturing. Some areas may see their prospects improve by making themselves more friendly and hospitable (and catering more explicitly) to the Latino migrants who have proved so important to the state's rural economy in recent decades. A number of declining small towns and rural communities in the Midwest have been brought back to life by such migrants, and in some ways the same process seems to be happening in places such as Siler City in Chatham County.

None of these strategies is foolproof, of course: Almost everyone by now has heard the sad developmental saga of the Randy Parton Theater in Roanoke Rapids in Halifax County. And alas, for some forlorn rural areas, the best development strategy might be one of exit for many—a ham sandwich and a one-way bus ticket, as one of our economist friends has put it. And these points hold more or less true in rural parts of other Southern states as well.

At the end of the day, it is hard to conclude that the South's 30-year rural crisis is nearing an end. Despite numerous good ideas, good policies, and good institutional developments and much goodwill, many of the same problems identified by the Southern Growth Policies Board and by MDC 25 years ago still plague the rural South today. Some grounds for hope exist, but the burden of the past is great in the rural South and cannot easily be vanquished, much less wished away.

REFERENCES

Carlton, David L., and Peter A. Coclanis, eds. *Confronting Southern Poverty in the Great Depression: The Report on Economic Conditions of the South with Related Documents.* Boston: Bedford/St. Martin's, 1996.

Carlton, David L., and Peter A. Coclanis. *The South, the Nation, and the World: Perspectives on Southern Economic Development.* Charlottesville: University of Virginia Press, 2003.

Coclanis, Peter A., and Louis M. Kyriakoudes. "Selling Which South?: Economic Change and Rural and Small-Town North Carolina in an Era of Globalization, 1940–2007." *Southern Cultures* 13 (Winter 2007): 86–102.

Daniel, Pete. *Breaking the Land: The Transformation of Cotton, Tobacco, and Rice Cultures since 1880.* Urbana: University of Illinois Press, 1985.

MDC. *Shadows in the Sunbelt: Developing the Rural South in an Era of Economic Change.* Chapel Hill: MDC, 1986.

MDC. *The State of the South 2002: Shadows in the Sunbelt Revisited.* Chapel Hill: MDC, 2002.

North Carolina. Department of Agriculture and Consumer Services. *North Carolina Agricultural Statistics*, 2010. http://www.ncagr.gov/stats/2010AgStat/index.htm.

North Carolina Rural Economic Development Center. *Choices for a New Century.* Raleigh: North Carolina Rural Economic Development Center, 1999.

North Carolina Rural Economic Development Center. *Living on the Margins: Rural North Carolina in the Aftermath of the Great Recession.* Raleigh: North Carolina Rural Economic Development Center, 2011.

Southern Growth Policies Board. *Halfway Home and a Long Way to Go: The Report of the 1986 Commission on the Future of the South.* Research Triangle Park, N.C.: Southern Growth Policies Board, 1986.

Walden, Michael L. North *Carolina in the Connected Age: Challenges and Opportunities in a Globalizing Economy.* Chapel Hill: University of North Carolina Press, 2008.

Wright, Gavin. *Old South, New South: Revolutions in the Southern Economy since the Civil War.* New York: Basic Books, 1986.

African American Economic Progress *and the* Post–Civil Rights South

GAVIN WRIGHT

comment by Arkansas Governor Bill Clinton in his introduction about having been inspired by Martin Luther King Jr.'s 1963 "I Have a Dream" speech. MDC's *Shadows in the Sunbelt* was only slightly more forthcoming, noting only that African Americans in the rural South were among the poorest people in the nation and that they had been especially hard hit by the decline of the rural economy. Even in the 1980s, it seems, Southern leaders preferred to consign the segregation era, along with slavery, to the "bad old days" now best forgotten.

The United States is now observing simultaneous commemorations of the 50th anniversaries of the landmark events of the civil rights revolution and the 150th anniversary of the outbreak of the Civil War. The ideals and accomplishments of the civil rights movement have now entered the civic culture of the nation, perhaps even more in the South than elsewhere. Yet discussions of regional economic performance and policy rarely mention this heritage as part of the present-day landscape. In 1986, *Halfway Home and a Long Way to Go* made no explicit mention of race except for one

This omission surely did not occur because the authors of these reports were unaware of the continued salience of race in the post–civil rights South. Instead, they believed that discussions of race were divisive and that the best path forward was to rally political and business leaders and public opinion behind policies to sustain economic development: promote local initiatives, engage citizens, invest in infrastructure and the environment, and upgrade education at all socioeconomic levels. This classic formula for New South politics was a profound if indirect achievement of the civil rights movement, which fostered significant economic progress throughout the region.

But race should not be ignored completely in these discussions. The past 50 years have constituted a remarkable economic success story for some African Americans in the South, though the strength and pervasiveness of this progress was not necessarily evident as of the 1980s. The Civil Rights Act of 1964 decisively abolished segregation in public accommodations, quickly improving the climate of race relations. But many observers believed at the time that the change had mainly secured rights that were largely symbolic, with little effect on economic well-being, especially for ordinary people. This impression was reinforced by urban racial violence and political splintering in the late 1960s and 1970s. Reports from southern cities confirmed this sense of pessimism, especially for black men. A 1978 study concluded that racial discrimination and educational deficiencies were generating "a widening of the gap between black and white incomes in the South."

But this conclusion was wrong. The overall picture is best conveyed in a pair of graphs showing median male income by region from 1953 through 2007. Median black male income in the South was declining until the early 1960s, reflecting the loss of agricultural employment and the absence of black opportunity in the Jim Crow era. Beginning in the 1960s, however, black male income grew faster in the South than in any other region. The biggest surge came during the boom of the 1990s. By the end of the decade, the Southern median virtually equaled that of the Northwest and Midwest, eliminating the historic regional income gap.[1]

The second graph compares black and white median male income within the South. The black relative gains are dramatic—from less than 40 percent of the white median in 1960 to nearly 60 percent in the 1970s and to 75 percent between 1990 and 2000—but at no time did Southern white incomes fall as black incomes rose. What we see, in other words, is not redistribution in the name of historical justice but an integration of the black population into the regional economy. When we add the consideration that the civil rights revolution invigorated the regional economy by opening it to inflows of capital, creativity, and new enterprises from around the world, it becomes clear that most Southern whites also benefited economically.

What mechanisms enabled this dramatic transformation? Most immediate was the opening to black workers of long-segregated industries such as textiles beginning in the 1960s. Employers at first resisted this change, often placing new black workers in the most menial and undesirable positions. With experience, however, firms revised these views. The manager of Erwin Mills, in the eastern North Carolina town of Erwin, told a reporter, "On turnover, absenteeism, and job performance, we can't tell the difference, really." According to a 1969 *New York Times* report, "Virtually all of the large companies have begun to preach a doctrine of equal, color-blind employment." In other industries, the integration process was more protracted and litigious, but the outcome was similar. According to economists John Donohue and James Heckman, the sharp rise in relative black incomes between 1965 and 1975 was exclusively a Southern regional phenomenon.

Because the textiles industry declined precipitously in the 1990s, it is tempting to view the gains from integration as transitory, a hollow prize. But black employment in the industry increased from virtually zero in 1965 to more than 220,000 in the early 1990s, providing an escape route from poverty for a full generation of African Americans. Speaking to interviewers years later, many black mill workers recalled with pride that their

[1] *Black median income in the West was reported as somewhat higher on average but fluctuated from year to year, presumably because of small sample sizes.*

> What we see, in other words, is not redistribution in the name of historical justice but an integration of the black population into the regional economy.

jobs enabled them to send their children to college. Industrial desegregation thus facilitated the transfer of improved economic potential across generations.

School desegregation was most extensive in the South. Recent economic research has identified significant gains for African Americans as a result of desegregation, including such indicators as educational attainment, test scores, earnings, occupational status, health, and probability of incarceration. In virtually every study, no adverse effects on whites were observed for these same outcome variables. It is often difficult to identify precise channels of influence, but the broad pattern shows complementarity between schooling and expanding economic opportunity. Tables 1.1 and 1.2 show that black educational advances in the South have exceeded those of other regions.

Perhaps the most decisive evidence of profound change in regional labor markets is the reversal of black migration flows. Table 1.3 demonstrates that since 1970, net black migration has been persistently southward, increasingly so over time. This "reverse" migration is remarkable not just for its direction but for the U-turn in educational selectivity. During the pre–civil rights era, additional years of schooling greatly increased the probability of black out-migration. By the 1990s, the typical black migrant was a young, educated person pursuing opportunities in the booming metropolitan areas of the New South. Although the region attracts white migrants as well, blacks are more likely than whites to choose the South. In interviews, migrants often emphasize family and cultural roots, but typically not at the expense of economic opportunity. When *Black Enterprise* magazine names the best cities for African Americans, the top spots are now always in the South.

Economic history rarely generates highly specific policy lessons because the context is always changing. The civil rights revolution was highly successful for African Americans in the South, but we no longer have opportunities for dramatic onetime gains merely by opening doors long closed by racial segregation. Furthermore, the demography of the regional labor market has changed fundamentally in recent decades. Latino in-migration is only the largest and most visible indication that the biracial model that has shaped so much of Southern history no longer matches the reality on the ground. Nonetheless, some broad principles shine through this historical record.

Whereas the authors of *Halfway Home* and *Shadows in the Sunbelt* urged Southerners to escape their past, the heritage of the civil rights revolution can be celebrated with pride and cultivated as the basis for social and economic policies. The revolution for African American rights has offered a model and an inspiration for social change and for liberation movements around the world. Surely it should be no less honored in the land of its birth, not just as a tourist attraction but as the foundation for inclusiveness in workplaces, schools, and communities throughout the region.

The other lesson of past economic success is the importance of investments in human skills and advanced education as a core part of state and regional development programs. The authors of *Shadows in the Sunbelt* already understood in 1986 that the era of growth on the basis of cheap, unskilled labor had passed. This perception is all the more true today. Higher educational attainment was essential for African American economic advancement in the 20th century, and it will be no less essential for all Southerners in the 21st century.[2]

---

[2] *Nothing in this review is meant to minimize the persistence of racial economic disparities in the South. These gaps would undoubtedly be larger if measured by wealth rather than income, because wealth accumulation tends to lag current income. But with all due qualifications, the long-term Southern record for African Americans is more hopeful than that of other regions.*

REFERENCES

Donohue, John, III, and James Heckman. "Continuous versus Episodic Change: The Impact of Civil Rights Policy on the Economic Status of Blacks." *Journal of Economic Literature* 29 (1991): 1411–31.

Frey, William H. "The New Great Migration: Black Americans' Return to the South, 1965–2000." In *Redefining Urban and Suburban America*, ed. Alan Berube, Bruce Katz, and Robert E. Lang. Washington, D.C.: Brookings, 2005.

Minchin, Timothy. *Hiring the Black Worker: The Racial Integration of the Southern Textiles Industry, 1960–1980.* Chapel Hill: University of North Carolina Press, 1999.

TABLES AND FIGURES

table 1.1 **PERCENTAGE OF THE BLACK POPULATION 25 YEARS AND OVER WITH A HIGH SCHOOL DIPLOMA OR HIGHER, 1940 TO 2009**

	1940	1950	1960	1970	1980	1990	2000	2009
UNITED STATES	7.7	13.7	21.7	31.4	51.2	63.1	72.3	80.0
REGION								
Northeast	11.7	20.6	27.6	37.8	56.4	65.3	72.1	80.3
Midwest	12.6	20.2	26.1	36.5	54.9	65.3	73.9	80.5
South	5.4	8.9	15.0	24.4	44.9	59.1	70.3	78.8
West	18.4	27.8	37.2	48.9	68.7	76.2	81.1	86.6

Source: U.S. Census Bureau, Decennial Census of Population, 1940 to 2000

table 1.2 **PERCENTAGE OF THE BLACK POPULATION 25 YEARS AND OVER WITH A BACHELOR'S DEGREE OR HIGHER, 1940 TO 2009**

	1940	1950	1960	1970	1980	1990	2000	2009
UNITED STATES	1.3	2.2	3.5	4.4	8.4	11.4	14.3	17.2
REGION								
Northeast	1.7	2.6	3.6	4.1	8.4	12.5	15.3	18.9
Midwest	1.8	2.5	3.4	4.0	7.9	10.4	13.3	15.6
South	1.1	2.0	3.2	4.4	8.0	10.7	13.7	16.6
West	2.3	3.3	5.4	5.9	11.4	14.8	17.4	21.0

Source: U.S. Census Bureau, Decennial Census of Population, 1940 to 2000

table 1.3 **NET MIGRATION INTO THE SOUTH, 1940–50 TO 2005–2010 (IN THOUSANDS)**

TIME PERIOD	WHITE	BLACK	HISPANIC
1940-1950	-866	-1581	
1950-1960	-234	-1202	
1960-1970	1807	-1380	
1970-1980	3556	206	
1980-1985	1808	83	
1985-1990	971	325	
1990-1995	1344[a]	358	282
1995-2000	1127[a]	347	256
2000-2005	1027[a]	318	275
2005-2010	731[a]	267	170

[a] Non-Hispanic White. A negative sign indicates net migration out of the South.

Sources: H.T. Eldridge and D.S. Thomas, Population Redistribution and Economic Growth Volume III (Philadelphia: American Philosophical Society, 1964), 90; U.S. Census Bureau, Historical Statistics of the U.S. to 1970 (Washington, D.C.: U.S. Goverment Printing Office, 1975), 94–95; J.D. Kasaida, M.D. Irwin, and H.L. Hughes, "The South Is Still Rising"; Isaac Robinson, "Blacks Move Back to the South," American Demographics (June 1986), 35, 43; U.S. Census Bureau, Current Population Reports: Geographic Mobility: Special Studies; Domestic Migration across Regions, Divisions, and States, 1980–85; Geographical Mobility: Special Studies, 1990–95; Migration by Race and Hispanic Origin, 1995–2000; CPS: Annual Social and Economic Supplement, 2005–2010. Figures for 1985–90: sums of the annual figures for 1985–86, 1986–87, and 1987–90.

THE Knowledge Economy *and the* the Crisis of Economic Development Policy *in* South Carolina, 1986-2011

LACY FORD

The relative stagnation of the South Carolina economy in recent decades has raised troubling questions about the state's overall approach to economic development. From 1950 through 1980, South Carolina enjoyed remarkable success in development, as per capita income not only increased by nearly 400 percent (in real terms) but also converged on the national average in impressive fashion, moving from just under 60 percent of the national average in 1950 to nearly 80 percent by 1980. Since 1980, however, that trend has stalled, leaving the Palmetto State regularly ranked among the nation's ten poorest states. South Carolina leaders have thus been left to ponder deep problems with the state's economic development policies.

The comparative stagnation of per capita income in South Carolina has raised questions about the state's traditional economic development strategy of recruiting existing industries form other states or overseas, an approach often referred to as "smokestack chasing" or "buffalo hunting." "Economic development is now struggling to find its way in South Carolina," observed respected College of Charleston economist Frank Hefner early in 2006. "More of the same is not going to work because you can only get so many BMWs."

Such a recruiting strategy, which relies heavily on attracting large manufacturing operations through the appeal of lower labor costs, has proven decidedly problematic in the age of economic globalization, in which low-wage industries have moved offshore to take advantage of even lower labor costs in Asia and other parts of the world. At the same time, South Carolina's relative lack of both venture and human capital has hindered the state's efforts to gain a foothold in the modern knowledge economy, where working smart is just as important as working hard. South Carolinians received only 3.6 patents per 10,000 workers in 2001, compared to a national average of 7.1. If patents serve as one proxy for overall inventiveness and creativity, South Carolinians apparently were only half as inventive as Americans as a whole. Moreover, venture capital funding stood at only $3 per worker in South Carolina in 2002, compared to a national average of $155 per worker, reflecting the state's long-term lack of indigenous capital.

At the heart of the slowdown in South Carolina's economic growth lies the shift of employment from the industrial sector to the service sector, where wages tend to be lower, and the dramatic retrenchment of government, a sector of the economy that grew rapidly during the postwar boom but has been shrinking over the past quarter century. A decade into the 21st century, South Carolina, like other textile states, has recovered only partially from the loss of tens of thousands of manufacturing jobs in bellwether industries such as textiles and apparel. Even though the state's maufacuring sector held its own between 1980 and 2000 in terms of total output, increasing its share of state domestic product slightly from 22.3 to 22.6 percent, manufacturing's share of total employment declined precipitously.

In 1977, manufacturing employed more than 27 percent of the Palmetto State's workforce; by 2001, that number had dropped to 14 percent. In fact, from 1993 through 2004, South Carolina employment in textiles declined by nearly two-thirds, from 120,000 jobs to approximately 40,000. The state's apparel industry was similarly devastated, with employment falling from just

 If patents serve as one proxy for overall inventiveness and creativity, South Carolinians apparently were only half as inventive as Americans as a whole.

over 38,000 in 1990 to 4,500 in 2004. The generally low-paying service sector increased its share of total employment from 16 to 25 percent between 1980 and 2000, even though the service sector's share of total state output increased only from 14.1 to 15.6 percent.

The other major shift in the Palmetto economy since 1980 has been the dramatic decline of the government sector share, which shrank from 24.3 percent of all output in 1977 to 14.5 percent in 2001, while government employment as a share of total employment declined more than 20 percent. Thus, as employment shifted out of manufacturing into the service sector, it moved from comparatively low manufacturing wages to even lower service wages, intensifying the state's tendency toward a low-wage economy and helping stymie the state's convergence on the national per capita income average. The problem in South Carolina has not simply been one of job growth or job loss but of the creation of jobs that pay good wages.

The most plausible remedy for the loss of manufacturing jobs is to create better-paying jobs in the technology and knowledge economies, which have grown rapidly since the mid-1980s. But South Carolina has proven poorly positioned to create or attract such industries as a result of the skill and educational levels of its workforce. When Google and Amazon come to South Carolina, they come for a server farm or a distribution warehouse, not a research complex.

Why? The answer lies largely in the state's staggering educational attainment shortcomings. South Carolina has the largest share of urban adults without a high school education of any of the nine southern states and ranks near the bottom nationally in terms of the proportion of adults with at least a high school diploma. In 2005, the state ranked 41st in the nation in the proportion of its adults with a

high school diploma, as roughly one in four Palmetto State adults had not completed high school. Less than 21 percent of all adult South Carolinians had a bachelor's degree or higher. Recent studies indicate that the two strongest contributors to the income gap between South Carolina and the national average were education-related variables: the low percentage of the population with bachelor's degrees, and the high proportion of residents over 25 who were not high school graduates. And South Carolina consistently ranks close to the bottom in the areas of K–12 education. In 1990, the state ranked 43rd, with only 68 percent of its population holding high school degrees. The southern states with lower percentages were Alabama, Mississippi, Tennessee, West Virginia, and Kentucky.

By 2007, South Carolina had increased its proportion of high school graduates to 82 percent, but it still ranked seventh from the bottom in terms of high school graduates, with Texas joining the list of states outperformed by South Carolina. At the other end of the education spectrum, just over 16 percent of the state's adult population had college degrees in 1990, leaving the state 43rd in the nation in that category. By 2007, that percentage had improved to 23 percent, and the state's ranking inched up to 40th in the nation, though it still remained in the bottom quartile.

But despite such across-the-board deficits in educational attainment, the state seems to lack the political will to provide resources to address the problem. Known nationally as a low-tax haven, South Carolina's state and local taxes stand at 30 percent below the national average. In 2001, South Carolinians paid 10.5 percent of their income in state and local taxes, placing the state in the bottom half of all states in terms of total tax burden. Moreover, South Carolina ranks 45th in terms of taxes per capita and 33rd in taxes as a share of personal income because incomes are low.

"Fostering a low-wage environment is one economic path, but it is not one that leads to rising standards of living for the population," one national consulting group told state business leaders, concluding that "as it now stands, South Carolina cannot compete vigorously in the new knowledge based economy with this mix of industries and this quality of economic foundations." Moreover, Harvard-based competitiveness expert Michael Porter also warned state leaders, "Competitiveness is not low wages or low taxes"; rather, "competitiveness is productivity." And productivity depends both on the value (quality) of inputs, including labor inputs, and the efficiency with which output is produced.

Productivity, as much as any other single item, influences the state's level of per capita income, and the availability of highly productive ("well-educated" or "well-trained") workers attracts new companies to an area. A partial key to South Carolina's ability to find the way again in the realm of economic development lies in preparing to compete effectively in the knowledge-based 21st-century economy. To do so, South Carolina must abandon its low-wage, low-tax strategy of development. It must also abandon the savaging of a public sector that creates the bulk of the state's human capital. Instead, the state must invest more heavily and patiently in the education and training of its citizens than ever before.

REFERENCES

Carlton, David, and Peter Coclanis. "The Uninventive South: A Quantitative Look at Region and American Inventiveness." *Technology and Culture* 26 (April 1995): 220–44.

Coclanis, Peter A., and Lacy K. Ford. "The South Carolina Economy Reconstructed and Reconsidered: Structure, Output, and Performance, 1670–1985." In *Developing Dixie: Modernization in a Traditional Society*, ed. Winfred B. Moore Jr., Joseph F. Tripp, and Lyon G. Tyler Jr. Westport, Conn.: Greenwood, 1988.

Ford, Lacy K., and R. Phillip Stone. "Economic Development and Globalization in South Carolina." *Southern Cultures* 13 (Spring 2007): 18–50.

Schunk, Donald. *The South Carolina Economy and Government Revenue: A Working Paper Prepared for the Palmetto Institute.* Clemson, S.C.: Strom Thurmond Institute of Government and Public Affairs, Clemson University, 2005.

Stone, R. Phillip. "Making a Modern State: The Politics of Economic Development in South Carolina, 1938–1962. Ph.D. diss., University of South Carolina, 2003.

25 YEARS LATER: REVISITING *HALFWAY HOME* AND *SHADOWS IN THE SUNBELT* / 1986–2011

Revisiting the 1986 Commission *on the* Future *of the* South's *Halfway Home and Long Way to Go*

JESSE L. WHITE JR.

Much was changing in the economy of the South in the 1980s, but less was understood about it. The decades-old landscape of row-crop agriculture, low-wage branch plant manufacturing, and extractive industries (coal, oil, timber) was fading and with it the pattern of vibrant small towns and a rural fabric of life. The brutal 1982 recession accelerated and highlighted these stresses, and Southern governors at the time were searching for answers. The Southern Growth Policies Board (SGPB) took the lead in providing them.

The original idea for the SGPB was Terry Sanford's. The board initially focused on managing the Sunbelt's burgeoning growth. The interstate agreement that created the board called for a statement of regional objectives every six years, and the mechanism for identifying objectives became known as the Commission on the Future of the South. The inaugural commission was convened in 1974 by Jimmy Carter, then governor of Georgia, and the second was appointed in 1980 by South Carolina governor Richard Riley. Both reports and sets of objectives reflect the times in which they were written: 1974 on growth management and quality of life, 1980 on governance, children, and human resources issues. The last six-year commission met in 1998, and the SGPB began to issue annual Future of the South reports in 2001. Each Commission on the Future of the South was freestanding and existed only until its report was complete. As one SGPB executive director has noted, "There was a disconnect and sometimes tension between the commissions and the board itself. When we made the change to annual reports in 2001, the board and its standing advisory councils began to take responsibility for the reports

> We remain on the road, with many promises still unfulfilled.

instead of that being assumed by commissions with limited life spans and almost no resources."

In the late 1970s, the SGPB opened up an office in Washington, D.C., to represent the South in the Sunbelt-Frostbelt wars over federal funding formulas, but many observers thought the move caused the board to lose its focus. When I took over as the SGPB's executive director in 1982, we closed the Washington office and focused on the economic growth and development issues facing the region in the deepening recession. Building a strong research capacity under Stuart Rosenfeld, the board conducted pioneering work on the industrial restructuring taking place in the rural and small-town South, resulting in a report, *After the Factories: The Changing Economy of the Rural South*. In addition to work on the importance of education and training to economic development, the board made the case to Southern policymakers that we had built our economy on the shifting sands of low human capital, cheap labor, and branch plants. This information led to the creation of *Halfway Home and a Long Way to Go*, one of the most significant documents in the history of the region and the report of the 1986 Commission on the Future of the South. Alumni Distinguished Professor Emerita Doris Betts of the University of North Carolina at Chapel Hill authored the report.

Bill Clinton, governor of Arkansas and chair of the SGPB, was determined that the commission would be a working body without external task forces or advisory groups, a trap into which the 1980 commission had fallen. He promised to stay involved and, equally important, appointed former governor William Winter of Mississippi to chair the commission. Commission members included three former governors, a former U.S. senator, two university presidents, several CEOs, state legislative leaders, and professors and nonprofit leaders. Clinton was deeply involved, especially at the penultimate meeting at the Graylyn International Conference Center in Winston-Salem, North Carolina, where the final recommendations were hammered out. Late one night, Clinton came up with the report's title: *Halfway Home and a Long Way to Go*.

Halfway Home and a Long Way to Go reported 10 objectives to be met by 1992:

1. provide a nationally competitive education for all students;

2. eliminate adult functional illiteracy;

3. prepare a flexible, globally competitive workforce;

4. strengthen society as a whole by strengthening at-risk families;

5. increase the economic development role of higher education;

6. increase the South's capacity to generate and use technology;

7. implement new economic development strategies aimed at homegrown business and industry;

8. enhance the South's natural and cultural resources;

9. develop pragmatic leaders with a global vision; and

10. improve the structure and performance of state and local governments.

The final report was delivered in Little Rock in November 1986 to Southern governors, legislators, and private-sector representatives. It made a huge impact. As William Friday, former president of UNC, told me, "This is the report I have been waiting for." Implementation was taken seriously, and Martha Layne Collins, 1987 SGPB chair and governor of Kentucky, devoted her term to promoting the report. She addressed a joint session of the North Carolina General Assembly, while Winter addressed a joint session of the Alabama legislature, and I addressed a joint session of the Mississippi legislature. The board also published reports on specific legislative follow-up to the commission recommendations.

It was a testament to the power of *Halfway Home* that the 1992 Commission on the Future of the South devoted much of its work to tracking progress on the objectives, something very rare in a politically led entity. The 1992 commission was appointed by Gaston Caperton (West Virginia governor and 1992 SGPB chair) and was chaired by Mississippi governor Ray Mabus. One of its two reports was titled *Heading Home: New Directions toward Southern Progress.*

This era was, in some ways, a golden age of Southern governors, a new generation of leadership trying to move the Deep South beyond the hysteria of the racial segregation fights. The governors were mostly progressive and almost all Democrats (Tennessee's Lamar Alexander was a notable and distinguished exception). They disagreed on some issues but were all devoted to moving the region ahead and securing its position as a full partner in the American economy.

As the report noted, this goal involved nothing less than changing many of the dynamics of Southern history. As Betts said, "Other self-proclaimed 'New Souths' have dragged behind them like long old chains the inevitable outcomes of the plantation system, secession and reconstruction, sharecropping, low-wage factories, and segregation. Decades after old economic systems have vanished, their high human cost remains." The 1986 commission found that investing in the people of the South was the only way to move beyond the often stifling past.

We remain on the road, with many promises still unfulfilled. One yearns for a bipartisan political consensus in our region to address the many problems still facing us. But it is not just nostalgia for the good old days of 1986. Investing in the people of the South still remains the only way forward.

The Southern "Consensus" on Education and Economic Development

DANIEL P. GITTERMAN

INTRODUCTION

Twenty-five years ago, the Southern Growth Policies Board (SGPB), with Arkansas governor Bill Clinton as chair, charged the 1986 Commission on the Future of the South with a goal: "Produce a short readable report to the people of the South" in an effort to mobilize support for public policies and public-private partnerships that could yield an increase in per capita income for Southerners. The resulting report, *Halfway Home and a Long Way to Go*, set forth objectives to be achieved by 1992 lest the South "stand still while a bustling world economy moves into the next century and leaves its citizens behind."

In May 1986, six months prior to *Halfway Home*'s release in November, the Chapel Hill-based MDC Panel on Rural Economic Development issued a report, *Shadows in the Sunbelt*, on the challenges facing the rural South. For years, the Southern strategy for economic development was simple: recruit new industry. The panel warned that "the rural South has traditionally been among the least educated regions in the nation" and called on states "to address the rural situation by broadening their economic development approach...and to develop broader indicators for assessing progress," such as median per capita income, educational attainment, and adult illiteracy. The 1986 SGPB commission and MDC panel, both chaired by Mississippi governor William Winter, highlighted a priority: ensure that all young adults enter working life with a minimum amount of human capital acquired through a quality public school education.

When *Halfway Home* and *Shadows* were released, Southern governors viewed themselves as a region apart and looked to one another rather than Washington, D.C., for policy ideas. The SGPB and MDC emerged as regional suppliers of policy knowledge, and their experts highlighted a link between education and economic development. The SGPB's 1985 *After the Factories* report noted, "Counties in the South which have shown the fastest growth are those whose workers are the best educated." A year later, *Shadows* concluded, "Only half of Southern adults have received high school diplomas, compared to an average of two-thirds in Southern cities and nationwide. Similar problems exist throughout the rural South." Twenty-five years later, it is time to reflect on the education and economy consensus, assess progress, and revise goals as we prepare today's students for tomorrow's labor market.

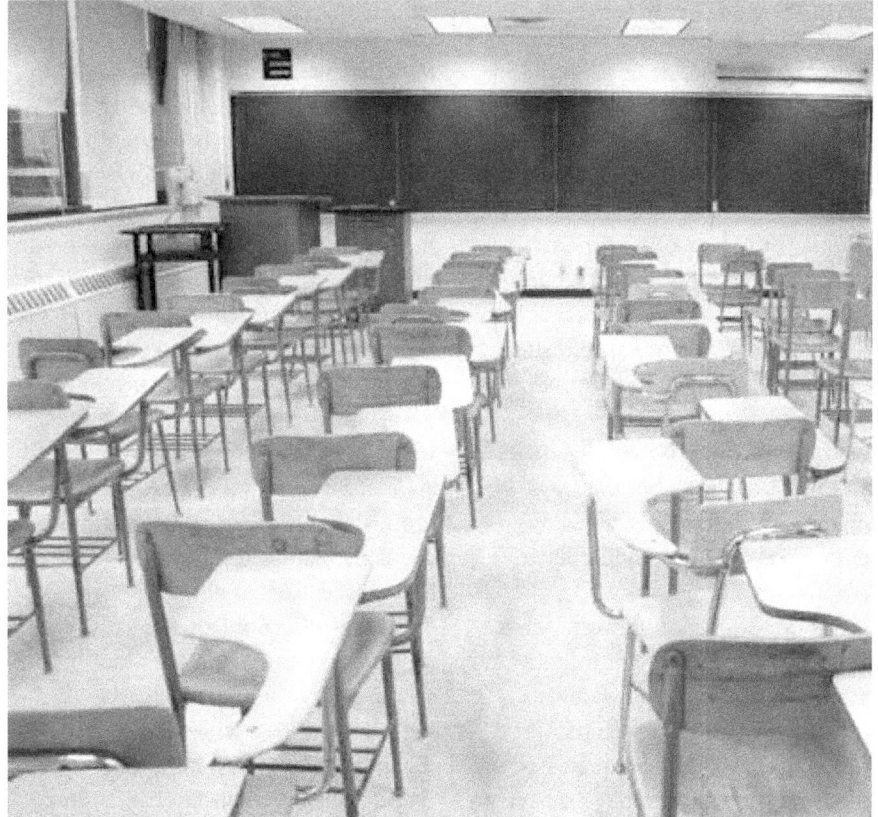

THE ORIGINS OF THE SOUTHERN "CONSENSUS" ON EDUCATION AND THE ECONOMY

For decades, Southern leaders had been engaged as collaborators in addressing the educational and economic challenges of the region. The Southern Regional Education Board (1948) and SGPB (1971) were formed under interstate agreements. The Southern Governors' Conference, which forged the compact to create the Southern Regional Education Board, affirmed that educational institutions "should make their full contribution to the social and economic development of the Southern region."

North Carolina governor Terry Sanford, who proposed the idea of the SGPB, viewed the interstate compact as a way "to harness the intellectual resources of our region to the problems of our region." At the 1982 SGPB annual meeting, attendees including governors William Winter of Mississippi, Lamar Alexander of Tennessee, Richard Riley of South Carolina, Jim Hunt of North Carolina, Bob Graham of Florida, and Chuck Robb of Virginia began to discuss the importance of educational reform to economic progress in the South.

The link between education and the economic development has been a theme for decades, but the ways in which Southern states acted on the premise varied considerably. In 1982, Winter led the way with the Mississippi Education Reform Act, a comprehensive package of initiatives that included mandatory statewide kindergartens, a new reading aide program that placed teaching assistants in the first three grades of elementary schools, and a compulsory attendance law. The reform was financed with more than a $110 million increase in sales and income taxes. Winter told a special legislative session, "The needs of education and the relationship of those needs to our future growth and progress cannot be put aside any longer…the south and 20th-century economic history[P]er capita income is tied directly, unequivocally, and irrefutably to education." Other Southern governors came to believe that they could increase per capita income only by facilitating higher levels of educational attainment—more and higher-quality public schooling.

Southern governors, motivated to spur economic growth, became the champions of improving public education in their states. Alexander explained the "consensus" on education and economy. "What has gotten the governors' attention?" he asked. "Jobs. More than anything, it is the threat to the jobs of the people who elect us. Better schools mean better jobs. Unless the states face these questions, we will forfeit our high standard of living. To meet stiff competition from workers in the rest of the world, we must educate ourselves and our children as we never have before." Much of the education reform leadership came from Southern governors and supportive legislators who called for tougher school standards, better pay for teachers, and more state funds for K–12 education. To overcome state legislators' reluctance to increase taxes to pay for reform, Southern governors attempted to mobilize the public on behalf of public school improvement.

In 1983, Hunt chaired the Education Commission of the States' Task Force on Education and Economic Growth. Several other Southern governors served as task force members, including Alexander, Graham, Robb, and Winter. The task force concluded that "technological change and global competition make it imperative to equip students in public schools with skills that go beyond the basic…This new era will radically change our concept of basic skills…necessary skills for a person's economic survival." Governors were encouraged to develop a plan to improve schools and acknowledge education's critical role in preparing people for the workforce.

Indeed, several decades ago, there was already a focus on the need for a globally competitive education system. This theme was magnified by the 1983 National Commission on Excellence in Education, which attempted to mobilize the public and policymakers in a crusade to reform education. As the *Nation at Risk* report concluded, "The world is one global village. We live among determined, well-educated, and strongly motivated competitors…These developments signify a redistribution of trained capability throughout the globe. Knowledge, learning, information, and skilled intelligence are the new raw materials of international commerce…the south and 20th-century economic historyrequired for success in the information age we are entering." Southern governors were among the first to respond to the *Nation at Risk* findings.

More specific to the region, a 1983 Southern Regional Education Board Task Force on Higher Education and the Schools affirmed that "Southern governors and many legislators must focus on the improvement of education as the underlying prerequisite for economic development." They warned that "if education is the South is to match the region's ambition for economic development, the task ahead is enormous.... [T]he South still lags in matters of educational achievement." For Southern governors, a central focus became public school reform and the identification of basic skills and competencies to prepare young adults for productive employment.

In August 1985, Alexander, who chaired the National Governors' Association and served as a member of the SGPB, established task forces on teaching, leadership and management, parent involvement and choice, readiness, technology, school facilities, and college quality to make recommendations to improve education in all states. The cochair was Clinton, who was also serving as vice chair of the National Governors' Association and the Education Commission of the States and who became chair of the SGPB in 1986. *The Governors' 1991 Report on Education* (released in 1986 but intended to show what the states should do for the next five years) suggested that governors "want to help establish clear goals and better report cards—ways to measure what students know and can do." The governors' association, the Education Commission of the States, and the Council of Chief State School Officers collaborated "to devise a system to keep with the results of this report on a yearly basis," but the governors opposed having the states directly compared with one another. To monitor progress, the governors' association decided to issue annual reports on states' advances for the next five years.

The 1986 commission embraced these prior calls for reform, recommending raising state and local investments in education, insisting on high-quality teachers, providing more and better preschool programs, and enforcing school attendance. The three leading education and economy objectives to be achieved by 1992 were: providing a nationally competitive education for all Southern students; mobilizing resources to eliminate adult functional illiteracy; and preparing a flexible, globally competitive workforce.

The commission believed that the region, though but "halfway home and a long way to go," could bring its people into the 21st century "and at long last achieve a standard of living that is equal to or beyond that enjoyed by the rest of this country." If the South was halfway home a quarter of a century ago, what has the path looked like as we moved out of the shadows and toward home?

FROM A NATIONALLY TO A GLOBALLY COMPETITIVE EDUCATION FOR ALL SOUTHERN STUDENTS

Historically, low educational attainment in the South was a cause and a consequence of the region's less-skilled economy and history of racial segregation. In earlier decades, the South marketed its lower-cost labor and low taxes to recruit low-skilled manufacturing firms. The less-educated workforce was a magnet for manufacturing plants in the South's small towns and rural areas, but it prohibited the region from attracting or developing higher-skilled jobs. The South was perceived as disadvantaged because of the overall low academic achievement of its students and its relatively underfunded state educational systems.

By the late 1970s, there was a belief that the deterioration of the nation's economy was caused by our lack of competitiveness internationally as a result of an inadequately trained labor force, especially in the South, which trailed the nation in school expenditures as well as student achievement. While the relationship between education and economic growth was complex, many Southerners concluded that improved education was essential for the region's economic progress. The SGPB came to embrace the premise that "education was both the seed and flower of economic development," or, as the commission concluded, "The South has begun to acknowledge and act upon the critical connection between human development and economic progress.... The new Southern economy will have to be built on the mental strengths of its labor force, and depend on the skills, knowledge, and creativity requirement for more technically sophisticated work stations."

By 1988, the Southern Regional Education Board Commission for Educational Quality invited its members to establish state standards and to meet or exceed national or international education standards. A *Charlotte Observer* editorial supported these goals, noting, "The citizens

> The overarching goal must not simply be more schooling but learning.

of this community—this state, this nation—must compare our educational accomplishments to what we know they must be, if our citizens are to intelligently exercise the duties of citizenship and successfully compete in a world economy."

By 1992, a newly appointed Commission on the Future of the South concluded that "a mere decade ago, too few in the South, much less the rest of the nation, were thinking about economic development and education in the same synapse." Many states, especially in the South, subsequently took up the cause of reforming education because of the "vital link to producing a workforce capable of the high quality jobs and preparing entrepreneurs equipped for the highly flexible enterprises that will secure our future prosperity." The new commission reaffirmed the 1986 objectives and concluded that "Southern education will become our greatest asset, helping our students and workers to compete internationally." The report noted that "high-productivity firms need all their workers to be more flexible, creative, skilled, and informed."

By the late 1990s, not only did the educational system of the South need to remain competitive with the rest of the nation, but now the region's educational system needed to keep pace with the rest of the globe. As a member of the 1998 Commission on the Future of the South, University of North Carolina at Chapel Hill chancellor Michael Hooker affirmed that the rules of economic activity had changed. He noted that knowledge had replaced energy as the primary means by which value is added to the economy and that "as a result, the only competitive advantage available to the South or to any region in the global economy is brainpower."

With its 2001 *Future of the South* report, the SGPB continued to highlight the necessity of a globally competitive education, recognizing that more would be required of workers in the 21st century than had been in the past. The report suggested that in today's economy, college attendance would not be sufficient and that the number of Southerners receiving high school diplomas, associate's degrees, bachelor's degrees, or higher degrees would increase regional competitiveness. There was still greater emphasis on degree attainment, with the recognition that the more education people receive, the better their options in the labor market.

A decade after *Shadows*, MDC's 1996 and 1998 *State of the South* reports called on the South to expand its discussion of education beyond elementary and secondary schools and to increase the number of people who continue education beyond high school. In its 2004 *State of the South* report, MDC concluded that although the South had made progress on the number of young adults with high school diplomas, Southern leaders still needed to consider new postsecondary goals.

MDC's 2011 *State of the South* report reiterated the ongoing "the more education, the better" theme, arguing that the South needed dramatically to increase the number of citizens earning bachelor's degrees, associate's degrees, certifications, or job-ready credentials. "Just as it is urgent that the South attack the too-high drop-out rate in high schools," the report stated, "so it is crucial that the region raise its completion rates in postsecondary education." While higher levels of educational attainment remained central to the economic development blueprint in all of the *Future of the South* and *State of the South* reports, the basic requirements to get out of the shadows and the distance to get home continued to change.

ELIMINATING YOUNG ADULT FUNCTIONAL ILLITERACY

Beyond just the level of educational attainment, basic functional literacy also emerged as key to the Southern economic progress. The 1986 commission concluded that the South "has even a higher proportion of adults who lack the basic skills to participate fully in the modern world—one in four Southern adults never went beyond the eighth grade." The focus on functional literacy addressed the issue of whether a young adult's reading and writing skills were sufficient to function in a modern society.

According to *Halfway Home*, the most pressing issue in the region and the impediment to retraining efforts was functional illiteracy. Former North Carolina governor Bob Scott, who led the North Carolina Community College System, claimed, "Illiteracy is a like a cancer. It's unseen and hidden, yet it's just eating away at the underbelly of the state." Although many Southerners were considered able to read and write, many lacked proficiency to function effectively in society and the economy. As one participant in the *Halfway Home* report explained, "The strongest and most specific recommendation of the 1986 commission was to reduce rates of adult literacy significantly. But much of what is happening is still a war of words. The level of resources is

Halfway Home noted, "Tomorrow's jobs will change from rural to urban settings, from old manufacturing methods to technological services, from low to high skill, from local to international competition. This increasing complexity means that every link in the chain of education, from preschool through graduate program, will be under strains as the South struggles to raise the standard of living by raising everyone's standard of thinking."

not nearly at the level of attention. It's a good start but only a start." In fairness, the objective was not to eliminate adult functional illiteracy by 1992 but rather to begin to mobilize resources to reduce it.

In 1988, the Sunbelt Institute, a nonprofit bipartisan research organization formed by regional policymakers, requested that MDC examine the literacy problem in the South as it related to the region's economic growth and productivity. MDC concluded that the "demand for increased literacy skills across the spectrum of occupation presents a critical challenge for our region. In an era where competitiveness is a national priority, functional literacy is the South's number one competitiveness issue." In identifying a Southern literacy gap, MDC argued that the South remains the nation's poorest and least educated region, while economic changes such as "automation, competition from low-wage plants in developing countries, and rapid shifts in employment from traditional goods-producing industries to more technologically advanced trade and services have significantly heightened the literacy skills demanded of the workforce."

MDC's 1988 report led to the creation of the Southern Regional Literacy Commission, chaired by former UNC president William Friday (with former North Carolina governor Jim Holshouser as a member). In 1990, the commission called for a permanent Southern Literacy Forum and requested that MDC prepare an additional report outlining the literacy challenges facing the South. Friday had hoped that the forum could "build a regional consensus among leaders in government, industry, education, and the media on the nature and importance of the South's literacy challenge—and on the need for concerted action." At a historic education summit between the nation's governors and President George H. W. Bush in Charlottesville, Virginia, the Southern regional objective became a national goal: one of six education goals stated that "by 2000, every American adult will be literate and possess the knowledge and skills necessary to compete in a global economy."

MDC reported its findings to the 1992 Commission on the Future of the South, illuminating the human and economic impact of the literacy crisis facing the South. Community colleges were seen to have a role in combating the literacy problem. Many Southern leaders felt that community colleges must bring their expertise in remedial instruction and student retention to ensure steady progress and forestall student frustration and withdrawal. However, by 1998, MDC's *State of the South* was responding to challenges to the value of adult literacy training: The "outbreak of anti-remediation rhetoric is unfortunate considering the South's legacy of under-education. Some see remediation as an unnecessary and wasteful expenditure of funds for students who should have been properly prepared for postsecondary education by the K–12 system." The report noted that without this support, Southerners would have limited employment and earning opportunities. With the 1992 National Adult Literacy Survey, states received an opportunity to participate in and obtain valid statewide literacy data. However, at a cost of $300,000 per state, only Mississippi, Florida, and

Texas agreed to take part. This low level of participation posed challenges to assessing progress on eliminating young adult functional literacy in Southern states.

EDUCATION AND PREPARING A FLEXIBLE, GLOBALLY COMPETITIVE WORKFORCE

Because the South lagged in shifting its regional economy toward information and technology, the 1986 commission suggested that states must not only develop new members of the workforce but retrain those who would need new skills. The commission also set forth the objective of preparing a flexible, globally competitive workforce. *Halfway Home* noted, "Tomorrow's jobs will change from rural to urban settings, from old manufacturing methods to technological services, from low to high skill, from local to international competition. This increasing complexity means that every link in the chain of education, from preschool through graduate program, will be under strains as the South struggles to raise the standard of living by raising everyone's standard of thinking."

Shadows also highlighted the new labor market dynamics of international competition. As the MDC task force reported, "The manufacturing economy of the rural South is almost exclusively tied to traditional industries, most notably textiles and apparel. Unfortunately, the market share for domestic producers of these goods has been eroding rapidly in recent years as international competition has increased. While workers in the rural South earn wages below the U.S. average, they cannot compete with the wage rates in several [developing] nations." The emerging focus was on public schools, which would teach flexibility and creativity, and two-year postsecondary and higher education, which could prepare students for the future growth occupations.

By 2004, Southern Growth's *Future of the South* report set forth a new objective beyond just more skills—internationalizing preschool through college and adult education. As stated in *The Globally Competitive South*, "Most exporters say that the language of global business is that of the customer. Some will add that the language of global business is also English spoken well—slowly and precisely. Either way, our workforce needs additional communication skills, not only the functional ability to speak excellent English and a foreign language, but a solid grasp of world geography, history, cultures and geopolitics." The new goal was to have students and workers who were both highly skilled and globally competent, again raising the bar for Southern students.

More than two and a half decades after the consensus on education and economic development, the race was on among nations to create "knowledge-fueled innovation economies," and educational attainment remained front and center in preparing young adults for a globally competitive workforce.

Since the *Halfway Home* report, new global economic realities have meant that states' performance relative to each other no longer matters; instead, what is important is how a state's students compare to those in countries around the globe. As part of a 2008 advisory group cochaired by Georgia governor Sonny Perdue, Hunt, Riley, and West Virginia's Bob Wise, the National Governors' Association and the Council of Chief State School Officers collaborated to provide to states a road map for benchmarking their K–12 education systems to those of top-performing nations and to help states take steps to ensure that students receive an education that positions them to compete and innovate in the 21st century. In outlining steps toward moving from a nationally to a globally competitive education, the group called for an upgrade of state standards by adopting a common core of international standards in math and language arts for grades K–12.

By 2010, as part of a state-led effort coordinated by the National Governors' Association and the Council of Chief State School Officers, the collaborators released a set of education standards, known as the Common Core State Standards, to define the knowledge and skills students should obtain in kindergarten through 12th grade so that they will graduate from high school fully prepared for college and careers. As Perdue noted, "When American students have the skills and knowledge needed in today's jobs, our communities will be positioned to compete successfully in the global economy." The standards were informed by those of other top-performing countries. All Southern states except Virginia and Texas have adopted and agreed to implement the common core standards.

In 2011, North Carolina governor Beverly Perdue, chair of the Southern Regional Education Board, led a commission to focus on improving student achievement in the middle grades, considered by many experts to be the weakest link in public education. The board's Middle Grades Commission concluded that states' goals of raising high school graduation rates, improving students' readiness for college and careers, and improving opportunities for earning degrees would be in jeopardy unless the middle grades were successful. But many challenges remain for states in the region: too many ninth-graders are not ready for high school, and too few students graduate. Even fewer go to and finish college. Twenty-five years later, Southern policymakers and education leaders continue to agree on the need to improve and prioritize all points in the education pipeline.

HUMAN CAPITAL: MOVING OUT OF THE SHADOWS AND CLOSER TO HOME

A quarter of a century after *Halfway Home* and *Shadows*, the link between education and economic growth is clearer than ever. Many policy-oriented academics affirm the importance of human capital, particularly as obtained through formal education, to economic progress. Educational advancements can contribute directly to economic growth by increasing the human capital—and thus the productivity—of the workforce and indirectly by increasing the rate of innovation and adoption of new technologies. Historically minded economists conclude that a greater level of education tends to foster a higher rate of aggregate growth. In simple terms, investing in education results in higher levels of technology and productivity as well as rapid economic growth and higher standards of living. However, experts also warn that economic growth is "not simply a matter of investing in education" and that the benefits may distribute unequally. A higher standard of living does not necessarily translate into gains for all.

If we are to move out of the shadows and forward on the long road home, boosting participation in formal education and training and the overall level of educational

attainment will remain a major element of any effective human capital skills-formation policy. However, the overarching goal must not simply be more schooling but learning. For too many students, more schooling has not resulted in more knowledge and skills. Too many young adults are leaving school and entering the workforce without the knowledge, skills, or competencies necessary to adapt to a competitive and increasingly globalized economy. The driver of future economic progress will ultimately be what individuals learn, both in and out of school, from preschool through the labor market. Education is about learning not only reading, writing, and arithmetic but also socialization, communication, teamwork, critical thinking, and problem solving skills—invaluable assets that people need to function well at home, in their communities, and at work. Today's students will be expected to use information in complex ways and to maintain and enhance their literacy skills to adapt to ever-changing technologies. For other young adults and older workers, specific technical or vocational skills will also be important for success in the labor market.

Governments and other stakeholders across the South must continue to assess young adults' skills to monitor their preparedness for the challenges of the modern knowledge-based society. According to the new World Bank Group Education Strategy, any new strategy must focus on learning for a simple reason: "Growth, development, and poverty reduction depend on the knowledge and skills that people acquire, not just the number of years that they sit in a classroom. At the individual level, while a diploma may open doors to employment, it is a worker's skills that determine his or her productivity and ability to adapt to new technologies and opportunities." As we look toward to the future of the South, learning must not stop once young adults have any particular diploma in hand.

If our future workforce can make adjustments to the new skills demanded, economic growth will be enhanced. If our workforce is less flexible in its skill set, then growth will be slowed. Those who can adjust will be rewarded; others will be left behind. We need to embrace the 1980s bipartisan consensus on education and economic development and make sure that all our young adults are out of the shadows and finally home.

REFERENCES

Alexander, Lamar. "Time for Results: An Overview." *Phi Delta Kappan* 68 (1986): 202–4.

Clinton, Jim. *The Globally Competitive South (under Construction): 2004 Report on the Future of the South*. Research Triangle Park, N.C.: Southern Growth Policies Board, 2004.

Goldin, Claudia, and L. F. Katz. *The Race between Education and Technology*. Cambridge: Harvard University Press, 2008.

International Bank for Reconstruction and Development/The World Bank. *Learning for All: Investing in People's Knowledge and Skills to Promote Development: World Bank Group Education Strategy 2020*. 2011. http://siteresources.worldbank.org/EDUCATION/Resources/ESSU/Education_Strategy_4_12_2011.pdf.

National Commission on Excellence in Education. *A Nation at Risk: The Imperative for Educational Reform*. Washington, D.C.: U.S. Government Printing Office, 1983.

National Governors' Association. *Time for Results: The Governors' 1991 Report on Education*. Washington, D.C.: National Governors' Association, 1986.

Rosenfeld, S., E. Bergman, and S. Rubin. *After the Factories*. Research Triangle Park, N.C.: Southern Growth Policies Board, 1985.

Southern Technology Council. *Invented Here: Transforming the Southern Economy: The 2001 Report on the Future of the South*. Research Triangle Park, N.C.: Southern Growth Policies Board, 2001.

Vinovskis, Maris A. *The Road to Charlottesville: The 1989 Education Summit*. 1999. http://govinfo.library.unt.edu/negp/reports/negp30.pdf.

PROVIDING A NATIONALLY COMPETITIVE EDUCATION FOR ALL STUDENTS

Southern Education Progress: Half Past Halfway, *but* Still a Ways to Go

TRIP STALLINGS

INTRODUCTION: EDUCATION REFORM IN THE SOUTH BEFORE 1986

As early as the mid-1960s and particularly between 1977 and 1985, systemic educational reform was an integral part of Southern policy and politics. Indeed, a series of South-focused reports set the education reform agenda for the decades ahead.

Throughout the 1970s, Southern states lagged behind other states in educational funding per capita, educational standards, and teacher competency despite these reports' and other observers' recognition of persistent problems with student achievement, poor teacher quality, and teacher shortages. At the time of the first state-level omnibus education reform passage in Mississippi in 1982, every Southern state spent less on education than did states in other regions, and in Mississippi the per-pupil expenditure rate was just over half the national average ($1,090 versus $2,010). Among the states ranking lowest, Georgia, Mississippi, and South Carolina almost always were near the bottom. Yet after less than a decade of work, Southern states were leading the way nationally in educational reform. A critical period of activity from 1977 to 1985, often called the "first reform wave" and fueled by a swelling tide of depressing information about how students in America stacked up against students across the globe, led to fundamental shifts that helped to move the South halfway home by the time of the 1986 reports.

The reforms that followed were game-changers: across-the-board raises and incentive pay plans for teachers and principals; expanded and more rigorous curricula, especially in science and mathematics; a renewed focus on programs that offered opportunities for academically gifted and vocational students; increases in graduation standards; early childhood programs and compulsory kindergarten; and overall increases in state education funding.

PROGRESS AND PERSISTENT CHALLENGES IN SOUTHERN EDUCATION

Since the "Southern education governor" era, the South has continued to tackle some—but certainly not all—of the educational disparities identified before and during that reform. While progress has never been steady or even consistent across the region, several positive trends have emerged in education between 1986 and the present; however, multiple challenges persist, and new ones continue to arise.

In our current era of accountability, the tendency to associate educational progress with direct measures of academic attainment (for example, test scores) is understandable, but discussions of progress too often are limited solely to measures of this kind. A more complete picture of educational progress includes consideration of measures such as school completion, dropout, and college attendance rates along with assessments of a state's financial investment in education. In all of these areas, the South has shown promise—sometimes significant promise—since 1986, though that overall promise often continues to be limited by stagnation or declines in specific states or on specific measures. Three measures of note—Southern student academic achievement relative to the rest of the nation, educational attainment beyond high school, and Southern states' fiscal commitment to education—indicate that despite some persistent lags, the South has held its own relative to the rest of the nation since 1986 and in some cases has even taken the lead, though for every two steps forward there often has been one step back.

> Ensuring that *every* student in the South gains equitable access to educational opportunities is critical to the region's efforts to remain competitive not only academically but also economically on both the national and international levels.

ADVANCES IN ACADEMIC ACHIEVEMENT: NATIONAL ASSESSMENT OF EDUCATIONAL PROGRESS

While trends in student achievement as measured by individual state tests can be useful for tracking changes over time at the state level, inevitable differences in test format, scoring procedures, and scale prevent these changes from being comparable across states. Since the early 1990s, however, results from the National Assessment of Educational Progress (NAEP) have made such comparisons possible. The assessment was designed primarily to provide a means by which student achievement could be compared across states. Before its development, no standard nationwide testing system existed. Though the program was initiated in 1963 and rolled out in 1969, the negotiations to get the assessment off the ground resulted in an agreement that results would not be identified by state. Not until the mid-1980s did politicians—including Governors Lamar Alexander of Tennessee and Bill Clinton of Arkansas and the members of the Southern Regional Education Board—begin calling for ways to compare results across states, and in 1986, eight Southern states agreed to participate in state-identified experimental administrations of the assessment. During the 1990s, the assessments became common across all states.

Indeed, in mathematics, results in most Southern states have trended up since 1990, with Virginia always ahead of the national average and North Carolina and Texas frequently ahead. Reading scores since 1990 have remained largely flat nationwide, but Virginia and Kentucky consistently outpace the rest of the nation in this area, and Delaware, Florida, and Maryland are not far behind.

Growth in student achievement as measured by the NAEP has been relatively uniform across the region as a whole, but the picture is not all rosy. Despite years of gains, the majority of Southern states post scores that consistently lag behind the national average; several states, such as Mississippi and Louisiana, are often noticeably below the national average, and gaps between student achievement in the District of Columbia and national student achievement are especially pronounced. In particular, reading scores for older students have changed little since the introduction of an eighth-grade NAEP test (though the same also has been true for the nation as a whole). Persistent and large gaps remain in NAEP achievement scores for whites and minorities across the region.

Growth in Higher Ed Measures: The College-Going Rate

In every Southern state, the chance that a student will enter college by the time she or he is 19 has risen—sometimes

considerably—since the mid-1990s, and a higher proportion of 18- to 24-year-olds were enrolling in colleges at the end of the last decade than did so in the 1990s. Furthermore, of those students in Southern states who graduate from high school, more enroll in college each year, and since 1998, these states appear to have closed the gap between themselves and other states. However, while more Southern students advance to postsecondary education opportunities, more also are finding that those opportunities are harder to afford, and in one critical link in the chain—high school graduation—Southern states continue to lag the rest of the nation.

State Fiscal Commitment to Public Education: Per-Pupil Expenditures
Except for Maryland, Delaware, and the District of Columbia (which has a unique financing system), Southern states do not receive or collect as much total revenue per student (funding from federal, state, and local sources) as do states in other regions. Therefore, most Southern states historically have spent less per student than the average state. However, beginning in the 1980s, most Southern states increased their per-pupil expenditures at a rate that exceeded the national average, with Arkansas, Georgia, and South Carolina leading. Also, most Southern states historically have provided more state-level support for K–12 education than have other states (though this trend appears to be ending in Florida, Georgia, Louisiana, and South Carolina).

The recent financial crisis and the resultant burgeoning debts now faced by many Southern states, coupled with already-low revenues, imperiled this trend of high state support after the 2008–9 fiscal year, and Southern state commitment to education declined.

THE "TWO-SOUTHS" CHALLENGES AHEAD: SEPARATION, ISOLATION, AND POVERTY

Many of these longer-term trends are good news, but recent declines and persistent problem areas have put some of these trends in jeopardy. In addition, targets for education are not stationary, and the South thus still may not be much more than halfway home. For educational opportunities to flourish across the region in the years ahead, the South not only must overcome the remaining problems of the past 25 years but also must be prepared to address what might be characterized as emerging "two-Souths dilemmas." Even as educational opportunities improve across the South, gaps between students with the greatest and least access to those opportunities persist and in some cases are widening. Ensuring that *every* student in the South gains equitable access to educational opportunities is critical to the region's efforts to remain competitive not only academically but also economically on both the national and international level. In particular, the South must address the challenges of the growing divide between rural and urban educational opportunities, the impact of escalating poverty on education outcomes, and the complexity of educating all students in the face of an increasingly diverse population.

The challenges of rural education and poverty are not new for the South, and though rurality and poverty are not synonymous, they often go hand in hand in the region, with rates of student poverty persistently higher in rural school districts than in urban districts. Evidence continues to grow for the links among rurality, poverty, and educational outcomes, with several recent reports showing significant impacts of both factors on student achievement. In its most recent ranking of states that need to address rural education issues, the Rural School and Community Trust ranked Alabama, Mississippi, Oklahoma, South Carolina, Louisiana, North Carolina, Kentucky, Florida, and Tennessee in the top quartile, with the majority of the nation's highest-need rural counties located in these states. What *is* new for the South is that these linked challenges are now complicated by growing urbanization (the 2010 Census reveals that a record low of 16 percent of the population now lives in rural areas) and a consequent growing social and cultural divide. For example, even as overall wealth increases across the region, impoverished students are now the new majority in Southern public schools.

Teacher- and principal-preparation programs frequently fail to provide specialized instruction in the unique needs of students in rural areas, and the out-migration of rural students to urban areas to attend college or pursue other opportunities can leave their communities hard-pressed to provide the teachers and workers necessary to maintain equitable educational opportunities and healthy economies. Furthermore, growing discrepancies in the electronic resources available to students are likely to result in vastly different economic outcomes for rural and urban localities in the burgeoning digital marketplace.

Two final and not insignificant pieces in this puzzle are the challenges of a rapidly diversifying population—the presence of Latino students alone has almost single-handedly transformed the composition of many Southern school districts—and the complexity of ongoing segregation. While the legal desegregation battle may have ended well before 1986, de facto segregation remains across the South and in some instances may be increasing. Such segregation appears to be less pronounced at the district level (between schools within a district) than is often assumed, but classroom-level data in North Carolina suggest that segregation may be happening in different ways—via within-school tracking at the secondary level and even as a result of an increase in the presence of private schools in the South.

EDUCATION AND THE SOUTH, 2012 AND BEYOND

Tremendous momentum in educational reform had been building in the South in the years leading up to *Halfway Home* and *Shadows*, but the promising advances that pushed the South "half past halfway" toward many of the goals outlined in those documents appear to have stalled somewhat in the face of disappointing retreats and the emergence of new challenges that defy single-solution responses. As fields such as business and medicine have learned over the past decade, without a move toward nimble and dynamic approaches to reform that provide flexible, context-specific solutions, the South is likely to remain stuck short of its education goals.

Some indicators seem to show that the region is on the verge of addressing its 21st-century educational problems with 21st-century answers. In 2010, 7 of the 12 winners of U.S. Department of Education Race to the Top grants were Southern states (Delaware, the District of Columbia, Florida, Georgia, Maryland, North Carolina, and Tennessee). These four-year awards, totaling more than $2.4 billion across the region, fund a comprehensive range of initiatives designed to transform teacher and leader distribution and effectiveness, turn around underperforming districts and schools, provide professional development opportunities for educators, and improve content standards and assessments. What is most promising about these states' plans is not the nature of any given initiative funded by the grants (many of which on their own are not much different from previous efforts) but the fact that for the first time since perhaps the reform period 25 years earlier, the concept of comprehensive plans in which outcomes are intended to be more than just the sums of their parts has returned to center stage in the South.

Other emerging responses across the region show signs of a growing awareness of the need to move away from one-size-fits-all reforms. Many Southern states are using technology to expand access to courses of study previously available only in urban areas, with all but two states in the region maintaining virtual public schools. Florida's and North Carolina's virtual public schools are two of the country's largest, with more than 120,000 students enrolled in 2009–10. Florida, North Carolina, Texas, and Virginia in particular also are exploring the potential of total classroom conversions that provide laptops for every student. Beyond just enticing effective educators to relocate to hard-to-staff rural or underperforming schools (a well-worn reform that has generated mixed results at best), aggressive, incentives-based educator recruitment efforts now prepare those educators for the specific challenges they will face. Equally impressive is the growth of cooperation between higher education and K–12 education, often in the form of no-cost programs that blur the lines between high school and postsecondary education in rural areas. North Carolina's Learn and Earn program, for example, enables students to earn credits toward a college degree while still in high school through partnerships with local community colleges.

These advances notwithstanding, Southern educational reformers must face the sobering realization that in the end, education-specific solutions are not likely to be enough on their own. Without a doubt, these initiatives will continue to move the South in the right direction, and the funding provided by Race to the Top offers welcome financial support in the midst of lean economic cycles that have seen state education budgets cut repeatedly and sometimes deeply. But in the end, the Race to the Top grants represent less than 1 percent of the winning states' educational budgets, and many of these reforms may not differ radically enough from their predecessors to help the region turn the final corner. Perhaps the most important lesson learned over the past 25 years—and one that is again a familiar echo from a previous era—is that educational reform is only as successful as the reforms in other social arenas that support it. In the next 25 years, the South may be served best not by focusing more resources on education reform in isolation but instead by focusing on a reform agenda that recognizes education as only one of a number of interdependent strands.

REFERENCES

Clotfelter, C. T. "Private Schools, Segregation, and the Southern States." *Peabody Journal of Education* 79 (2004): 74–97.

Clotfelter, C. T., H. F. Ladd, and J. L. Vigdor. "Federal Oversight, Local Control, and the Specter of Resegregation in Southern Schools." *American Law and Economics Review* 8 (2006): 1–43.

Clotfelter, C. T., H. F. Ladd, and J. L. Vigdor. "Segregation and Resegregation in North Carolina's Public School Classrooms." *North Carolina Law Review* 81 (2003): 1463–1511.

Dahl, G., and L. Lochner. *The Impact of Family Income on Child Achievement*. Discussion Paper 1305-05. 2005. http://www.irp.wisc.edu/publications/dps/pdfs/dp130505.pdf.

Harris, A. "Mississippi Gropes for a Way to Get Schools 'Off Bottom.'" *Washington Post*, December 13, 1982, A1, A4.

Hawley, W. D. "Missing Pieces of the Educational Reform Agenda; or, Why the First and Second Waves May Miss the Boat." *Educational Administration Quarterly* 24 (1988): 416–37.

Johnson, J., and M. Strange. *Why Rural Matters 2009: State and Regional Challenges and Opportunities*. Arlington, Va.: Rural School and Community Trust, 2009.

Lacour, M., and L. D. Tissington. "The Effects of Poverty on Academic Achievement." *Educational Research and Reviews* 6 (2011): 522–27.

Mackun, P. J. *Population Change in Metropolitan and Micropolitan Statistical Areas: 1990–2003*. Washington, D.C.: U.S. Census Bureau, 2005. http://www.census.gov/prod/2005pubs/p25-1134.pdf.

Mackun, P. J., and S. Wilson. *Population Distribution and Change: 2000 to 2010*. Washington, D.C.: U.S. Census Bureau, 2011. http://www.census.gov/prod/cen2010/briefs/c2010br-01.pdf.

McDonnell, L. M., and S. H. Fuhrman. "The Political Context of School Reform." In *The Fiscal, Legal, and Political Aspects of State Reform of Elementary and Secondary Education*, ed. V. D. Mueller and M. P. McKeown. Cambridge, Mass.: Ballinger, 1986.

Peevely, G., and J. R. Ray. "The Relationship of Rurality and Education Accountability Outcomes." Paper presented at the annual meeting of the American Educational Research Association, Seattle, April 10–14.

Proceedings: Tenth Anniversary Conference of the Southern Growth Policies Board: Cooperative Growth Strategies for the 80's. Research Triangle Park, N.C.: Southern Growth Policies Board, 1982.

Southern Regional Education Board. *State Virtual Schools*. 2009. http://www.sreb.org/page/1331/state_virtual_schools.html.

Vinovskis, M. A. "Overseeing the Nation's Report Card: The Creation and Evolution of the National Assessment Governing Board (NAGB)." Paper presented to the National Assessment Governing Board, 1982.

Yen, Hope. "Rural U.S. Disappearing? Population Share Hits Low." Associated Press, July 27, 2011.

TABLES AND FIGURES

table 3.1a AVERAGE SCALE SCORES FOR MATHEMATICS, GRADE 4, 1992 TO 2009

	1992[1]	1996[1]	2000	2003	2005	2007	2009
Alabama	208	212	217	223	225	229	228
Arkansas	210	216	216	229	236	238	238
Delaware	218	215		236	240	242	239
D.C.	193	187	192	205	211	214	219
Florida	214	216		234	239	242	242
Georgia	216	215	219	230	234	235	236
Kentucky	215	220	219	229	231	235	239
Louisiana	204	209	218	226	230	230	229
Maryland	217	221	222	233	238	240	244
Mississippi	202	208	211	223	227	228	227
North Carolina	213	224	230	242	241	242	244
Oklahoma	220		224	229	234	237	237
South Carolina	212	213	220	236	238	237	236
Tennessee	211	219	220	228	232	233	232
Texas	218	229	231	237	242	242	240
Virginia	221	223	230	239	240	244	243
West Virginia	215	223	223	231	231	236	233
Nation (Public Schools)	219	222	224	234	237	239	239

[1] Accommodations were not permitted for this assessment.
Sources: U.S. Department of Education, Institute of Education Sciences, National Center for Education Statistics, National Assessment of Educational Progress (NAEP), 1990, 1992, 1996, 2000, 2003, 2005, 2007, and 2009 Mathematics Assessments;

table 3.1b AVERAGE SCALE SCORES FOR MATHEMATICS, GRADE 8, 1990 TO 2009

	1990[1]	1992[1]	1996[1]	2000	2003	2005	2007	2009
Alabama	253	252	257	264	262	262	266	269
Arkansas	256	256	262	257	266	272	274	276
Delaware	261	263	267		277	281	283	284
D.C.	231	235	233	235	243	245	248	254
Florida	255	260	264		271	274	277	279
Georgia	259	259	262	265	270	272	275	278
Kentucky	257	262	267	270	274	274	279	279
Louisiana	246	250	252	259	266	268	272	272
Maryland	261	265	270	272	278	278	286	288
Mississippi		246	250	254	261	262	265	265
North Carolina	250	258	268	276	281	282	284	284
Oklahoma	263	268		270	272	271	275	276
South Carolina		261	261	265	277	281	282	280
Tennessee		259	263	262	268	271	274	275
Texas	258	265	270	273	277	281	286	287
Virginia	264	268	270	275	282	284	288	286
West Virginia	256	259	265	266	271	269	270	270
Nation (Public Schools)	262	267	271	272	276	278	280	282

[1] Accommodations were not permitted for this assessment.
Sources: U.S. Department of Education, Institute of Education Sciences, National Center for Education Statistics, National Assessment of Educational Progress (NAEP), 1990, 1992, 1996, 2000, 2003, 2005, 2007, and 2009 Mathematics Assessments;

table 3.2 CHANGE IN PROSPECTS FOR COLLEGE, COLLEGE ENROLLMENT, AND COLLEGE AFFORDABILITY, EARLY 1990S TO 2008

	Chance for college by age 19		18- to 24-year-olds enrolled in college		Percentage of income a family needs to pay for one child at a community college	
	1990s	2008	1990s	2008	2000	2008
Alabama	37%	39%	32%	35%	20%	25%
Arkansas	36%	45%	24%	32%	11%	17%
Delaware	40%	45%	34%	36%	18%	26%
Florida	30%	32%	28%	33%	18%	25%
Georgia	35%	38%	23%	29%	16%	20%
Kentucky	34%	44%	28%	35%	19%	21%
Louisiana	29%	38%	27%	30%	18%	19%
Maryland	43%	48%	28%	32%	22%	23%
Mississippi	38%	45%	28%	32%	14%	20%
North Carolina	34%	43%	29%	33%	16%	22%
Oklahoma	39%	44%	36%	33%	18%	20%
South Carolina	25%	36%	26%	32%	18%	21%
Tennessee	32%	42%	26%	32%	19%	22%
Texas	29%	35%	28%	30%	15%	21%
Virginia	38%	46%	28%	35%	16%	21%
West Virginia	38%	42%	31%	39%	20%	29%
Tops in U.S.	58%	59%	50%	42%	10%	17%

Note: Data not available for District of Columbia.
Source: National Center for Public Policy and Higher Education. (2008). Measuring Up 2008: The National Report Card on Higher Education. http://measuringup.2008.higereducation.org.

table 3.3 PERCENTAGE OF HIGH SCHOOL GRADUATES GOING DIRECTLY TO COLLEGE, 1992 TO 2008

	1992	1994	1996	1998	2000	2002	2004	2006	2008
Other States	55.8	59.0	60.6	58.1	56.6	56.5	55.1	61.4	63.7
South	51.1	53.3	54.4	55.5	57.0	56.7	56.9	61.8	62.5
Change (Points)		2.2	1.0	1.2	1.4	-0.3	0.2	4.9	0.7
Gap	-4.7	-5.7	-6.2	-2.6	0.4	0.1	1.8	0.3	-1.2
Alabama	56.5	64.1	59.8	58	58	55.2	60.6	62.7	66.7
Arkansas	45.7	48.2	51.5	53.7	52.9	57.2	55.9	56.6	62.5
Delaware	57.7	65.1	66.5	62.2	59.9	40.8	54.4	64.1	66.2
Florida	45.4	49.2	50.3	49.5	57.5	55.4	53.5	60.2	58.8
Georgia	55.1	59.4	55.6	60.4	60.4	59.4	64	68.2	69.6
Kentucky	48.9	49.4	52.9	54.7	58.7	62.4	57.4	61.4	60.9
Louisiana	54.2	53.4	54.2	63	59.2	57.6	54.5	65.5	65.3
Maryland	55.9	55.2	58.2	57.6	54.7	56.5	58.7	65.6	62.9
Mississippi	61.9	68.6	63.5	59.7	63.4	65.1	59.9	76.1	77.4
North Carolina	50	51	53.8	64.5	65.4	63.6	64.3	65.6	66
Oklahoma	50.6	49.3	47.6	50.7	49.7	51.2	52.9	59.2	56
South Carolina	43.4	58.4	59.1	61.2	66.3	59.6	67	63.9	70.1
Tennessee	46.7	53.5	53.8	55.6	62.2	61.8	62	63.5	61.6
Texas	52.5	50.4	54.1	51.2	52.5	53.4	51.9	55.2	56.9
Virginia	51.7	53.3	54.5	56.1	53.1	54.4	57.6	67.2	68.7
West Virginia	49.1	49.5	50.1	53.4	52.4	54	53.3	57.8	59

Note: Number of first-time freshmen who graduated from high school in the past year from state X enrolled anywhere in the U.S. / Public and private high school graduates.
Sources: Tom Mortenson, Senior Scholar, Pell Institute for the Study of Opportunity in Higher Education in Washington, DC; The Mortenson Seminar on Public Policy Analysis of Opportunity for Postsecondary Education, http://www.postsecondary.org.

table 3.4 REVENUES PER STUDENT, ALL SOURCES, 1986–1987 TO 2008–2009

	86-87	93-94	00-01	07-08	08-09
All Other States*	4,322	6,420	9,093	12,706	13,819
Alabama	2,822	4,251	6,503	10,356	10,165
Arkansas	2,541	4,535	6,250	9,758	10,978
Delaware	4,548	6,484	9,701	13,792	14,738
D.C.	5,137	9,119	15,128	17,394	24,121
Florida	4,113	5,844	7,338	10,995	10,665
Georgia	3,202	5,368	8,437	11,319	11,478
Kentucky	2,577	4,875	6,773	9,848	11,342
Louisiana	3,039	4,507	6,810	11,543	12,701
Maryland	4,693	6,659	9,200	15,471	16,509
Mississippi	2,158	3,715	5,832	8,880	9,463
North Carolina	3,201	4,907	7,160	8,439	9,695
Oklahoma	2,876	5,095	6,475	8,539	9,496
South Carolina	3,248	4,972	8,059	10,913	11,632
Tennessee	2,523	4,212	6,283	8,535	9,252
Texas	3,708	5,195	7,506	9,749	10,688
Virginia	N/A	5,895	8,135	11,803	12,960
West Virginia	3,581	5,978	8,296	11,207	12,170

*All Other States = Revenue per student for all other states (estimated) — derived from total revenues for all non-Southern states divided by total enrollment for all non-Southern states

TREADING WATER: K-12 Educational Attainment *in the* South and North Carolina

LANCE D. FUSARELLI

INTRODUCTION AND BACKGROUND

Providing a nationally competitive education for all students by 1992—a key objective of the *Halfway Home and Long Way to Go* report—remains an elusive goal that has largely been unmet. While the South has changed in many significant ways since the 1980s, a systematic review of state performance data, including high school graduation and dropout rates, demonstrates that many Southern states, even comparatively wealthy higher per capita income Southern states, have made only marginal progress in education. The South generally and North Carolina specifically have a long way to go to produce well-educated students prepared to enter the workforce, job training, or higher education.

Shrinking state revenue, coupled with a severe and lingering economic recession, disproportionately affects those with the least amount of education. The unemployment rate of high school dropouts is more than three times that of those possessing bachelor's degrees or higher. States with high dropout rates produce citizens who earn significantly less over the course of their lifetimes, spend less, invest less, buy less expensive homes and autos, work less, and generate significantly less tax revenue per year than people who complete high school. Over time, the multiplier effect of low educational attainment is substantial and significantly hinders state, regional, and national economic growth.

HISTORICAL/EMPIRICAL TRENDS IN EDUCATIONAL ATTAINMENT

First the bad news. Not surprisingly, low-performing schools have a disproportionate number of dropouts; approximately 50 percent of the nation's dropouts are concentrated in fewer than 13 percent of high schools nationwide. Some states in the South have disproportionately large numbers of low-performing schools, defined as high schools in which 60 percent or less of freshmen progress to their senior year on time. One-fifth of high schools in North Carolina are among the lowest-performing in the nation; In terms of highest percentage of low-performing schools, North Carolina comes in 8th among the 12 Southern states in the study (Louisiana, Florida, Alabama, Georgia, South Carolina, North Carolina, Virginia, Tennessee, Mississippi, Arkansas, Oklahoma, and Kentucky). More than one-third of Florida's high schools are among the nation's lowest-performing schools, with fewer than 60 percent of freshmen progressing to their senior year on time and fewer than two-thirds of students graduating. Nearly half of South Carolina's high schools are considered among the country's lowest-performing, while Georgia comes in third in the study at 32 percent. One-fifth of the nation's lowest-performing high schools are concentrated in these three states. Conversely, only 4 percent of high schools in Arkansas are ranked among the lowest in the nation, followed closely by Oklahoma and Virginia, at 5 and 8 percent, respectively.

Nationally, only just over two-thirds of students graduate from high school. Of the 12 Southern states, North Carolina falls in the middle of the pack—tied for 6th in high school graduation rate. Eight of the 12 Southern states have graduation rates below the national average; 3 of the 5 states with the lowest high school graduation rates are located in the South—South Carolina, 55 percent; Louisiana, 57 percent; and Georgia, 58 percent—as well as 6 of the bottom 9. In the South, only Kentucky (+3 percent), Oklahoma (+3 percent), and Virginia (+1 percent) are above the national average.

Persistent gaps in educational attainment exist among ethnic and racial groups, and states are making little progress in reducing, let alone eliminating, those gaps. Of the 12 states in the study, Tennessee has the smallest gap between white and African American students in high school graduation rates (11 percent) while Oklahoma has the largest gap (26 percent); 6 of the 12 states have gaps of at least 20 percent. Particularly distressing is the fact that 3 of the 6 states with the lowest percentage of black males completing high school are located in the South. Louisiana, South Carolina, and Florida graduate only 38 percent of black males from high school, compared to Arizona at 81 percent and New Jersey at 74 percent. Only Michigan at 33 percent and Wisconsin at 36 percent graduate lower percentages of black males. Estimates show that dropouts cost the South between $3.5 and $34 million in lost state revenue each year.

Now for the good news. The South is not falling behind the rest of the country in educational attainment. It started behind and has been treading water since 1986, a pattern that is consistent with national trends. Nationally, the average college freshman graduation rate increased only 1 percent from 1990 (cohort began in 1986) to 2008. Eight of the 12 states in the study matched or beat the national trend: Florida (+1 percent), Kentucky (+1 percent), Mississippi (+1 percent), North Carolina (+2 percent), Oklahoma (+1 percent), and Virginia (+1 percent); Louisiana (+6 percent) and Tennessee (+5 percent) showed the greatest improvement in graduation rates from 1990 to 2008. Conversely, Alabama and Arkansas fell slightly (–1 percent), while Georgia (–5 percent) and South Carolina (–8 percent) declined significantly. Louisiana and Tennessee made the greatest improvements, having been among the furthest behind in 1986.

In addition, roughly half of the population age 25 and older in the rural South in 1986 had completed high school, compared to a national average of 67 percent. By 2008, the gap had closed considerably: 82 percent of the population age 25 and older had completed high school, close to the national average of 85 percent; however, only one state, Virginia, had a completion rate that exceeded the national average—and by only 1 percent. North Carolina's rate of 83 percent remains slightly below the national average. None of the 12 Southern states placed in the top half nationally; Virginia was highest at 31st; 7 of the 12 ranked in the bottom 11 states in high school completion, including Louisiana at 46th, Alabama at 47th, Kentucky at 48th, and Mississippi at 50th. North Carolina ranked 37th in the percentage of the population that completed high school.

Much of the recent policy debate about cuts in education spending concerns whether the South as a whole and North Carolina in particular will lose ground relative to other states/regions of the country. The data presented here suggest that is indeed the case; at best, the South is treading water, despite significant investment in education over the past two decades. From 1984 to 2008, total expenditures per pupil increased 69 percent nationally. All of the Southern states except Oklahoma and Florida met or exceeded this increase, and the average increase was 73 percent. Per-pupil spending in North Carolina increased 70 percent over this period, consistent with the national average. Some changes in state ranking in per-pupil expenditures occurred between 1984 and 2008; Florida dropped from 1st (highest) to 5th among the Southern states, while Virginia increased from 3rd to 1st in the rankings. Alabama made the greatest jump in the rankings, going from 12th place to 4th place; Oklahoma dropped the most, going from 2nd to 12th in the rankings. In 1984, North Carolina ranked 6th in per-pupil expenditures; in 2008, it had fallen to 11th.

The average national increase in the percentage of state and local taxable resources spent on pre-K–12 education was 3.8 percent; in the South, only Alabama, Arkansas, Georgia, Mississippi, and South Carolina exceeded the national average. North Carolina's percentage decreased slightly during the period. From 1991 through 2009, Arkansas experienced the greatest increase in ranking, moving up from 23rd to 10th in per-pupil state spending on pre-K–12 education, while Florida fell from 16th to 49th. North Carolina dropped from 15th to 23rd among states.

LOOKING BACK AND PROJECTING FORWARD

In sum, Southern states have made little progress in improving the educational attainment of students, and the South continues to lag the rest of the nation in the effort to produce well-educated students prepared to enter the workforce, job training, or higher education. In many respects, the South has never really caught up with the rest of the nation in terms of educational attainment. The South was one of the last regions of the country to extend schooling through high school. With a high percentage of African Americans, segregation and limited educational opportunities further hindered educational attainment and economic growth. Southern states' rural, agricultural makeup has also been offered as a partial explanation for lower levels of educational attainment. Several other social, demographic, and economic factors, including poverty and unemployment, play roles as well.

One thing is fairly certain: we cannot expect significant increases in spending on K–12 education in the next decade; per-pupil expenditures are expected to increase only 12 percent, much less than the 69 percent increase that occurred between 1984 and 2008. Further, as a result of migration and immigration, enrollment in public schools in the South is projected to increase by 13 percent through 2019; North Carolina (23 percent) and Georgia (16 percent) will see the greatest increases, while Mississippi (–5 percent) and Alabama (–2 percent) will see decreases in enrollment. The percentage of high school graduates in the South is projected to increase 13 percent by 2019, compared to only 9 percent in the West, with decreases of 14 percent in the Northeast and 7 percent in the Midwest. North Carolina (+33 percent) and Georgia (+22 percent) will lead the way. This enrollment growth will place additional burdens on local and state educational systems as they seek effectively to educate increasing numbers of students amid turbulent economic times.

RECOMMENDATIONS FOR POLICIES

If the South is to make significant improvements in increasing educational attainment and lowering the dropout rate, policymakers should focus limited resources on

- providing greater access to high-quality early childhood education programs, as research demonstrates that children who enter school behind leave school behind or drop out altogether;
- focusing on intensive literacy instruction in the early grades, as research demonstrates that reading comprehension is the key to success in all other subjects, including math and science, particularly in elementary school, with multiplier effects well beyond;
- redoubling efforts to improve teacher and school leader accountability by using value-added metrics directly tied to student performance to more effectively evaluate teachers and school principals and by streamlining the process for removing ineffective personnel;
- creating more incentives to reward highly effective teachers and school leaders;
- expanding the school day to increase instructional time, although since 11 of the 12 states are projected to have significant revenue shortfalls (including 4 states with 20 to 30 percent deficits), the current economic situation makes this recommendation impractical at the present time; and
- considering efforts to more effectively integrate social and health services into schools, especially in high-need, high-poverty areas, including efforts to streamline the bureaucracy so that disparate social service agencies can work more effectively together with schools.

While the historical effects of regional education attainment trends may linger, they cannot be used as an excuse for the South to continue to lag behind the rest of the nation in educational attainment, particularly given the increasingly globally competitive nature of the workforce and the needs of society in the next quarter century.

REFERENCES

"Diplomas Count." *Education Week*, June 10, 2010.

Fusarelli, L. D. "School Reform in a Vacuum: Demographic Change, Social Policy, and the Future of Children." *Peabody Journal of Education* 86 (2011): 215–35.

Goldin, C., and L. F. Katz. *The Race between Education and Technology*. Cambridge: Belknap Press of Harvard University Press, 2008.

National Center for Education Statistics. *The Condition of Education*, 1986–Present. Washington, D.C.: U.S. Government Printing Office, multiple years.

National Center for Education Statistics. *Projections of Education Statistics to 2019*. Washington, D.C.: U.S. Government Printing Office, 2009.

Assessing Progress: Almost Home?

DANIEL P. GITTERMAN AND BRITTANY L. REID

INTRODUCTION

The 1986 Commission on the Future of the South concluded that by increasing investment in education, "we can make Southern students nationally competitive as thinkers and doers in the next century's workplace, one which will be as intricate as a microchip and as far-reaching as the globe." Assessing progress on *Halfway Home*'s educational objectives, the 1992 commission asked, "Has there been genuine progress? The truth is we're not really sure how much has happened since 1986; we just know it's not enough." Their report, *Measure by Measure*, recommended that the Southern Growth Policies Board help states develop benchmarks "not only for individual states, but for the region as a whole. It's time for an assessment." Indeed, 25 years later, it's time for another assessment.

The appropriate metric is not just local, regional, and national but global. This essay assesses educational progress (educational attainment and young adult literacy) and places the measures in comparative perspective. These trends offer a big-picture analysis of educational progress and act as reasonable proxy for the stock of human capital in individual states, the region, and the nation. Human capital is the notion that individuals acquire skills and knowledge to increase their value in labor markets. Experience, training, and education are the mechanisms for acquiring human capital, with formal education being primary for most individuals. Education facilitates the acquisition of new skills and knowledge that increases productivity.

Educational attainment refers to the highest level of education that an adult has completed.[1] The percentage of state, regional, or national population over the age of 25 that has completed a given level of schooling is a way to show a subgroup's attainment of skills and knowledge associated with a particular level of education. A number of factors can influence levels of educational attainment, including the availability of educational services, the quality of those services, and the responsiveness of educational institutions to the particular needs of a state or region, affordability, regional or state culture, economic opportunity, and migration into and out of the state.

LEVEL OF EDUCATIONAL ATTAINMENT

First, we place the South in historical perspective. During the first half of the 20th century, the educational attainment of young adults greatly increased: more than half of that increase resulted from the rise in high school graduation rates. The increase in secondary schooling from 1910 to 1940 was extremely rapid, especially for regions outside the South. The South was a laggard: Young adults in most parts of the South had the lowest rates of high school enrollment in the nation, a finding that holds true even if one excludes the African American population, whose schooling rates were extremely low: The schooling rates for white young adults also stood far below those in other regions. The South continued to rank far behind the North and West in secondary schooling until the 1970s. U.S. regions also differed in their support for higher education. Southern states had a

---

[1] *Information on educational attainment of the U.S. population has been collected in every decennial Census since 1940. Since 1990, the Census has asked a single question: "What is the highest grade of school...has completed, or the highest degree...has received?" Between 1940 and 1980, respondents were asked a two-part question: What was the highest grade they had attended, and did they complete that grade?*

disproportionate share of the earliest public universities. While 57 percent of the higher education institutions founded before the Civil War were in the South, by the 1930s, almost all of the states reporting lower levels of college attendance were Southern.

Second, we offer a snapshot of educational attainment and place North Carolina's measures in a regional (and national) context. North Carolina ranked 37th in high school educational attainment, placing it in the bottom third of the nation (figure 3.1a). North Carolina ranked 26th in terms of bachelor's degree education attainment. Of the South (Census) region, only the District of Columbia, Maryland, Virginia, and Delaware did not rank in the bottom two quintile categories nationally, making the South far and away the lowest-ranking region in postsecondary school attainment (figure 3.1b). In 2009, only four Southern states had higher percentages than the U.S. average for population 25 years and older with at least "some college" education. More than half of North Carolina's population 25 and over had at least some college. Kentucky, Arkansas, and West Virginia trailed the pack in percentage of population attending some college.

Third, we use 1980 as the baseline for assessing educational progress since the 1986 *Halfway Home* report. In 1980, North Carolina and the South trailed the U.S. average in percentage of population 25 years and older with at least a high school diploma. By 2009, North Carolina and the South had converged on the U.S. average (85.3 percent) (figure 3.2). We also take a wider historical snapshot by assessing educational progress since 1940. Since 1940, North Carolina and the South had trailed the U.S. average

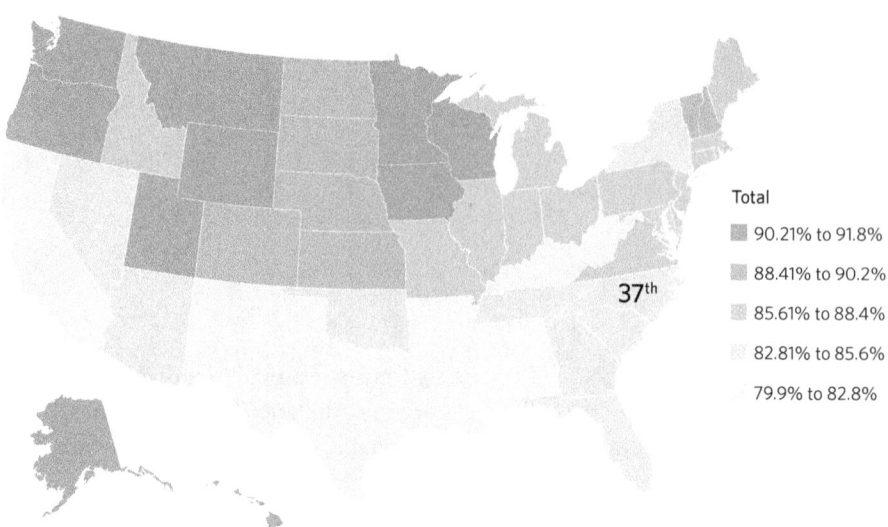

figure 3.1a HIGH SCHOOL ATTAINMENT, AGE 25+, 2009

Source: State of Metropolitan America *Interactive Indicator maps Brookings Institution Metropolitan Policy Program*

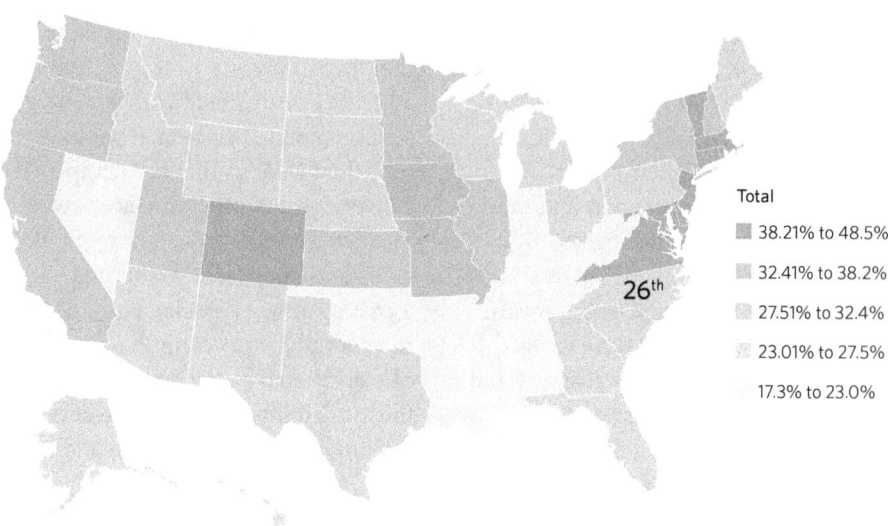

figure 3.1b BACHELOR'S DEGREE ATTAINMENT, AGE 25+, 2009

Source: State of Metropolitan America *Interactive Indicator maps Brookings Institution Metropolitan Policy Program*

in the percentage of the population over age 25 with a high school degree or more, with North Carolina falling significantly below the U.S. average in 1970. Yet by 2000, North Carolina and the South had almost converged on the national average of 80.4 percent (table 3.5). From 1940 to 2009, the South was consistently the lowest of the regions in percentage of the population over age 25 with a high school diploma or higher. Though the South remained a little behind, it almost reached parity with the Northeast in 2009 (table 3.5).

Between 1940 and 2009, North Carolina and the South also topped the national average in percentage of the population over age 25 with less than a high school education. In 2009, the South fell below the national average, although North Carolina still remained above average (a bad thing). With the exception of 1960 (when its rate was barely lower than that of the Northeast), from 1940 to 2009, the South led all other regions in percentage of the population over age 25 with less than a high school education. In 2009, the South converged on the other regions, trailing only the West.

YOUNG ADULT FUNCTIONAL LITERACY

Young adult literacy can be an alternative measure of human capital. *Halfway Home* reported that the South "has a high proportion of adults who lack the basic skills to participate fully in the modern world—one in four Southern adults never went beyond the eighth grade." A primary means of transmitting literacy to succeeding generations is the public school system. As many scholars have observed, the

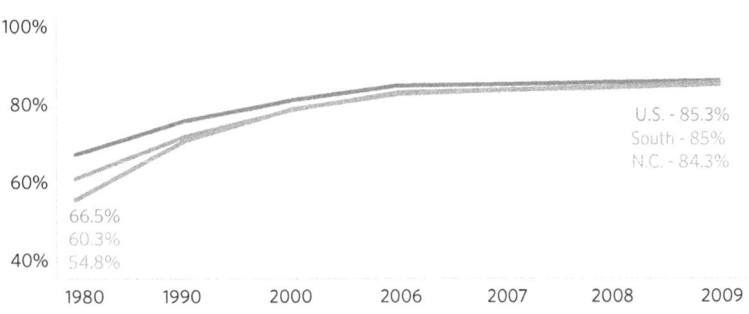

figure 3.2 PERCENTAGE OF POPULATION AGE 25+ WITH A HIGH SCHOOL DIPLOMA OR HIGHER: NORTH CAROLINA, SOUTH REGION, AND THE UNITED STATES, 1980 TO 2009

Source: U.S. Census Bureau, 1990 Census of Population, CPH-L-96; 2000 Census of Population, P37; "Sex by Educational Attainment for the Population 25 Years and Over," using American FactFinder; 2008 American Community Survey, R1501, "Percent of Persons 25 Years and Over Who Have Completed High School"; American Community Survey 2009 (1-Year Estimates) (SE), ACS 2009 (1-Year Estimates), Social Explorer; U.S. Census Bureau.

relationship between schooling and literacy is complex. Schooling increases an individual's skills, but individuals with higher proficiencies are more likely to extend their schooling. Functional literacy measures can give an important indication of the basic skills of the young adult population in individual Southern states, the region, and the nation.

In the early 1980s, no standard definition of literacy or illiteracy existed, although there was a consensus that literacy should not be defined as a particular level of educational attainment or any specific set of skills. However, educational attainment was the only proxy available to estimate functional literacy, reported by the Census as percentage of adults with eight years of education or less. The 1985 National Assessment of Educational Progress yielded the best literacy assessment—measuring young adults on scales of prose, document, and quantitative literacy. This focus on functional literacy addressed the issue of whether a young adult's reading and writing skills were sufficient to function in modern society.

With the 1985 Young Adult Literacy Assessment, experts defined literacy as "using printed and written information to function in society, to achieve one's goals, and to develop one's knowledge and potential." Using a combination of reading questions and questions designed to simulate literacy activities that adults encounter in daily life, the assessment surveyed the extent and nature of the literacy problem among young adults (a national sample of 21–25-year-olds). The report concluded, "Concerns over skill deficiencies come at a time when the nature of working is changing. The continued shift in our society from manufacturing to information and service job market, combined with foreign competition and accelerating technological change

▷ **Southern states had a disproportionate share of the earliest public universities. While 57 percent of the higher education institutions founded before the Civil War were in the South, by the 1930s, almost all of the states reporting lower levels of college attendance were Southern.**

has made literacy skills increasingly important for more workers."[3]

The 1992 National Adult Literacy Survey (NALS) and 2003 National Assessment of Adult Literacy (NAAL) produced estimates of prose, document, and quantitative literacy based on four performance levels: below basic, basic, intermediate, and proficient. The measure chosen to assess literacy is the percentage of adults lacking basic prose literacy skills. Some young adults who lack basic prose literacy skills are unable to read or understand any written information in English, while others can locate easily identifiable information in short, commonplace prose text but can do nothing more advanced. According to 1992 NALS results, young adults in the Northeast and South demonstrated lower proficiencies, on average, than adults living in the Midwest and West. No single variable accounted for the regional variations in literacy proficiencies. Only 12 states (including only Florida and Texas from the South) chose to participate in the 1992 State Adult Literacy Survey, designed to provide state-level results that were comparable to the national data. States that chose to participate in the State Adult Literacy Survey had to pay for any additional state-specific costs.

In 2003, only six states (and only Kentucky from the South) participated in the NAAL. The National Center for Education Statistics subsequently produced estimates of the percentage of adults lacking basic prose literacy skills for all U.S. states and counties in 1992 and 2003.[4] By comparing these results, we can assess progress in levels of young adult literacy.

In 1992 and 2003, only two states from the South, Delaware and Maryland, scored below the national average (a good thing) in population lacking basic prose literacy skills. In 2003, six Southern states reported that more than 15 percent of their young adult populations lacked prose literacy skills. Every state except Florida and Texas reported decreases in the percentage lacking basic skills (see figure 3.3a). North Carolina was higher than the U.S. average (14 percent) in 1992, but by 2003, both the state and the South slouched toward the U.S. average of 12 percent (figure 3.3b.) Figure 3.4 shows the 10 North Carolina counties with the highest percentages of the population lacking basic literacy skills; all had at least one in four young adults lacking basic skills.

AN EDUCATED AND "GLOBALLY COMPETITIVE" SOUTH

Halfway Home also recommended that Southern states prepare a "globally competitive" workforce, concluding, "Every link in the educational chain from preschool through graduate program can raise the standard of living by raising everyone's standard of thinking." So how does the United

---

[3] *The 1985 results suggested that young adults' educational attainment had a strong and positive relationship with performance on each of the three literacy scales. Each succeeding category of educational attainment was related not only to significantly higher performance but also to the magnitude of the difference. The average performance of young adults in the Northeast, Central, and West regions exhibited no significant differences, but the mean of the Southeast was significantly lower than that for each of the other three regions. Overall, adults with relatively few years of education were more likely to perform at lower literacy levels than those who completed high school or received some type of postsecondary education. Not surprisingly, the level of education attainment had the strongest relationship with demonstrated literacy proficiency. Young adults with higher levels of education were likely to demonstrate much higher average proficiencies than those with fewer years of schooling.*

[4] *In the 1992 NALS, 14.7 percent of adults lacked basic prose literacy skills; the 2003 NAAL put that number at 14.5 percent. In the 1992 NALS, 13.8 percent of adults scored below basic in prose literacy; the corresponding number in the 2003 NAAL was 13.6 percent. Estimates from the 1992 NALS offer a local, regional, and national snapshot of the condition of literacy, while the 2003 NAAL provides an updated picture of adult literacy skills, revealing changes over the preceding decade.*

figure 3.3a PERCENTAGE LACKING BASIC PROSE LITERACY SKILLS: SOUTH REGION, 1992 AND 2003

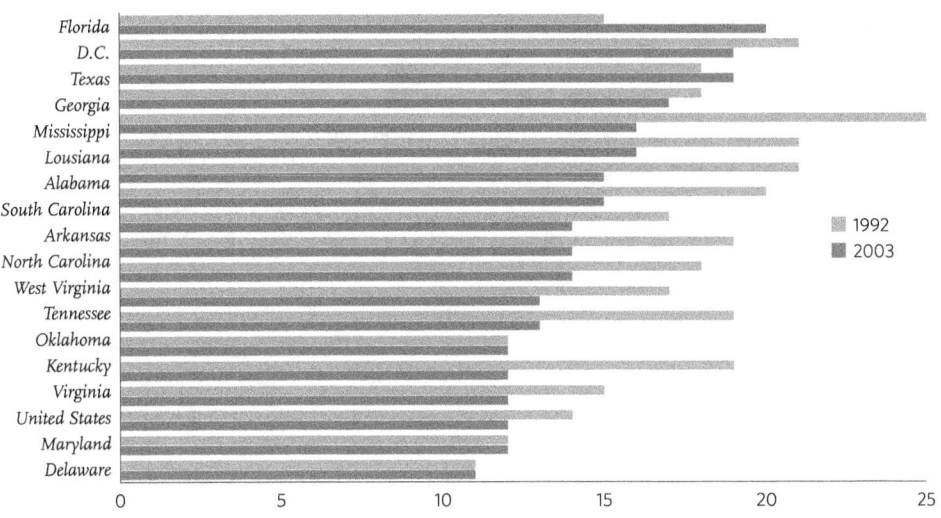

Source: U.S. Department of Education, Institute of Education Sciences, National Center for Education Statistics, 1992 National Adult Literacy Survey and 2003 National Assessment of Adult Literacy.

figure 3.3b PERCENTAGE LACKING BASIC PROSE LITERACY SKILLS: NORTH CAROLINA, SOUTH REGION, AND THE UNITED STATES, 1992 AND 2003

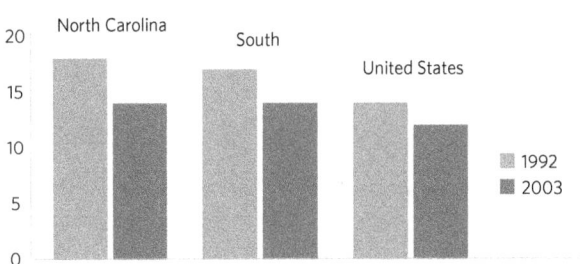

Source: U.S. Department of Education, Institute of Education Sciences, National Center for Education Statistics, 1992 National Adult Literacy Survey and 2003 National Assessment of Adult Literacy.

figure 3.4 HIGHEST NORTH CAROLINA COUNTIES: PERCENTAGE OF THE POPULATION AGE 25+ LACKING BASIC PROSE LITERACY SKILLS, 2003

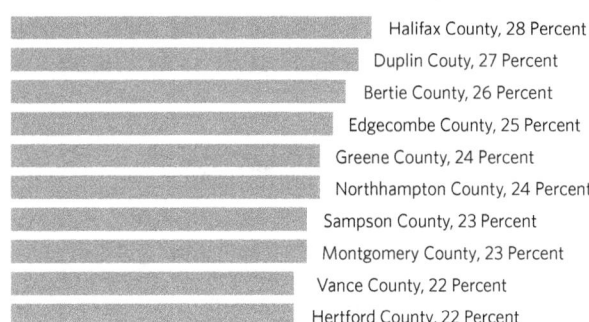

Source: U.S. Department of Education, Institute of Education Sciences, National Center for Education Statistics, 2003 National Assessment of Adult Literacy.

States compare globally in terms of levels of educational attainment? Of all of the countries in the Organization for Economic Cooperation and Development (OECD), the United States ranked second-highest, behind Norway, in percentage of population over age 25 with a bachelor's degree or higher in 2008. The South and North Carolina ranked significantly higher than the average (figure 3.5).

How does the United States compare globally in terms of levels of adult literacy? The OECD Program for International Student Assessment reports measures of international literacy of 15-year-old students in reading, mathematics, and science (based on a 1,000-point scale). The United States scored slightly higher than the OECD average for 15-year-old students on the combined reading literacy scale in 2009 but still trailed 13 of the 34 countries (figure 3.6). In 2009, the United States scored below the average for 15-year-old students on the combined mathematics literacy scale (see 3.6) and just above the average on the combined science literacy scale. Sixteen countries reported higher scores than the United States (figure 3.6).

CONCLUSION: ALMOST HOME?

Between 1940 and 1990, the South made significant educational progress: the percentage of the population with a high school degree or higher increased from 20.3 to 60.2 percent in the region, compared to 24.5 to 66.5 percent for the United States as a whole. By 2009, 85 percent of South's total adult population had obtained at least a high school diploma, in line with the national average of 85.3 percent. By the 1980s, therefore, the South and North Carolina were indeed halfway home, having increased the 19 percent rate of 1940 to 54.8 percent. By 2009, the region and state had continued to progress on the long road home, reaching 84.3 percent.

So, are we almost home? We don't think so. The most recent snapshot of the percentage of the population with less than a high school education suggests the hard work ahead. Almost 16 percent of North Carolinians cannot lay claim to a high school diploma. Moreover, in seven Southern states, more than 17 percent of the adult population lacks a high school degree. And in today's globally competitive economy, where there is a premium on a postsecondary education, only about 25 percent of the South's adult population reports obtaining a college degree. There is plenty of work still to be done.

Many observers emphasize the importance of human capital, particularly as gained through formal education, to economic progress. Indeed, policy-oriented social scientists have reached a consensus that education is an important determinant of individual earnings as well as economic growth. The amount of education an individual receives affects not only earnings but also the quality of employment. Moreover, although educational attainment has a positive effect on workers' earnings, the types of knowledge required in an occupation also play an important role in shaping future labor market success. Because human capital is multifaceted and includes a complex set of human attributes, the stock of human capital held by individuals is hard to assess precisely with any quantitative measure. Thus, the level of educational attainment is at best a proxy for the component of the human capital stock obtained through formal education.

By focusing on level of educational attainment and the receipt of a high school or college degree, we emphasize how long a student spent acquiring human capital as opposed to exactly what he or she knows. As a recent report put it: "What d'ya know? We toss out this casual greeting all the time, not really inviting a serious response." What do you know? How we answer it—as a state, as a region, as a nation—holds the key to future progress. A formal education can serve as the foundation for productive work. Job experience and training can build on it. But learning cannot stop once we have any diploma in hand.

The amount of education an individual receives affects not only earnings but also the quality of employment.

REFERENCES

Goldin, Claudia, and Lawrence F. Katz. "Why the United States Led in Education: Lessons from Secondary School Expansion, 1910 to 1940." *Journal of Economic Perspectives* 13 (1999): 37–62.

Schultz, Theodore W. "Investment in Human Capital." *American Economic Review* 51 (1961): 1–17.

Southern Growth Policies Board. *Measure by Measure: The South Will Lead the Nation.* Research Triangle Park, N.C.: Southern Growth Policies Board, 1992.

What D'Ya Know? Lifetime Learning in Pursuit of the American Dream. Dallas: Federal Reserve Bank of Dallas, 2004.

TABLES AND FIGURES

table 3.5 PERCENTAGE OF THE TOTAL POPULATION AGE 25+ WITH A HIGH SCHOOL DIPLOMA OR HIGHER: SOUTH REGION, 1940 TO 2009

LOCATION	1940	1950	1960	1970	1980	1990	2000	2009
United States	24.5	34.3	41.1	52.3	66.5	75.2	80.4	85.3
Northeast	24.0	35.7	41.0	52.9	67.1	76.2	81.6	88.3
Midwest	25.0	35.4	41.7	53.7	68.0	77.1	83.5	88.9
South	20.3	26.7	35.3	45.1	60.2	71.3	77.7	85
West	34.8	45.6	50.8	62.3	74.5	73.7	79.9	87.9
Alabama	15.9	21.9	30.3	41.3	56.5	66.9	75.3	82.1
Arkansas	15.1	21.5	28.9	39.9	55.5	66.3	75.3	82.4
Delaware	23.9	34.8	43.3	54.6	68.6	77.5	82.6	87.4
D.C.	41.2	50.2	47.8	55.2	67.1	73.1	77.8	87.1
Florida	26.6	35.8	42.6	52.6	66.7	74.4	79.9	85.3
Georgia	17.4	20.8	32.0	40.6	56.4	70.9	78.6	83.9
Kentucky	15.7	22.3	27.6	38.5	53.1	64.6	74.1	81.7
Louisiana	17.7	22.5	32.3	42.2	57.7	68.3	74.8	82.2
Maryland	21.1	32.1	40.0	52.3	67.4	78.4	83.8	88.2
Mississippi	16.2	22.0	29.8	41.0	54.8	64.3	72.9	80.4
North Carolina	19.0	20.9	32.3	38.5	54.8	70.0	78.1	84.3
Oklahoma	24.5	33.8	40.5	51.6	66.0	74.6	80.6	85.6
South Carolina	18.4	19.0	30.4	37.8	53.7	68.3	76.3	83.6
Tennessee	18.1	24.6	30.4	41.8	56.2	67.1	75.9	83.1
Texas	24.7	30.7	39.5	47.4	62.6	72.1	75.7	79.9
Virginia	21.6	29.4	37.9	47.8	62.4	75.2	81.5	86.6
West Virginia	17.8	24.9	30.6	41.6	56.0	66.0	75.2	82.8

Source: U.S. Census Bureau, Decennial Census of Population, 1940–2000; American Community Survey 2009 (1-Year Estimates) (SE), American Community Survey 2009 (1-Year Estimates), Social Explorer; U.S. Census Bureau.

figure 3.5 PERCENTAGE OF THE POPULATION AGE 25+ WHO HAVE ATTAINED A BACHELOR'S DEGREE OR HIGHER

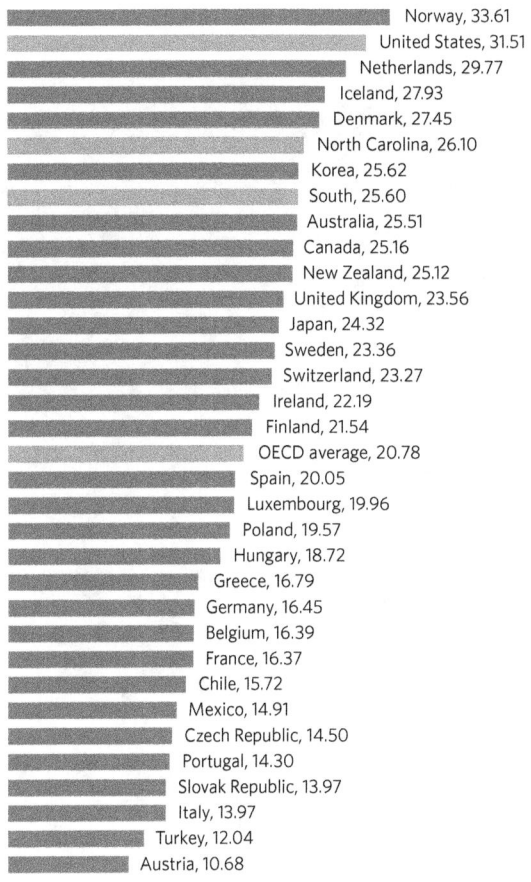

Source: U.S. Census Bureau, 2008 American Community Survey and OECD Fact Book 2009

figure 3.6 AVERAGE SCORES OF 15-YEAR-OLD STUDENTS ON COMBINED READING, MATHEMATICS, AND SCIENCE LITERACY SCALE

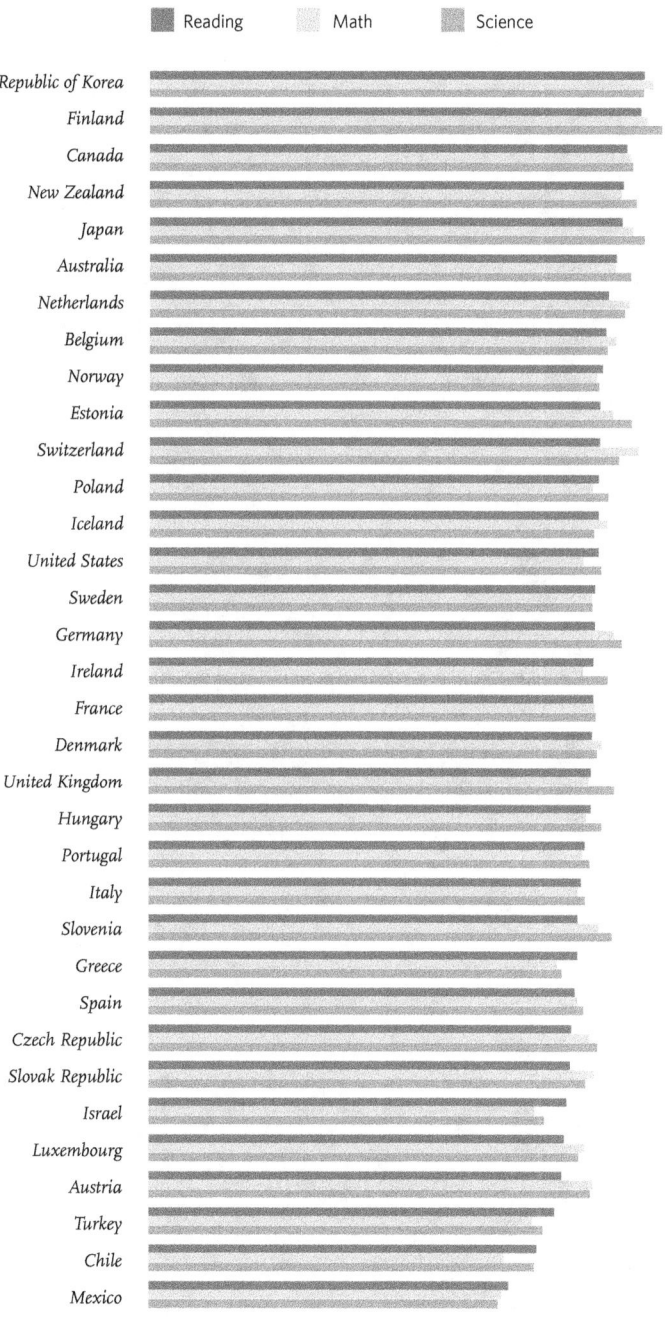

Source: OECD, Program for International Student Assessment 2009: What Students Know and Can Do—Student Performance in Reading, Mathematics, and Science, Vol. 1.

PREPARING A FLEXIBLE, GLOBALLY COMPETITIVE WORKFORCE

Toward a "Globally Competitive" Southern Workforce

PATRICK J. CONWAY AND DANIEL P. GITTERMAN

INTRODUCTION

In North Carolina and throughout the South, globalization has increased competition for jobs as workers around the world participate in the constant flow of goods, services, and information. The growth of a global economy can be seen in reduced trade barriers, increased trade, highly mobile capital, and rapid transmission of technology across national lines. Back in 1986, the Commission on the Future of the South set forth the regional objective: "preparing a flexible, 'globally competitive' workforce" by 1992. As the *Halfway Home* report diagnosed the problem; "A flash-flood of change rushing over the South has left many workers stranded. The opportunity offered by world markets is balanced by the challenge of world competition—it is urgent that the Southern people recognize their interdependence with one another and the world." In preparing young adults for an uncertain labor market, the commission called on states to invest in programs to "prepare students for occupations while helping them learn and apply basic skills." Over the past 25 years, we have come to understand that a new "globally competitive" workforce requires Southern workers with higher skills than in the past.

The working definition of a "globally competitive" workforce has changed over time, and it includes ever-increasing skill levels. The term *knowledge-based economy* has also emerged in recognition of the place of knowledge and technology in modern Southern regional economies. Almost every report of future developments in the labor market, including the 2009 President's Council of Economic Advisers report, highlights the preparations necessary to develop this "well-trained and highly skilled" 21st-century workforce. Introducing his National Graduation Initiative, President Obama reaffirmed the goal of ensuring that we are educating and preparing Americans for 21st-century jobs in a global economy.

Key questions remain since the 1986 *Halfway Home* recommendation: What is a "flexible, globally competitive" workforce, and how do we prepare one? The 2002 Southern Growth Policies Board (SGPB) *Future of the South* report concluded that "while the demands of the knowledge economy for educated, skilled, flexible workers have grown exponentially, the South has made only incremental progress in improving its workforce." By 2003, the SGPB's newly formed Southern Global Strategies Council recommended "a pattern of actions that will lead to a rational, policy-based approach to creating a globally educated, engaged, and competitive South." The council called on all Southern states to teach the future workforce the skills and instill the confidence needed to interact productively with people from other countries, get more students through postsecondary education, and encourage colleges and universities to reexamine their mission statements and strategic plans in light of the new global challenges and opportunities. Public policies will need more emphasis on upgrading human capital by promoting access to a range of skills.

This essay offers a typology of a "globally competitive" worker (or workforce) and examines what role public policy can play in preparing a critical mass of what we call "globally ready" students and workers. It is difficult to argue with this aspiration for all North Carolinians, for all Southerners, and for all Americans: Everyone, given the opportunity, will choose to be "globally competitive," and policymakers and educators will attempt to prepare adaptable, "globally ready" workers for this uncertain future. The 2007 University of North Carolina Tomorrow Commission recommended that "UNC should educate its students to be personally and professionally successful in the 21st century, equipping them with the tools they will need to adapt to an ever-changing world, and should enhance the global competitiveness of its institutions and their graduates." The North Carolina Board of Education affirmed a similar goal with its mission: "Every public school student will graduate from high school globally competitive for work and postsecondary education and prepared for life in the 21st century." But what does the goal of a "globally competitive" or "globally ready" workforce really mean?

THE TYPOLOGY AND VARIETIES OF A "GLOBALLY COMPETITIVE" WORKFORCE

Understanding the Metaphor: The Globally Competitive Worker
Policymakers use *globally competitive worker* metaphorically: In nearly all cases, Southern workers do not compete directly for employment with workers from foreign countries. However, the phrase invites a thought experiment: Suppose we take a high school graduate from North Carolina and drop her into a competition for employment in France, Brazil, or China. Will she get the job?

Setting aside language difficulties or requirements, the employer will weigh our North Carolina applicant on two dimensions. First, how productive will the applicant be in the workplace? Second, what wage is the applicant demanding? If the first is high enough or the second low enough, our North Carolina applicant is "globally competitive" and will secure the job.

Making a "Globally Competitive" Product
It is rare for a North Carolina worker to compete directly in a foreign workforce, but workers across the South always have competed to secure and to keep their jobs. The Southern workforce now competes globally through the goods and services it produces. If a local plant cannot produce a globally competitive product, it will shut down. If there is no local plant but there is the opportunity to produce a globally competitive product, a plant will be built and jobs created—perhaps by a foreign investor. International trade theory teaches us that a globally competitive product is defined at the firm level. Those that are competitive, ceteris paribus, will have either a price advantage over equal-quality competing goods or a quality advantage over similarly priced competitors.

Given the choice, workers will prefer to work for firms with "globally competitive" products attributable to a quality advantage. The reason is simple: Firms with a price advantage can only maintain it in the face of increased competition by lowering product price, a situation that puts downward pressure on wages. Firms with a quality advantage are less susceptible to this pressure, as their quality advantage makes their goods less substitutable for competing products. The SGPB made this point early and often. The South originally grew as a manufacturing base through its promise of lower production costs: lower wages, nonunion workplaces, lower business taxes. This promise attracted firms wishing to maintain a price advantage and promised for the future a scenario of wage compression should these firms face increasing global competition. The SGPB counseled Southern states to assist firms in establishing quality advantages and in becoming less reliant on price-based competition.

The Worker's Role in Making a "Globally Competitive" Product
Global competition sets a maximum price at which the firm can sell its product as currently configured. This also sets limits on what the firm can pay to its workers. Consider a producer of UNC–Chapel Hill Tarheel T-shirts. The maximum sales price may be one dollar per shirt, of which 50 cents is paid for yarn, elastic, and other inputs. Normal profits, rental, and back-office expenditures take up about 20 cents of the price. That leaves 30 cents per shirt to compensate labor.

This situation disciplines the firm but does not preclude increasing labor compensation. The first option for raising compensation is by raising worker productivity. If one worker at the firm can produce 20 shirts per hour, $6 per hour is available for compensation. If another worker can produce 60 shirts per hour, then $18 per hour is available for compensation. As a general rule, more productive workers can be paid more. The second option for raising compensation is through increasing the quality of the product. If the T-shirt can be differentiated from others, it will command a higher price—say, $1.20 per unit. This higher price also will increase the share per unit available for compensation.

What Worker Skills Translate into Higher Productivity?

Higher-productivity workers are critical to success of a "globally competitive" firm given current U.S. wages: Such workers are "globally competitive." A worker's "productivity" is not a readily observable characteristic; it depends on the worker's background and experience and how they match with the firm's productive needs. The worker's education and training have not taught productivity but have taught occupations and skills; linking the two is crucial to understanding the globally competitive worker. The 2009 Council of Economic Advisers report summarizes recent research linking productivity with occupations and skills and establishes an important historical regularity.[1] Declining (and by implication low-productivity) industries are those that are more likely to employ workers to do routine tasks. Growing (and by implication high-productivity) industries are significantly more likely to employ workers in nonroutine tasks. Thus, we prepare globally competitive workers by providing them with the skills needed effectively to perform these nonroutine tasks. Doing so has a range of implications for state policy.

Identifying the Skills of a Globally Competitive and Globally Competent Worker

Many observers suggest that building a globally competitive workforce depends on an identification of the basic skills required for a globally ready worker. According to Michael Porter, a globally competitive workforce has the "knowledge, skills, attitudes, and behaviors to continually adapt to ever-changing and escalating labor market requirements." Globally competitive workers must have the ability to integrate and apply their academic, technical, and practical knowledge and skills to solve real-world problems; to

continue learning in formal and informal ways throughout their lifetimes on the job, in schools, and in their communities; and to interact effectively with other people as customers, coworkers, and supervisors. The knowledge and skills required to improve one's global competitiveness will differ from industry to industry and with the level of sophistication of the goods and services being produced.

Indeed, employers demand workers who can think critically and solve problems. These job-based educational requirements reflect a need for highly skilled workers who can perform complex, ever-changing tasks. Evidence indicates that both cognitive and noncognitive skills affect labor market outcomes. To define cognitive skills, it is important to know that they include a wide variety of abilities. These abilities are necessary for analyzing sounds and images, recalling information, making associations between different pieces of information, and maintaining focus on a given task. These skills include literacy, numeracy, and an ability to solve abstract problems. Although "interactive" skills, such as effective communication and the ability to work well with others, have not traditionally been highlighted or perhaps valued by educators, there is growing awareness of their importance for young adult success.

Economist James Heckman suggests that academic discussions of skill and skill formation almost exclusively focus on measures of cognitive ability and ignore

---

[1] The Council of Economic Advisers report defines "routine" tasks as those with repetitive demands on the worker: for example, repeating a task on an assembly line. In contrast, "nonroutine" tasks are those that can vary and require creativity in thought during the course of a day on the job: for example, a software engineer or a production worker responsible for varying the product to fit individual demands. In the empirical results reported, declining industries rely significantly more heavily on routine tasks, while growing industries rely more intensively on nonroutine tasks. Similarly, Oldenski (2010) reports the results of comparing export firms with those that outsource production. Those firms choosing to export their products had a higher intensity of nonroutine tasks, and those firms choosing to set up foreign plants had a higher intensity of routine tasks. The top 10 occupations ranked by nonroutine tasks are services (export) industries; the bottom 10 occupations are drawn from traditional (import-competing) manufacturing.

noncognitive skills. Researchers, however, have suggested the importance of noncognitive skills in the labor market, including characteristics across multiple domains (social, emotional, personality, behaviors, attitudes) not included under cognitive skills. These noncognitive skills include work habits such as effort, discipline, and determination; behavioral traits such as self-confidence, sociability, and emotional stability; and physical characteristics such as strength, dexterity, and endurance. Globally competitive skills are those combinations of cognitive and noncognitive skills used to accomplish specific tasks.

Beyond just specific skills, other observers conclude that we also need to ensure that our high school (and college) graduates are globally competent. This global competence skill would include knowledge of other world regions, cultures, languages, economies, and global issues; the ability to work in cross-cultural teams; the ability to assess information from different sources around the world; and respect for other cultures. As former North Carolina governor Jim Hunt concluded, "If we do not reinvent education for a new era, our children will simply not be able to compete in the global economy. As never before, education must prepare students for a world where the opportunities for success require the ability to compete and collaborate on a global scale." In sum, public education systems will need to adapt to these changes so that they can produce the skilled, globally informed citizens needed in this environment.

Preparing Workers for a "Globally Secure" Occupation?
Recent policy debates about the negative effects of offshoring have introduced the idea of a "globally secure" worker. This worker is one whose job is protected from foreign competition as a result of the lack of international competition in the product she produces. This is viewed as an alternative to the "globally competitive" worker.

International trade economists typically conceptualize the world's goods and services as falling into one of two categories: tradable or nontradable. As economist Alan Blinder explains, traditionally, any manufactured item that can be put in a box and shipped was considered tradable, while anything that cannot be put in a box, such as services, or was too heavy for shipping, such as a home, was thought of as nontradable. At any point in time, the available technology—especially transportation and communications technologies—largely determines which goods and services are easy to trade internationally and which are difficult or impossible to trade. An interesting policy question follows: Can we prepare our workers for jobs that are "globally secure"?

The logic of foreign offshoring, an extension of specialization according to comparative advantage, suggests that the answer is no. As Blinder concludes, "Because technology is always improving and transportation is becoming cheaper and easier, the boundary between what is tradable and what is not is constantly shifting. And unlike comparative advantage, this change is not kaleidoscopic; it moves in only one direction, with more and more items becoming tradable." Because packets of digitized information can play the role that boxes used to play, many services are tradable, and many more will become so. But as the domain of tradable services expands, many service workers also will have "to accept the new, and not very pleasant, reality that they too must compete with workers in other countries. And there are many more service than manufacturing workers." Blinder predicts that jobs that are "globally secure" will dwindle in number over time. The more educated will not be the more "globally secure"—the most offshorable jobs include high-skill and low-skill jobs, and many of the most secure will be the most basic and mundane.

State industrial recruitment policies have faced the difficulty of defining secure jobs for some time—What is unique about the state that will tether jobs to our location? Answering this question has proved a difficult except in the area of tourism-related jobs. Those lessons are relevant here—there are few globally secure jobs, and aside from tourism, it is futile to design state policies to promote such jobs.

Designing a "Globally Competitive" Education and Training Policy
In *Halfway Home*, the commission made several recommendations for creating a globally competitive workforce, concluding, "Every link in the educational chain from preschool through graduate program can raise the standard of living by raising everyone's standard of thinking." In the intervening years, we have learned more about what we call globally ready workers. This learning leads to a number of new recommendations, divided here by level of education:

- Early investment in children through universal preschool programs is an important common feature in effective public policies to build human capital. An investment made while a student is young pays repeated benefits over a lifetime, as the future worker builds on the strengths and skills he or she has developed during childhood.

- Primary and secondary schools can create globally ready students by teaching and practicing the skills that are needed to perform nonroutine tasks. While schools cannot teach creativity, they can provide and enhance opportunities for students to apply principles they have learned to new, different situations.

- On their own, workers are generally unable to generate high and rising productivity in their firms. High and rising labor productivity is observed when labor is using effective complementary inputs, such as high-tech machinery and information technology. Schools must provide the math and science training necessary for workers to understand and use effectively these complementary inputs. It is also important where possible to provide hands-on training with these productivity-enhancing tools.

- Community colleges in the South have taken on the dual role of providing technical training in specific occupations and of providing additional education and retraining for those with outdated or insufficient skills.[2] For students to become globally ready, community colleges must
    + offer occupational courses in those occupations intensive in nonroutine tasks;
    + structure curricula in these courses to stress those nonroutine tasks; and
    + build group problem solving into the curriculum, because creativity, innovation, and increased productivity in the workplace are often the product of redesigning the ways in which workers interact, and this interaction is a skill that should be practiced.

- Universities also have a responsibility in creating these skills. They must
    + provide repeated opportunities for nonroutine problem solving to promote and foster adaptive expertise, cognitive flexibility, creativity, and innovation;
    + avoid developing a single math and a single writing curriculum but rather uncover themes and patterns that lead to measurably stronger student learning; and
    + support curricula that bring students to high levels of cognitive development by exposing them to real-world problem solving.

[2] Community colleges also have a third important role, providing an alternative set of entry courses toward a university degree. We address this role in the context of universities.

CONCLUSION: PREPARING ADAPTABLE, GLOBALLY READY STUDENTS AND WORKERS

For decades, there has been a remarkably simple conclusion for public policy: The more educated worker is the more "globally competitive" worker. Indeed, the positive link between schooling and productive skills is not perfect but remains a starting point for consideration. However, too many people assume that the critical labor-market divide in the new global economy is (and will remain) that between highly educated people, who will flourish under globalization, and less-educated people, who will suffer. We disagree. The South's efforts to encourage a "globally competitive" workforce must focus on particular skills and not just on the level of education attainment. Moreover, our formal education system must produce graduates with knowledge and skills relevant to market demand. This trend is a powerful argument for aligning public-school curricula with labor-market needs.

> The South's efforts to encourage a "globally competitive" workforce must focus on particular skills and not just on the level of education attainment.

Thus, we offer a clarification of the popular "higher educational attainment for global competitiveness" hypothesis: The type of specific skills facilitated by educational attainment will matter. Given the wide range of knowledge and skills that are important to job performance, the number of years of formal education provides too simplistic a view of human capital. Research findings show that although educational attainment has a substantial positive effect on the earnings of workers, the types of knowledge required in an occupation play an equally important role. So the answer is simple: To create a "globally ready" workforce, improve the nonroutine cognitive skills associated with high-performing occupations.

Skills for nonroutine employments and jobs with in-person skills will remain the most globally secure. For children and young adults, it will be important to define the curriculum for primary and secondary schools, community colleges, and universities to reinforce the acquisition and practice of nonroutine cognitive skills. If past trends hold, the growth occupations in the future will be those that intensively use those nonroutine skills. For those older adults needing retraining to transition from a sunset occupation, community colleges also will need to create a curriculum that supports nonroutine cognitive skill development. It will be important to redefine retraining programs to facilitate learning to think as opposed to learning to do.

While most governments consider education and training part of their mandates, learning opportunities—from preschool to universities and training programs—are not provided and supported only by state governments. The federal government, the private and nonprofit sectors, and philanthropy are all involved and can all help guide the way. If we continue to invest in education and training and if current workers are flexible in their skill sets today, we can prepare the adaptable, globally ready students and workers that are demanded tomorrow.

REFERENCES

Blinder, Alan S. "Offshoring: The Next Industrial Revolution?" *Foreign Affairs* 85 (2006): 13–28.

Clinton, Jim, and Carol Conway. "The Mercedes and the Magnolia: Preparing the Southern Workforce for the Next Economy." In *Report on the Future of the South*, ed. Scott Doron, Linda Hoke, and James Keecia. Research Triangle Park, N.C.: Southern Growth Policies Board, 2002.

Heckman, James J. A Research Agenda for Understanding the Dynamics of Skill Formation. 2010. In American Economic Association, *Ten Years and Beyond: Economists Answer NSF's Call for Long-Term Research Agendas*. http://ssrn.com/abstract=1889178.

North Carolina Public Schools. "State Board of Education." http://www.dpi.state.nc.us/stateboard/.

Oldenski, Lindsay. *Export versus FDI: A Task-Based Approach*. Mortara Working Paper 2011-1. Washington, D.C.: Mortara Center for International Studies, 2010.

University of North Carolina Tomorrow Commission. *UNC Tomorrow Commission Final Report*. 2007. http://www.northcarolina.edu/nctomorrow/execsummary.pdf.

U.S. Council of Economic Advisers. *Preparing the Workers of Today for the Jobs of Tomorrow*. 2009. http://www.whitehouse.gov/administration/eop/cea/Jobs-of-the-Future/.

THE American South *in the* Global Economy

THOMAS KEMENY

INTRODUCTION

The 1986 Commission on the Future of the South observed a "flash-flood of change rushing over the South…leaving many workers stranded." That flood was globalization. Since then, the floodwaters have only risen. Merchandise imports have grown faster than domestic output, and close to half the value of all imports comes from developing countries such as China. Most experts consider that trade helps the United States on the whole, but we also recognize that it rewards certain workers while hurting others. There is reason to think that the pains of adjustment may be borne disproportionately by workers and firms in the South. As the commission noted, workers in many Southern industries were focused on comparatively low-skill and routine activities—precisely the kinds of tasks most likely to be offshored to developing countries. Conversely, some entrepreneurs undoubtedly responded to these challenges by creating innovative products that have spurred economic opportunity in the South.

This essay examines how globalization has affected the economic vitality of North Carolina and the South. It seeks answers to three main questions. First, how has global integration affected employment in major industries in North Carolina? Second, how has North Carolina's response differed from that found in the South as a whole as well as the entire United States? Third, based on current conditions, what can we expect from work in tradable sectors over the next 25 years?

Trends, 1980-2008

To understand the impact of foreign competition, this essay focuses on employment in domestic tradable industries. An industry is tradable to the extent that its production and consumption can practically be performed across national borders. Today, many but not all industries are tradable. For example, China is a reasonable location to have your iPad assembled, but it is a less practical place to send your dry cleaning. To identify tradable industries, this article relies on Bradford Jensen and Lori Kletzer's observation that tradables tend to be geographically concentrated, while nontradables are ubiquitous. The realm of tradables is always growing as a result of technological change. Every town has dry cleaning establishments and hair salons; these are nontradables. But only a few places assemble televisions; these are tradable sectors that serve world demand. Some large sectors, such as agriculture, are fully tradable. Others, such as finance and insurance, contain tradable and nontradable components. Using data from the Census and following Jensen and Kletzer's approach, employment in tradable industries is calculated for 1980, 1990, 2000, and 2008 (the most recent year for which these data are available).

Table 4.1 provides a snapshot of tradable employment in North Carolina, the South, and the United States in 1980. The overall tradable employment patterns are reasonably similar across regions, though North Carolina is particularly focused on agriculture and lower-sophistication manufacturing, such as textiles and food processing (Manufacturing 1). In 1980, North Carolina also was less specialized than the South and the United States as a whole in a range of specialized tradable services, such as finance, accounting, and several information technology sectors.

How have these patterns changed since 1980? Like the country as a whole, North Carolina and the South have suffered declines in agriculture and routine manufacturing jobs. Many routine manufacturing jobs moved from the Rustbelt to the Sunbelt in the 1960s, 1970s, and 1980s in search of cheap, unskilled labor and land. But as the Commission on the Future of the South observed, these jobs were increasingly being offshored by the mid-1980s. New trade deals, cheap shipping, and information technology rendered many industries footloose that were once place bound, and firms found cheaper locations for production in the developing world.

The top row of Figure 4.1 shows a pattern of decline in low-skill manufacturing and agricultural production, but it also reveals some interesting nuances. North Carolina was particularly hard hit by declines in these two sectors, which dominated its tradable economies as recently as 1980. Employment in North Carolina's textile, footwear, tobacco, and food-production sectors declined by 68 percent between 1980 and 2008, as

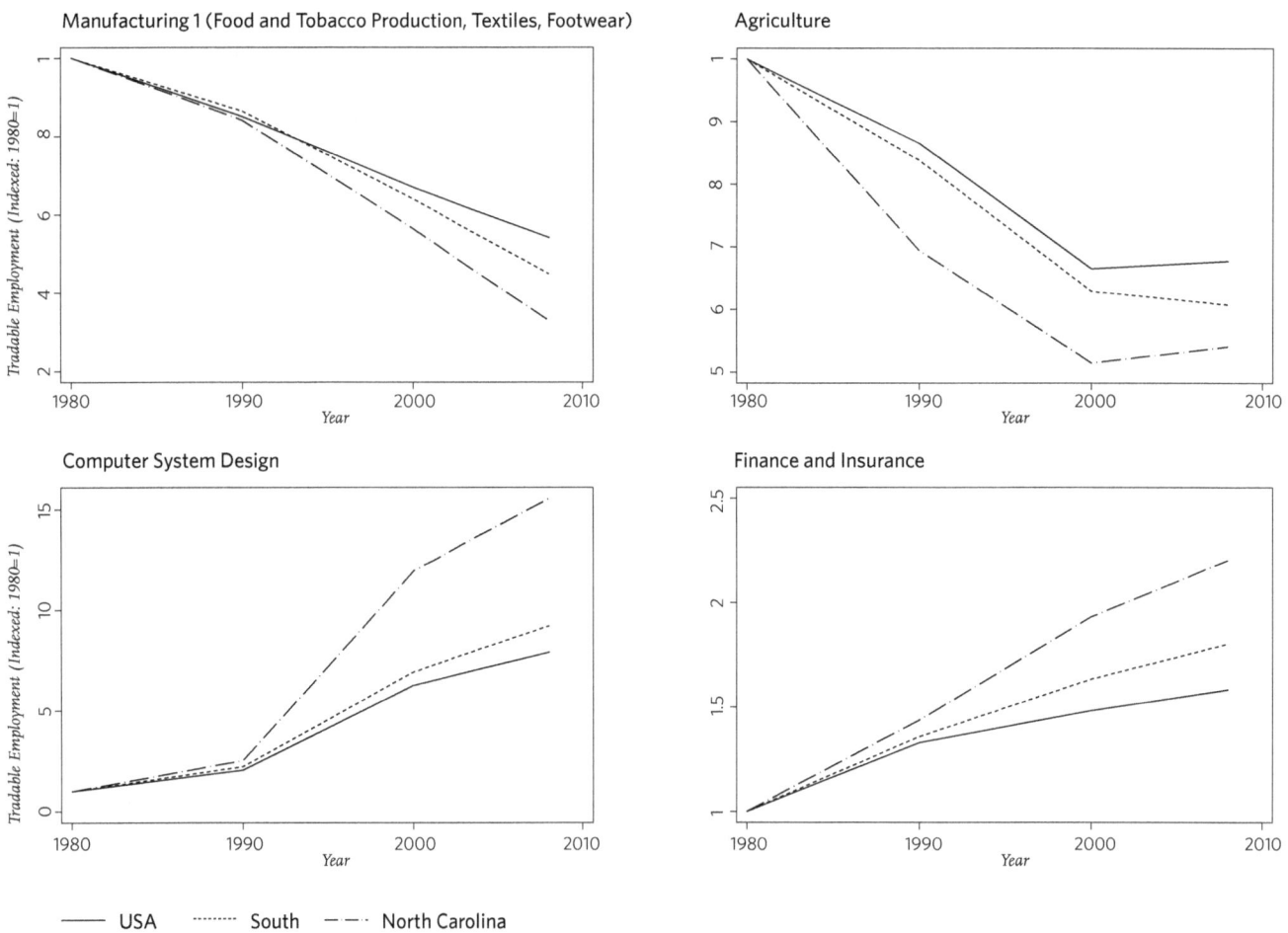

figure 4.1 PERCENTAGE CHANGE IN TRADABLE EMPLOYMENT, 1980 TO 2008

Source: Author's calculations based on Integrated Public Use Microdata Series (IPUMS) Decennial Census 1980 5 percent sample and American Community Survey S 2006–8 3 percent sample.

compared with 55 percent in the South and 46 percent in the country as a whole. North Carolina's agricultural workforce shrunk by almost half, whereas elsewhere declines were only a third, largely because of the decline of tobacco.

The other half of the national story also is reflected in North Carolina and the South, again with some instructive differences. U.S. tradables have increasingly come to reflect the country's

> Since 1986, the floodwaters of globalization have only risen.

comparative advantage in high-skill technical and business services. Overall, employment growth has shifted from routine manual and cognitive work to jobs that demand more abstract and analytical thinking. This trend appears magnified in North Carolina. The bottom row of figure 4.1 shows changes in employment in two new economy sectors: computer systems design and finance and insurance. Employment growth in these two industries in North Carolina far outstrips the national growth rate. In computer-systems design, employment in North Carolina has grown by a factor of nearly 15, while in the United States as a whole, it grew by a factor of 7.

As table 4.2 indicates, North Carolina's (and to a lesser extent the South's) push into higher-sophistication tradable work includes additional sectors, such as scientific research and development services, technical consulting, and accounting services. Unlike the South and the entire United States, North Carolina has also leveraged its know-how into higher-sophistication activities in wood, paper, and chemicals manufacturing. And it has weathered the storm in electrical and machinery manufacturing better than other parts of the country have.

The Next 25 Years

Can this transformation be sustained going forward, or will computer design go the route of textiles? The answer is probably yes to both. Locational patterns in these sectors are likely to fracture, with some activities remaining while others peel off. As in 1986, today's conventional wisdom says that routine activities are most offshorable; today, this process is likely to occur not just among industries but within them as firms focus on subsets of larger goods and services whose production involves linked firms and subsidiaries located in many different countries. Are North Carolina and the South especially vulnerable to this kind of offshoring? Within the overall context of the United States, have they shifted to less sophisticated subsets of activities within sectors such as computer systems design? We can get some clues by looking at the average level of schooling among employees in such sectors. Workers in North Carolina's computer-systems-design sector had, on average, three years of college education—the same level found among workers in this industry in the United States as a whole as well as in the South. As table 4.3 shows, there are no meaningful differences in average education in finance and insurance as well as other selected sophisticated tradable sectors. Based on this snapshot, North Carolina and the South do not appear to be repeating the previous pattern of specialization within the United States on lower-sophistication work. From the evidence, these regions are no more vulnerable than is the nation as a whole.

North Carolina and to a lesser degree the entire South have made progress in transitioning away from sectors that do not fit with what America does best. The economic future of these regions ultimately depends less on particular sectors and more on residents' continued ability to engage in entrepreneurial and innovative activities.

REFERENCES

Jensen, B., and L. Kletzer. "Measuring Tradable Services and the Task Content of Offshorable Services Jobs." In *Labor in the New Economy*, ed. K. G. Abraham, J. Spletzer, and M. Harper. Chicago: University of Chicago Press, 2010.

Ruggles, S. J., T. Alexander, K. Genadek, T. Goeken, M. B. Schroeder, and M. Sobek. *Integrated Public Use Microdata Series: Version 5.0* [machine-readable database]. Minneapolis: Minnesota Population Center, 2010.

Spence, M., and H. Hlatshwayo. *The Evolving Structure of the American Economy and the Employment Challenge*. New York: Council on Foreign Relations, Maurice R. Greenberg Center for Geoeconomic Studies, 2011.

TABLES AND FIGURES

table 4.1 ESTIMATED EMPLOYMENT SHARES FOR SELECTED TRADABLE SECTORS, 1980

INDUSTRY	NORTH CAROLINA	SOUTH	UNITED STATES
Agriculture	4.1%	3.3%	3.3%
Manufacturing 1 (textiles, tobacco, food)	16.5	7.0	4.7
Manufacturing 2 (wood, paper, chemicals)	3.3	3.3	3.3
Manufacturing 3 (electrical, machinery)	7.2	5.7	7.2
Wholesale	2.2	2.4	2.3
Electronics	1.6	1.2	1.9
Finance and Insurance	2.3	2.8	3.1
Accounting Services	0.4	0.4	0.5
Computer System Design	0.1	0.2	0.2
Research and Development	0.1	0.2	0.3
Management, Scientific, and Technical Consulting	0.2	0.3	0.3

Notes: Author's calculations based on Integrated Public Use Microdata Series (IPUMS) Decennial Census 1980 5 percent sample.

table 4.2 PERCENTAGE CHANGE IN EMPLOYMENT, 1980 TO 2008, SELECTED TRADABLE SECTORS

INDUSTRY	NORTH CAROLINA	SOUTH	UNITED STATES
Agriculture	−46%	−39%	−32%
Manufacturing 1 (textiles, tobacco, food)	−68	−55	−46
Manufacturing 2 (wood, paper, chemicals)	26	2	−10
Manufacturing 3 (electrical, machinery)	−6	−8	−30
Wholesale	25	18	7
Electronics	−17	−6	−25
Finance and Insurance	120	80	58
Accounting Services	129	132	105
Computer System Design	1455	823	691
Research and Development	658	149	129
Management, Scientific, and Technical Consulting	350	298	218

Notes: Author's calculations based on Integrated Public Use Microdata Series (IPUMS) Decennial Census 1980 5 percent sample and American Community Survey S 2006–8 3 percent sample.

table 4.3 AVERAGE SCHOOLING, SELECTED TRADABLE SECTORS, 2008

INDUSTRY	NORTH CAROLINA	SOUTH	UNITED STATES
Finance and Insurance	8.4 Years	8.0 Years	8.2 Years
Accounting Services	8.5	8.5	8.7
Computer System Design	9.2	9.0	9.1
Research and Development	9.3	9.2	9.3
Management, Scientific, and Technology Consulting	9.2	9.1	9.3

Notes: Author's calculations based on Integrated Public Use Microdata Series (IPUMS) American Community Survey 2006–8 3 percent sample. Figures do not directly correspond to schooling years. Six is equal to high school graduate, with subsequent increments equal to one year of college.

PUBLIC UNIVERSITIES IN A NEW ECONOMIC ERA

A WAY FORWARD: BUILDING A GLOBALLY COMPETITIVE SOUTH

Our Southern Universities as Engines of Innovation

HOLDEN THORP AND BUCK GOLDSTEIN

Public and private research universities have been important contributors to the rise in the South's prosperity in the 20th and 21st centuries, propelling it out of an agrarian economy and making it one of the most dynamic regions of the country in population and job growth over the past 20 years. Yet as we face the challenges of economic constraints, shifting demographics, and worldwide competition, what should we expect of these institutions? The research university has proven to be one of our society's most durable institutions, and it is reasonable to expect that those in the South will continue their traditional missions of research and teaching. But the status quo is not enough. We believe that these institutions have the capacity to do much more—to help find the answers for the region's and the world's biggest problems.

The idea of the modern American research university with its emphasis on applied as well as theoretical knowledge grew out of the Morrill Acts of 1862 and 1890. For the South, a region struggling to modernize its economy and infrastructure, such institutions attracted the people, businesses, and financial capital that helped build the economy and grow metropolitan areas. Over time, ecosystems of innovation developed around these research universities, resulting in an intense concentration of talented people interacting in an open atmosphere that encouraged the generation of new ideas and new enterprises.

Consider the member institutions of the Association of American Universities (AAU), which represents public and private research universities in the United States and Canada. The association's 61 members, which represent the leading edge of innovation, scholarship, and knowledge creation, award more than half of all U.S. doctoral degrees and 55 percent of those in the sciences and engineering. They educate more than 1 million undergraduates, employ nearly 800,000 people, and have combined annual operating budgets of about $121 billion. They are responsible for significant new discoveries—more than 70 percent of Nobel Prize winners at U.S. institutions have been affiliated with AAU universities.

The AAU has 13 member institutions (21 percent of its total) in the South (see table 5.1). Five of these institutions have joined the AAU since 1985, an indication of the region's recent economic growth and investment in higher education. These 13 institutions have a combined endowment of more than $47 billion and annual research expenditures of more than $7.3 billion. Many are at the heart of significant clusters, such as the biomedical concentration in northeast Maryland around Johns Hopkins University and the University of Maryland, the high-tech concentration in Austin around the University of Texas and Texas A&M, and the life sciences/medical concentration in Research Triangle Park (RTP), clustered around Duke University and the University of North Carolina at Chapel Hill (UNC).

Southern research universities, whether or not they are members of AAU, are significant to their local economies. They attract government and private research dollars to the area, a phenomenon that has a multiplier effect resulting in increased commercial activity. Research also means jobs. Duke is the second-largest private employer in North Carolina, for example, while Johns Hopkins is the largest private employer in Baltimore and in combination with the Johns Hopkins University Health System is the largest private employer in Maryland. The University of Texas is the largest employer in Austin, and Tulane University is the largest private employer in New Orleans.

These institutions are not only employers but also incubators for new companies. In the RTP, North Carolina State's discoveries have resulted in

more than 660 patents and more than 70 companies created. UNC and Duke can make similar claims. The RTP-based Council for Entrepreneurial Development boasts a membership of more than 5,500 people representing more than 1,000 companies, making it one of the most successful organizations of its kind.

By virtually any measure, government support and private funding have made southern universities among the most affluent institutions in the region. In these extraordinarily difficult times, it is not surprising that those who have supported (and passionately believed in) higher education now expect a greater return on their investment. To some, this means preparing the next generation for an uncertain and increasingly competitive economic environment. Others expect universities to be engines of economic development, spinning out knowledge-based businesses that create jobs. Still others have loftier goals and believe that our institutions of higher learning should have a bigger impact on the problems of their home states, the nation, and the world.

Conversations on the UNC campus and throughout the nation since the publication of our book, *Engines of Innovation—The Entrepreneurial University in the 21st Century,* convince us that such goals are attainable if we pay attention to the critical intersection between innovation and execution and introduce entrepreneurial thinking as a complement to traditional academic dialogue. In terms of practical implementation, we can think of no magic bullets, and one size does not fit all, but our campus work and multiple conversations with others suggest some broad guiding principles that we believe can help southern universities respond to the increasing demands of their multiple constituencies.

First, construct a university-wide vision or strategy for innovation, not one identified with one particular college or school. We have found that encouraging innovation and entrepreneurial thinking in the arts and sciences, often the heart of a campus, paves the way for similar initiatives throughout the institution. If such efforts are coupled with a broad definition that includes social, scientific, and economic entrepreneurship, it is possible to enlist a wide array of faculty and student interest in learning more about entrepreneurial thinking. This constituency can be a stepping-stone toward the professional schools and departments that are already oriented toward an entrepreneurial point of view.

Second, entrepreneurs must be invited inside the walls of the university as an important component of the academic dialogue. As it turns out, this is not a new idea. Many of the most distinguished universities in the United States were conceived as partnerships between entrepreneurs and academics. The recent partnership between Michael Bloomberg and Johns Hopkins University is a contemporary example of the impact of such relationships. At UNC, our entire innovation agenda has been shaped by such partnerships. A team of academics and entrepreneurs designed and teaches our entrepreneurship curriculum. Similarly, academics

> The research university has proven to be one of our society's most durable institutions, and it is reasonable to expect that those in the South will continue their traditional missions of research and teaching.

and entrepreneurs working together developed our innovation road map, a plan to make entrepreneurship part of the university's culture. The concept of entrepreneur in residence has spread throughout the university, where it has been embraced not only by the College of Arts and Sciences but also by the schools of medicine, public health, and business.

The fundamental change in the academic conversation that takes place by welcoming entrepreneurs and other outside voices leads us to our third point. Focusing on transforming the culture of southern research universities will have a greater impact than tinkering with their structures. This point was strongly reinforced during an interview for our book when Stanford University professor James Spudich recounted the genesis of Bio-X, a remarkable interdisciplinary effort to address complex problems of human health at the intersection of chemistry, physics, medicine, and engineering. The Bio-X building, designed by world-class architect Norman Foster to facilitate multidisciplinary dialogue, was halfway done when President John Hennessey called Spudich to tell him there was a funding shortfall and to suggest that the downstairs cafeteria might be eliminated. Spudich, who believed deeply in interdisciplinary dialogue, replied, "Eliminate the laboratories and keep the cafeteria." Over and over again, we learned from our experience and conversations with others that a culture that focuses on problems and enlists a diverse set of participants and points of view has the greatest likelihood of achieving the results that Southern universities are being asked to deliver. Such a culture encourages ad hoc team building around specific problems rather than establishing institutes and schools with an indefinite life span. It also encourages experimentation with the understanding that failure is an acceptable outcome as long as the lessons learned are applied to the next undertaking. In the current financial situation faced by virtually all public universities, such a flexible culture that embraces innovation and entrepreneurship is best equipped to turn a crisis into an opportunity and undertake change that has long-term positive impact on the institution and the community.

Just as we advocate a broad-based, problem-centered dialogue as a means of maximizing the impact of the South's great research universities, we also suggest that such dialogue is critical among universities throughout the region if they are to play the role that is expected of them. We know all too well how difficult it is to actualize collaborative efforts even when geography is not an excuse—our own home turf includes three of the South's great universities, all within a 30-mile radius, and the level of cooperation among us, though improving, is nowhere near what it could be. But the same constituencies that expect more from their flagship institutions also expect these institutions to cooperate more and to rationalize the available resources if they are effectively to shape the region's future.

Only a few years ago, entrepreneurship at most great universities was relegated to the halls of the business school. Increasingly, however, entrepreneurial thinking—the ability to take ideas and turn them into reality—is being embraced by members of university communities with diverse values and points of view. This process has only begun, and we look forward to being part of the regional and national conversation about how the crown jewels of our society, our great universities, can have an even greater impact on their region and the nation as a whole.

REFERENCES

Association of American Universities. Website. http://www.aau.edu/about/default.aspx?id=5476.

"College and University Endowments, 2008–2009." *Chronicle of Higher Education.* http://chronicle.com/premium/stats/endowments/results.php?year=2010&state=Michigan&sort=market.

National Science Foundation. *Academic Research and Development Expenditures: Fiscal Year 2009.* NSF 11-313. July 2011. http://www.nsf.gov/statistics/nsf11313/pdf/nsf11313.pdf.

Thorp, Holden, and Buck Goldstein. *Engines of Innovation—The Entrepreneurial University in the 21st Century.* Chapel Hill: University of North Carolina Press, 2010.

TABLES AND FIGURES

table 5.1 AMERICAN ASSOCIATION OF UNIVERSITIES MEMBERS IN THE SOUTH
(RANKED BY MARKET VALUE OF ENDOWMENT)

INSTITUTION	ENDOWMENT (FY2009) IN THOUSANDS OF DOLLARS	RESEARCH EXPENDITURES (FY2009) IN THOUSANDS OF DOLLARS
University of Texas at Austin	12,163,049	506,369
Texas A&M University	5,083,754	630,655
Duke University	4,440,745	805,021
Emory University	4,328,436	449,419
Rice University	3,612,884	78,745
University of Virginia	3,577,266	261,604
Vanderbilt University	2,833,614	431,673
Johns Hopkins University	1,976,899	1,856,270
University of North Carolina at Chapel Hill	1,905,081	646,011
University of Florida	1,010,590	592,082
Georgia Institute of Technology	944,346	561,361
Tulane University	807,859	155,139
University of Maryland at College Park	167,995	409,190

Source: "College and University Endowments, 2008–2009." Chronicle of Higher Education. http://chronicle.com/stats/endowments/; National Science Foundation. "Academic Research and Development Expenditures: Fiscal Year 2009." NSF 11-313. July 2011. http://www.nsf.gov/statistics/nsf11313/.

THE Relevant University

RANDY WOODSON

It is no secret that North Carolina's economic landscape—as embodied by the array of businesses and industry sectors that flourish in our state—has changed dramatically over the past 25 years. With the benefit of hindsight, we should not be surprised by the astonishing speed with which emerging technologies and globalization have brought about that change. But who could blame us for being a bit stunned and perhaps even nostalgic as we reflect on a bygone time when the furniture industry, tobacco, and textiles were the engines of our economy?

Reflection aside, if we have learned anything, it is that the landscape continues to change and the pace of change is accelerating. That future, sitting like a speck on the horizon, is going to be nose-to-nose with us soon. We cannot wait for it to arrive to make our adjustments.

As we think about the role universities can play in the South's economic future, we could do worse than to consider the land-grant university model. The land-grant concept came into being as a response to industrialization, with an array of disciplines and a mission that were directly relevant to the needs of a rising middle class.

In the roughly 150 years since its inception, the land-grant concept has matured and expanded. Land grants have lived up to the late-1800s vision of "educating the working classes" but also have honed an ability to move knowledge swiftly to those who can best use it and have developed a capacity to be engines of economic development and upward mobility.

In thinking about the future, three ideals come to mind in regard to how universities can support a healthy, economically prosperous North Carolina. All three are squarely in the wheelhouse of the nation's land-grant universities.

- We need to continue supporting existing business and industry while anticipating future needs and building a vision for meeting them.

- Partnerships and collaborations will support our ability to be prescient about emerging needs and assist the state's growth.

- Institutions of higher education can open pathways for individual innovation and entrepreneurship.

SUPPORTING THE PRESENT, ANTICIPATING THE FUTURE

While many of the state's traditional business sectors have suffered in the age of globalization, pockets of success continue to exist in the fields of agriculture and manufacturing. For example, few people realize that North Carolina is home to thousands of manufacturers.

In 1988, the Industrial Extension Service became the lead state agency for the federal government's Manufacturing Extension Partnership. Its technical assistance and training programs are evaluated quarterly by the National Institute of Standards and Technology (NIST), which recently reported the highest economic impact for the Industrial Extension Service since the surveys started in 2000. According to the NIST survey, moreover, total impact in the past four years exceeded the goal of $1 billion and 4,549 jobs created or retained for North Carolina.

Agriculture (and its cousin, aquaculture) remain viable contributors to the state's economy. While agriculture remains one of our most popular academic disciplines, our research contributes to value-added agriculture. For example, North Carolina leads the nation in sweet potato production. It is a crop that is emblematic of the broad reach of university-based agriculture research, which extends from enriching the nutritional components of crops to biofuels. We recently licensed faculty research results to local farmers in Snow Hill, allowing them to open a 100 percent farmer-owned plant that created 60 badly needed jobs. The plant produces a sweet potato product that is shelf stable without refrigeration.

The lesson here is somewhat analogous to the conventional wisdom in economic development circles, which says we cannot spend so much time recruiting new firms to the state that we forget about the assets that are already here. Agriculture and manufacturing still support a significant number of jobs, especially in rural areas. Even as we pursue a vision that continually brings new players to the table, there is much promise in nurturing existing assets. Because of their mission, their historic contributions, and the presence of strong research enterprises, our land-grant universities are best positioned to strike that balance.

About 25 years ago, North Carolina State University, in partnership with the state, embarked on a task to create the preeminent university research park. Centennial Campus has subsequently grown and recently was recognized by the Association of University Research Parks as the Research Science Park of the Year. It is to North Carolina State what Research Triangle Park is to the Triangle region (and to the state of North Carolina).

The campus is organized into educational neighborhoods to stimulate creativity and innovation. Its 36 corporate and government research partners, 26 incubator companies, and 75 campus units are integrated into research and development neighborhoods in advanced materials, communication technologies, environmental science, biosciences, and education. We require business and government entities seeking space on the campus, particularly those that support scholarship and research, to incorporate formal plans for partnerships with the university.

Anticipating the needs of the state and university and providing a physical and philosophical launching pad for

A WAY FORWARD: BUILDING A GLOBALLY COMPETITIVE SOUTH

people with ideas, research acumen, and a predisposition to collaborate and with an eye toward economic development, Centennial Campus continues to flourish, in keeping with its creators' vision. It is the embodiment of the university's land-grant mission, which calls us to respond to the state's needs through engagement and the delivery of relevant solutions.

Centennial Campus also is home to our College of Textiles, one of the country's few remaining textile programs. As the nation's textile industry began to founder, universities across the country significantly decreased or even eliminated their textile programs. Instead, we worked with industry to move in a different direction and led revitalization by emphasizing new-wave textiles. The shift has kept the industry relevant and led to the development of fabrics that are treated to kill disease-carrying bacteria; clothing and fabrics that are cooler, lighter, and less costly to produce; and lightweight turnout gear for firefighters that provides even greater protection.

As the textile industry was remaking itself, North Carolina's biotechnology sector was taking off. Research shows that start-up biotech companies tend to begin their lives in proximity to major research universities, where they can work with research faculty to develop business ideas and further hone research. Those companies then move to more rural areas, closer to the crop that is the source of their bioproduct. Biolex, for example, began as a start-up at North Carolina State, then moved to Pittsboro.

North Carolina's biotechnology industry is third in the nation, behind only California and Massachusetts. But as every solution generates its own set of problems, a burgeoning biotech sector needs a growing pool of workers. To accommodate that need, North Carolina State worked with the Golden LEAF Foundation, North Carolina Central University, the state's community colleges, and industry partners to create the Biomanufacturing Training

> The strength of the partnership allows us to anticipate the state's growing biotech needs and exemplifies the type of collaboration that will be relevant now and into the future: It is a participatory and anticipatory effort.

and Education Center. The center is the largest pilot-plant facility of its kind in the world, providing hands-on training for students and retraining for those already working in the industry. The students work on the same equipment used in the biotech field. Graduates have a more than 90 percent placement rate. And we have just added a master of biomanufacturing/master of business administration degree designed to prepare students to work as managers in the industry. The strength of the partnership allows us to anticipate the state's growing biotech needs and exemplifies the type of collaboration that will be relevant now and into the future: It is a participatory and anticipatory effort.

TAKING AN INTENTIONAL APPROACH TO PARTNERSHIPS AND COLLABORATIONS

Across North Carolina State and many of the nation's other universities, there are numerous partnerships and collaborations that include government agencies, business and industry, other higher-education institutions (including international institutions), community groups, and individuals. We have a clear understanding of our land-grant mission

and a focus on connecting that mission to North Carolina's people. Our partnerships and collaborations deliver mutual benefits. To ensure that engagement and economic development remain core objectives, we included them in recently revised guidelines for faculty evaluation, tenure, and promotion.

Partnerships and collaborations are the linkage between our primary mission of student success and our historic frontline support of economic development. Having done the heavy lifting of codifying how we go about collaborating and building this work into our mission, we have the pathways for partners to come into the university and for students and faculty to reach out.

Our partnerships extend to the recruitment effort. Strong universities attract businesses to the state. The typical approach of land grants is to provide active assistance in the state's recruitment efforts. The Economic Development Partnership with the state recently played a prominent role in helping North Carolina attract two significant corporate headquarters: IEM, with about 430 jobs located in the Research Triangle Park, and HCL America, which opened its regional headquarters in Cary's Regency Park with 225 new jobs.

Recognizing that in many ways we are still having the same conversation about rural North Carolina that we had 25 years ago—How do we support education and economic opportunity there?—it is important that universities continue actively to reach out to rural and often distant sections of the state. The Northeast Leadership Academy benefits rural northeastern North Carolina teachers and central office staff. The curriculum is tailored for future leaders of high-needs rural schools. After graduation, all members of the academy make three-year commitments to work in the region's schools.

A university-wide emphasis on collaboration is mirrored in the current generation of students, who are predisposed to seek out and respond to opportunities to collaborate with each other. Especially in light of the growing use of technology in the classroom—and even as a substitute for the classroom—higher education

> **The charge for colleges and universities is to seek ways intentionally to encourage students who have an entrepreneur's mind-set and to awaken it in students with that potential.**

institutions must continue to anticipate and employ collaborative learning.

The Student-Centered Active Learning Environment for Undergraduate Programs (SCALE-UP) approach, first introduced at North Carolina State, establishes a highly collaborative, hands-on, interactive learning environment for large-enrollment courses. Students are placed in small groups and collaborate to deliver detailed reports on hypothesis-driven labs. Data on more than 16,000 students show that SCALE-UP improves students' ability to solve problems, increases conceptual understanding, and reduces failure rates. More than 100 institutions across the country now employ the SCALE-UP approach.

FROM GROUP COLLABORATIONS TO INDIVIDUAL ENTREPRENEURSHIP

Even as we embrace the collaborative spirit among our faculty, staff, and students, universities should not lose sight of the innovation and economic development potential to be found in the entrepreneurial spirit. Successful start-ups evolving into larger, successful businesses are among our biggest drivers of job growth. Many of those start-ups begin as an entrepreneurial vision.

In many ways, colleges and universities encourage entrepreneurship simply by opening the doors to the learning environment. In some respects, however, our universities are tradition-bound, slower-moving organizations—the antithesis of an entrepreneurial environment. The charge for us is to seek ways intentionally to encourage students who have an entrepreneur's mind-set and to awaken it in students with that potential. We have pockets of both these types of students on our campus but only recently have raised the bar, making entrepreneurial education a university-wide, multidisciplinary effort.

Technology Entrepreneurship and Commercialization is an example of an intentional effort. It teaches graduate students from business and technical disciplines the innovation and entrepreneurial processes necessary to transform new technology platforms into successful businesses. A team-based approach utilizing emerging technologies and a proprietary commercialization methodology provide the students with an opportunity for hands-on commercialization experience. The approach has produced a new corporation, Tec-Cel, which has obtained a grant to underwrite a search for venture capital based on a faculty-developed technology for the next-generation lithium-ion battery capable of storing up to 10 times the energy of conventional batteries. The U.S. Department of Energy provided $1.35 million to optimize the technology, and a leading computer manufacturer has offered to test the battery in its laptops.

The Technology Incubator, established in 1999, creates an entrepreneurial environment for technology start-ups. About 30 companies have graduated from the incubator, creating 894 jobs and generating $75 million in gross state product.

We should not overlook the entrepreneurial, innovative work of our faculty, whose research routinely delivers relevant solutions for North Carolina's needs. Since 1980, North Carolina State faculty have generated

732 active U.S. patents, with 196 applications pending review and 150 products licensed and on the market. Eighty-one start-up companies representing more than $750 million in venture-capital investment and 3,000 jobs have been created. Research and outreach expenditures have increased dramatically, growing from $128 million in fiscal year 1987 to $380 million in fiscal year 2010, providing a solid base for future technological innovations.

ANTICIPATING THE NEXT 25 YEARS

The recommendations from the Southern Growth Policies Board's *Halfway Home and a Long Way to Go*, MDC's *Shadows in the Sunbelt*, and more recently the President's Council on Jobs and Competitiveness (2011) and the North Carolina Commission on Workforce Development Board (2011) argue for a closer connection of universities with the private sector to deliver regional innovation. The council specifically called for a private consortium with university partners to graduate 10,000 more engineers and to build workforce skills in advanced manufacturing. The role of higher education is only becoming more relevant to economic development.

Higher education can be the catalytic change agent in creating the talent base and educating the future workforce—through degrees and lifelong learning—to maintain the edge in innovation and competitiveness. Land-grant universities are well positioned to lead the effort. We should welcome the opportunity. We should ask not only how we will affect the state but how the changing landscape will affect us. Universities tend to move slowly. The state's needs and our appropriations-dependent funding likely will require us to be more nimble and agile in our organizational approach. In short, while we focus on developing innovative research, supporting existing and developing industry sectors through collaboration, and encouraging entrepreneurship, our business-planning processes—from which all our work proceeds—need to be in sync with the fast-moving future that is heading our way.

REFERENCES

Brown, John Seely, Ann Pendleton-Jullian, and Richard Adler. "From Engagement to Ecotone: Land-Grant Universities in the 21st Century." *Change: The Magazine of Higher Learning*, November–December 2010.

MDC. *Shadows in the Sunbelt—Developing the Rural South in an Era of Economic Change*. Chapel Hill: MDC, 1986.

North Carolina Commission on Workforce Development. *State of the North Carolina Workforce, 2011–2020: Preparing North Carolina's Workforce and Businesses for the Global Economy*. Raleigh: North Carolina Employment Security Commission, 2011.

North Carolina State University. *Strategic Plan, 2011–2020*. http://info.ncsu.edu/strategic-planning/.

President's Council on Jobs and Competitiveness. *Progress Report*. Raleigh: President's Council on Jobs and Competitiveness, 2011.

RTI. *Economic Impact Analysis of the North Carolina State Technology Incubator*. Research Triangle Park, N.C. : RTI, 2007.

Southern Growth Policies Board. *Halfway Home and a Long Way to Go*. Research Triangle Park, N.C.: Southern Growth Policies Board, 1986.

North Carolina Community Colleges *and a* New Economic Landscape

SCOTT RALLS

> Our citizens must realize that skill-based technology often drives the new job inequality, suggesting that insufficient educational levels should receive a portion of the blame. Indeed, growing wage differentials and trade practices distract us from what should be our greatest concern—the growing education gap between ourselves and our worldwide competitors.

INTRODUCTION

When W. Dallas Herring, former chair of North Carolina's State Board of Education, joined Governor Luther Hodges (1954–61) to pioneer the introduction of Industrial Education Centers across the state in 1957 and then encouraged Governor Terry Sanford (1961–65) to transform those centers into the system of community colleges in 1963, he did so in great part to provide the majority of North Carolinians access to the broad benefits of higher education as well as an opportunity for a brighter economic future. Herring and Sanford had plotted the locations of the community colleges, sitting down together on the floor of the governor's mansion with a map of the state. The efforts of these leaders enabled North Carolina to become one of the first southern states to be prepared for a changing economic landscape, at that time dominated by a burgeoning manufacturing sector. As a result, per capita income for North Carolinians quickly gained ground on the national average, causing other states to look to our success in an effort to replicate our economic progress.

Herring would want us to spend little time celebrating what a long road we have traveled. He would rather we keep our eyes on the future—an economic future that for too many North Carolinians is as uncertain today as it was in the 1950s and 1960s. He would be concerned that in a world economy where what you earn increasingly is based on what you learn, too many North Carolinians fail to appreciate the value of postsecondary education. Now, 50 years later, with tremendous recent advances in technology, this story is being played out on a global scale at a phenomenal pace. As Herring said, "We must take the people where they are and carry them as far as they can go."

FACING THE BRUTAL FACTS OF A NEW ECONOMIC LANDSCAPE

Too frequently, we assume that job losses in North Carolina result from unfair trading practices and low international wages, not fully realizing that job losses are not confined to low-wage production jobs. Our citizens must realize that skill-based technology often drives the new job inequality, suggesting that insufficient educational levels should receive a portion of the blame. Indeed, growing wage differentials and trade practices distract us from what should be our greatest concern—the growing education gap between ourselves and our worldwide competitors.

Ongoing discussions also concern the potential division into two North Carolinas: rural and urban, poor and rich. Such economic disparities are seen increasingly along racial lines in rural areas, where education varies with race. The negative correlation between educational achievement and poverty ultimately exacerbates the division. When combined with the slowing of educational attainment levels, the increasing economic disparities along racial and poverty lines evince the ever increasing economic benefits of higher education. Unless our state's policymakers and educational leaders confront new economic and educational realities, our next 50 years are not likely to see the same level of progress as did the previous 50.

Four brutal facts must be recognized before we can introduce innovations to our educational system and modify our perspective on community colleges' role in our economic future.

1. The Emerging "Nontraditional" Student and the Vanishing African American Male Student

Nationally, only 20 percent of undergraduates conform to the traditional stereotype of a recent high school graduate enrolled as a full-time residential student. Nontraditional students are the new norm, including students who are older, work full-time, take classes part-time, or have children. The 72 percent national increase in undergraduate students over the past 35 years has been caused primarily by an influx of nontraditional students, with community colleges chosen as their most common educational path. The more nontraditional a student is, the likelier it is that he or she will attend community college, with 64 percent of highly nontraditional students attending community colleges.

At the same time that nontraditional community college undergraduates are filtering into postsecondary ranks, African American males are vanishing. The number of African American male community college graduates has declined each of the past several years even as the benefits of education are rapidly growing. To combat the division into two North Carolinas, our state must address this predicament.

2. Facing the Consequences of North Carolina's Community College Completion Rates and the Costs of Remediation

Increasing postsecondary enrollment is necessary but not sufficient to the task of fending off two North Carolinas and bolstering the economy; the state also must retain those enrolled students. To understand the low completion rates in community colleges, one must first understand that "community colleges often serve students who have the fewest options and the greatest challenges"—61 percent of U.S. community college students attend school part time, 57 percent work more than 20 hours per week, 34 percent spend 11 or more hours per week caring for dependents, and 21 percent spend between 6 and 20 hours per week commuting to and from class.

Among nontraditional community college students nationwide, 46 percent leave during their first year (48 percent in North Carolina), compared with 23 percent of traditional students. Nationwide, community college completion rates are improving, while North Carolina's are worsening, a condition brought on by five primary factors: the lack of intent to earn a degree, work recruitment prior to graduation, financial pressures, inability to qualify for financial aid, and a lack of academic preparedness.

With regard to financial pressures, data from the American Council on Education indicate that community colleges are the most likely to benefit from financial aid but are the least likely to apply for it. The lack of academic preparedness also is of great concern, as the state often ends up "paying double" for high school graduates to take remedial courses before working on college credits; since 1999–2000, the percentage of North Carolina community college students requiring remediation has ranged from 48.6 percent to 54.3 percent.

3. North Carolina's Looming Workforce Shortage, the Emerging Role of Immigrants, and the Consequences of Low College-Going Rates

Between 2006 and 2016, North Carolina's population is predicted to increase by 15 percent, much higher than the overall U.S. growth rate of 9 percent. Demographic trends suggest that this significant growth will heighten rather than alleviate workforce shortages. So where will we find workers to provide the necessary health care and other services for a booming retirement population?

No state has seen a greater percentage influx in foreign immigration than North Carolina. With such significant increases and the beginnings of labor shortages in a number of occupational areas, the foreign-born immigrant population has assumed an increasingly prominent role in the North Carolina workforce. The growth of illegal immigration is a particularly emotional issue in states such as North Carolina that have dealt simultaneously with significant job losses as a result of foreign competition and the rapid influx of new foreign-born workers. Admission of undocumented immigrants into community colleges is obviously a legal and political issue, and many native North Carolinians see inequity in offering jobs and services to new arrivals while longtime citizens see record numbers of pink slips.

On the one hand, in addition to the law-and-order argument, those who oppose the admission of illegal immigrants to community colleges can ask a number of valid questions from a strictly economic perspective. For example, given the community college workforce development mission, why invest resources in individuals not legally eligible to participate in North Carolina's workforce? On the other hand, there exists our brutal economic dilemma. New immigrants to our state, including undocumented immigrants, are part of our current workforce. Consequently, our state faces a challenging macrolevel question similar to one posed to a business leader: "What if I train them and they leave?" His response: "What if they are not trained and they stay?"

4. Balancing Rising Enrollments, Lagging Faculty Salaries, and Inadequate Equipment Funds with Expanding Needs for Graduates

Increased enrollment pressures community colleges' resources at a difficult time. North Carolina's community colleges cannot remain competitive either with other community colleges nationally or with other postsecondary institutions in our state with regard to teacher salaries and equipment. Without the necessary funding increases, the workforce and economic development consequences of uncompetitive salaries and outdated equipment manifest themselves in the elimination of high-cost vocational and technical programs that could provide good-paying jobs. In addition, community colleges should not just keep pace with today but also should prepare for tomorrow, such as in developing programs to address North Carolina's current nursing shortages.

CONCLUSION

In 1963, when Sanford called on the North Carolina General Assembly to create the North Carolina Community College System, he stated, "Much remains to be done, to provide better educational opportunities for the competition our children will surely face, to encourage broader economic development so everybody will have a better chance to make a better living. Now is the time to move forward. Now is no time to loaf along."

To ensure that our next 50 years are as productive and beneficial as our last 50, North Carolina's leaders must not only recognize these facts but also act to enable community colleges to provide the access and opportunity capable of bridging the education and economic gaps that threaten to divide our state.

THIS IS EXCERPTED from an article in *North Carolina Insight*, the journal of the North Carolina Center for Public Policy Research. To download the article free of charge, go to http://www.nccppr.org/drupal/content/insightarticle/84/facing-brutal-facts.

THE Unique Role of Southern Historically Black Colleges and Universities in ECONOMIC DEVELOPMENT

CHARLES NELMS

My life would have been profoundly different had it not been for the open access of a low-wealth historically black college or university (HBCU). I am just one of hundreds of thousands of HBCU success stories. My test scores did not suggest that I was leadership material when I entered the Arkansas Agricultural, Mechanical, and Normal College (now the University of Arkansas at Pine Bluff) in 1965. I shall never forget my academic adviser, Gladys McKindra Smith, who said to me on a hot July day in a non-air-conditioned auditorium, "Mr. Nelms, your scores are sort of low, but if you follow this plan, you'll be all right." She handed me a schedule that included remedial English and remedial math.

Three years later, Arkansas AM&N College graduated a more confident young man with a degree in agronomy and chemistry who was able to compete successfully at Indiana University and the Teachers College at Columbia University with graduate students from some of the nation's best colleges and universities. The institution that ensured my entrée to the middle class was a poorly resourced, 1890 land-grant college.

A distinct and distinguished set of colleges, HBCUs were forged in racial segregation and struggled against deprivation, unfair competition, and open hostility to lift up a race through education. Defined by the Black College and University Act as those schools founded before 1964 to educate blacks, the HBCUs' unique culture, social significance, and educational utility ensure their continued relevance in American higher education. Rather than recede quietly into the annals of history, HBCUs stand ready to assume a leadership role in increasing the educational attainment of African Americans in the 21st century.

President Barack Obama has been quoted as saying, "The achievement gap is going to be an albatross around the neck of our economy if we don't solve it. You're increasingly seeing a mismatch between the jobs that are being created and the skill sets that are available."

In the National Urban League's *The State of Black America 2010 Jobs: Responding to the Crisis* report, U.S. secretary of education Arne Duncan wrote, "The achievement gap is unacceptably large. The average black child is two or three grade levels behind the average white child…. Only one in five blacks over the age of 25 has a bachelor's degree." Partly as a consequence of this systemic disparity in education, African Americans in 2010 were almost twice as likely to be unemployed — 15.8 percent of blacks were jobless, compared with 8.5 percent of whites, according to the U.S. Department of Labor — and three times as likely to live in poverty, according to the National Urban League. A clear explanatory factor in this discrepancy is that whites are more than 1.5 times likelier than blacks to hold bachelor's degrees. Even in the midst of this Great Recession, the unemployment rate for bachelor's degree holders was only 5.2 percent. College graduates earn an average of $22,000 more per year and maintain healthier lifestyles than those with only high school diplomas. Is there any wonder why Duncan has called education "the civil rights issue of our generation?"

> Rather than recede quietly into the annals of history, HBCUs stand ready to assume a leadership role in increasing the educational attainment of African Americans in the 21st century.

All Southerners (and Americans) should be concerned that the nation is not living up to its ideal of equal opportunity; however, where cries for social justice fall on deaf ears, there is always the dollars-and-cents argument that closing the achievement gap could raise the gross domestic product in this country by more than a half trillion dollars per year.

The nation's 105 HBCUs, 11 of which are in North Carolina, confer degrees on African Americans in disproportionate numbers. According to the National Center for Education Statistics, they enroll 11 percent of all African American students but are the source of 22 percent of all bachelor's degrees awarded to black graduates; 35 percent of astronomy, biology, chemistry, mathematics, and physics graduates; half of all black teachers; and 24 percent of all black science and engineering graduates. In 2006, one-third of all black holders of doctoral degrees in science and engineering had received their baccalaureate degrees from HBCUs. HBCUs are critical not only to degree attainment but also to the maintenance of America's global leadership role. The return path to world leadership in health, prosperity, and education should include the financial and programmatic stabilization of the HBCUs.

However, HBCUs must respond to the dynamic changes taking place in our society and economy. To become a force, HBCUs must make critical changes in a number of key areas. First, these institutions must become more competitive and responsive in their curricular offerings. The trend toward online education, for example, requires that institutions explore more contemporary modes of instruction delivery, inter-institutional collaboration, and research in emerging fields. The need for such a paradigm shift is critical to HBCUs.

Second, HBCUs also must diversify curricula to include more contemporary offerings reflective of the dynamic social, economic, national, and international landscapes and to include offerings in areas such as entrepreneurship, health disparities, environmental technologies, mass communication, and information management. These should be experiential programs that emphasize hands-on laboratory research, industry internships, and real-life problem solving to ensure that graduates will be job-ready on Day 1.

For example, at North Carolina Central University, a century-old HBCU, the state has invested in the development of the Biomanufacturing Research Institute and Technology Enterprise (BRITE), where students work in laboratory settings that rival those in industry. BRITE is an education, training, and research center for workforce development to support the state's pharmaceutical and biotechnology industries. Students engage in state-of-the-art procedures such as protein separation and molecular cloning. Coursework in biomanufacturing prepares students for work in quality assurance and quality control, process development, and validation. BRITE's short-term goal is to meet the region's need for scientists at biotechnology, biomanufacturing, and pharmaceutical companies, but the institute's long-term goal is to develop new technologies that will attract new companies to North Carolina.

Third, HBCUs possess the requisite experience and skills to assist communities in addressing issues related to K–12 education, law and criminal justice, health education, entrepreneurship, and economic development. Many HBCUs have created community development corporations that purchase and restore houses and finance homeownership for low-income residents in the university environs. HBCUs and majority institutions need to do a better job of seeking out collaborations and establishing consortia to address these broad societal needs.

Fourth, HBCUs are working to ensure students' competitiveness by raising expectations for success. For more than four decades, the focus has been on student access, with student success gaining momentum in more recent years. Many institutions, including HBCUs, have retention and graduation rates that are unacceptably low. Knowing that retention is a prerequisite for graduation, colleges and universities must significantly increase support services and enhance teaching effectiveness. The goal of all higher education must be the graduation of students well prepared for their chosen careers. It is often said, accurately, that students of the 21st century must be able to learn, unlearn, and relearn.

CONCLUSION

While it is imperative that HBCUs remain true to their unique missions, it is important for them to consider their role in a changing society and economy. Current and projected demographics confirm ethnic population shifts. These changes are beginning to emerge in university enrollments nationwide. For their benefit, HBCUs must expand inclusiveness to meet the needs of Latinos and other groups seeking a college education. A richer ethnic fabric will only enhance the HBCU experience and result in an expanded opportunity to serve. Globalization must be reflected throughout the curricula and not relegated to supplemental coursework or fragmented study abroad activities. Students and faculty need opportunities to participate in international studies and to learn Chinese, Arabic, and other critical languages.

The future of HBCUs will be determined by their competitiveness, responsiveness, and relevance. A commitment by public and private funding sources to support HBCUs must be orchestrated as part of a regional strategy to develop intellectual capital to sustain our economy. If state and federal governments, private corporations, and foundations came together to coordinate a National HBCU Reinvestment Act to encourage the development of these institutions in these strategic areas, they could more significantly contribute to the economic well-being of this region and nation. HBCUs have demonstrated capacity, resolve, and results. We must embrace and empower these institutions: The magnitude of the issues confronting us is too great to leave any of the nation's talent pool untapped. At North Carolina Central University, we are prepared to do our part to ensure economic vitality through workforce development.

REFERENCES

Barnett, A. D. and K. Chappell. "Education Nation," *Ebony*, September 2010, 70.

Duncan, Arne. "Education: The Path to Success for African Americans" In *The State of Black America 2010 Jobs: Responding to the Crisis*. New York: National Urban League, 2010, 94.

"NAFEO, the Membership Association of the Nation's Public and Private 2- and 4-Year HBCUs and PBIs, Responds to Jason Riley's 'Black Colleges Need a New Mission: Once an Essential Response to Racism, They Are Now Academically Inferior.'" http://www.nafeo.org/community/web2010/news_vedder.html.

Burrelli, J. and A. Rapoport. *Role of HBCUs as Baccalaureate-Origin Institutions of Black S&E Doctorate Recipients.*" NSF 08-319, 2008. http://nsf.gov/statistics/infbrief/nsf08319/.

INCREASING THE ECONOMIC DEVELOPMENT ROLE OF HIGHER EDUCATION

Shadows and Light on the Way Home:

The University of North Carolina's Role in Higher Education and Economic Development

LESLIE BONEY

INTRODUCTION

Halfway Home and a Long Way to Go took a full frontal whack at higher education in the South, stating bluntly that the region "doesn't get its money's worth" out of higher education, charging politicians with "adding programs with little regard to cost, merit or duplication," accusing education administrators of focusing more on growing enrollment than on "increasing quality or relevance of the education and research they administer," and calling on higher education to align course offerings more closely with workforce demand. The report recommended five areas of focus: deepening linkages between higher education and the private sector; increasing remedial education in higher education; increasing access for underrepresented groups; focusing campus missions more carefully; and linking funding growth to improvements in quality.

Shadows in the Sunbelt took its whacks at higher education from the side, but it too called on campuses to work more intentionally on economic-development-related activities: "conducting market research, applying technological innovation, and providing expert advice to local businessmen and developers" as well as recruiting and training students "for careers related to engineering, computer science and other disciplines that expand the knowledge base and enhance the area's development potential." In sum, both the Southern Growth Policies Board and MDC agreed that Southern states needed to find ways to "increase the economic development role of higher education."

Over the past 25 years, reaction to these ideas has moved from "Why?" to "How?" as public university systems across the South and across the nation have been called on to increase activity in economic development and have begun to make efforts to respond to a growing drumbeat of demand. The University of North Carolina's history in creating and adapting a public higher education system to the needs of the state is illustrative of the approach of many public universities: While the system may have been halfway home in 1986, we are heading—slowly—toward home.

THE "SHADOWS" BEFORE "HALFWAY HOME"

North Carolina's first constitution, written in 1776, called on the state to create a university that would deliver "all useful learning." In the 200 years following, as the University of North Carolina grew into a system of sixteen four-year universities, campus activity intentionally focused on economic development was intermittent and anecdotal at best. Faculty expressed significant ambivalence about universities working directly with economic development partners. Over time, university leaders concluded that collaboration was possible: Research Triangle Park was off and running, with universities as key partners.

UNC and Economic Development, 1986–2007

By the time *Halfway Home* and *Shadows* were released, the success of the Research Triangle Park was apparent, but many in higher education remained skeptical about a broader commitment to economic development. Meaningful progress by UNC campuses in addressing the higher education and economic-development recommendations has come in two distinct stages, one incremental and one fundamental.

In the mid-1980s, the UNC system had four state-serving, economic development-oriented organizations: the Cooperative Extension Service, based out of North Carolina State University and North Carolina A&T State University; the Institute of

Government at UNC-Chapel Hill (now the School of Government); the Industrial Extension Service, based out of N.C. State's School of Engineering; and the Small Business Technology Development Center (then based out of the system offices of UNC General Administration and now administered through N.C. State). Since the 1980s, each organization's economic development capacity has grown impressively. The North Carolina Cooperative Extension Service has increased its responsiveness to demand for more assistance with value-added agriculture, food safety, and environmental issues. To its traditional education of state and local government officials, the School of Government added training modules and short courses on economic and community development. The Industrial Extension Service set new and ambitious goals for its work in business-efficiency consulting and has recently taken on high-profile work making the case for the value and future of North Carolina manufacturing. The Small Business Technology Development Center added to its hands-on work with small technology-based businesses to lead high-profile statewide programs on capital access and entrepreneurial development and has assisted businesses statewide in reworking business plans, particularly in the wake of the 2008 recession. Executive director Scott Daugherty simultaneously runs the organization and serves as the state's first-ever small-business commissioner.

Between 1986 and 2007, UNC campuses began developing their own centers, institutes, and organizations to work on economic-development-related issues, with work ranging from advocating regional and statewide economic development strategies to analyzing economic data to leading community development projects.

UNC and Economic Development, 2007–2011

What was missing was an organizing theory, a cohesive perspective on why and how universities might do this work. UNC got that in 2007 through UNC Tomorrow, a nine-month effort by the university to listen to what people across North Carolina wanted UNC to be and do over the next 20 years. Through a series of 39 meetings, with feedback from more than 10,000 people, a group of 15 UNC faculty members (the Scholars Council) worked with 25 commission members to recommend steps that the university should follow to meet the state's needs.

Three of the recommendations — that UNC do a better job of preparing students for the global economy, that it more intentionally work on community and economic development, and that its students, faculty, and staff should in general be more directly concerned with the communities and regions that surround them — provided a specific platform for campuses to increase their economic development work. The commission's recommendation that campuses actively look for ways to increase access to historically underserved regions and populations reaffirmed *Halfway Home*'s call for increased access and indirectly more remediation. And recommendations that UNC campuses strengthen programs in growing sectors such as health care and the green economy encouraged the synching of degree production with economic demand.

Since the UNC Tomorrow Commission reported its

recommendations in December 2007, campuses have mounted clear responses in each of these areas, stepping up efforts to connect students, faculty, and staff to the international economy, increasing student internships with businesses and nonprofits and government agencies, boosting enrollment in health care and environmental disciplines, and joining state efforts to increase the number of science, technology, engineering, and math graduates.

As the UNC School of Government, the Industrial Extension Service, and the Small Business Technology Development Center have launched increased economic development efforts, system campuses and administration have developed a series of regional responses.

- Five campuses have launched extensive rural community development projects, deploying students, faculty, and staff to work hand in hand with rural economic developers and planners to overcome challenges.
- Campuses have started or strengthened entrepreneurship centers designed to help increase the success of regional entrepreneurial efforts, whether they begin on campus or in the community. Each campus has formed a team to determine how it can work with businesses to more effectively and efficiently move intellectual property — technology and services — out of the laboratory and into the economy.
- Seven UNC campuses, including N.C. Central, N.C. State, and UNC-Chapel Hill, have joined Duke University, Rowan Cabarrus Community College, and 10 private companies at the N.C. Research Campus in Kannapolis as part of a public-private partnership to discover commercially viable solutions to nutritional and disease challenges.
- All UNC campuses, as a consequence of a memorandum of understanding with the N.C. Department of Commerce, meet regularly with state and regional economic developers to improve communication and collaboration.
- Responding to a series of recommendations developed in collaboration with IBM and other businesses, each UNC campus has formed a team to determine how to make it easier to transfer their technologies and discoveries out of labs and into commercial use. Working with campuses, General Administration also has developed a first-of-its-kind electronic portal that enables developers to find technology, research, and subject matter experts throughout the UNC system. REACH NC is intended to deepen partnerships between UNC and the business and economic development community.

The collective impact of the UNC system in economic development work is substantial. Beyond the work of UNC's statewide entities, beyond the impact of campus spending in communities, beyond the impact of each year's graduating class on the economy, beyond the impact of research spending and discoveries, more than 11,000 UNC students completed internships at more than 2,000 businesses, donating more than 800,000 hours of service to those businesses in 2010.

UNC and Economic Development, 2012–2036

The current and ongoing response to UNC Tomorrow represents an important step for the UNC campuses in approaching home and becoming the sort of public university system that *Halfway Home* and *Shadows* imagined. Safely reaching home will depend on UNC's ability to continue to make progress in three key areas:

Leadership: At least one person at each public university must be regularly examining the assets the campus can bring to bear on economic development and finding ways to deploy them. While each UNC chancellor has appointed a lead representative on "economic transformation," the amount of time those people are able to devote to this responsibility varies widely, from full-time leadership at East Carolina University to people wearing multiple hats on other campuses.

Mission: Campuses need to find ways officially to acknowledge the value of economic development work. So far there are some hopeful signs from campuses. East Carolina has revamped its mission statement, aspiring to become a "national model for public service and innovation." N.C. State's rewritten mission statement calls for the university to provide "leadership for...economic...development across North Carolina and around the world."

Recognition: Talking a good game about economic development and having programs and anecdotes to document good work can be useful. But taking the next steps to recognize and reward this activity makes the most significant difference. At Western Carolina, the school's adoption of the Carnegie Foundation for the Advancement of Teaching "Boyer Model" permits faculty to be promoted and granted tenure based on their work in engaged scholarship, including work in economic development, technology transfer, and applied research. UNC-Wilmington's new tenure guidelines note that as a public university, the school has a responsibility to engage aspects of the public and private sectors to enhance economic, social, and cultural development. At UNC-Greensboro, decisions regarding promotion and tenure can consider "business creation, growth or assistance activities" and "leadership in or making significant contributions to economic and community development activities." And as N.C. State describes what faculty must do, it encourages them to use their "knowledge and imagination" to "drive the economic and social systems of the state, the nation, and the world."

As more UNC campuses integrate the principles laid out in *Halfway Home* and *Shadows* into their core philosophy, they are likely to receive substantial encouragement from nonuniversity policymakers who believe universities can and must do more to help the economy. The devil comes in the details not addressed in the 1986 reports: How can we ensure that higher education is specific and responsive enough to be useful in preparing students for the job market while being broad and general enough to be relevant to the economy as it changes in ways we cannot predict? How can we continue to increase access when there is little will to increase investment in higher education? How do we define and evaluate quality in higher education? Even if we are most of the way home, we still have a long way to go in addressing those issues in the next 25 years.

REFERENCES

Link, Al. *From Seed to Harvest: The Growth of the Research Triangle Park*. Chapel Hill: University of North Carolina Press, 2002.

University of North Carolina Tomorrow Commission. *UNC Tomorrow Commission Final Report*. 2007. http://www.northcarolina.edu/nctomorrow/UNCT_Final_Report.pdf.

Western Carolina Quality Enhancement Plan and Boyer Model. http://www.wcu.edu/23521.asp

STATE INVESTMENT *in* Higher Education: *Rethinking the Impact on Economic Growth*

JAY SCHALIN

INTRODUCTION

Humanity has long sought a philosopher's stone—a magic mechanism that creates riches out of simple materials. From ancient mythical kings with the "golden touch" through medieval alchemists attempting to turn base metals into gold and silver and Goethe's Faust and Mephisto producing unlimited wealth through confidence-backed credit money, the search continues.

In recent years, many influential people believe they have at last found the key to guaranteed wealth creation: investment in higher education. Former Iowa governor Tom Vilsack illustrates the widespread faith in this belief: "We need to invest more…to spur innovation and creativity. If we endow chairs and recruit great faculty to our universities, the brightest and best minds can be attracted to Iowa. If we expand lab space and incubator space, those bright minds can transfer into new products and new opportunities for Iowa."

Advocates justify public spending on higher education by citing close correlations between wealth and education levels and by pointing to successful high-tech clusters near major research universities. Economic studies abound showing that each public dollar invested in higher education is multiplied two or more times as it wends its way through the local or regional economy. Policymakers in particular perceive universities as some sort of field of economic dreams—fund them, and prosperity will come.

But the fundamental relationship between education and economic growth requires much more scrutiny. One question especially needs asking: "Does increased state support for higher education lead to economic growth?" The answer does not come easily.

THE LINK BETWEEN HIGHER EDUCATION AND ECONOMIC GROWTH?

Some things stand out clearly. We can be fairly certain that gains in knowledge—improvements in job skills, education levels, technology levels, innovation, and so on—contribute to rising living standards. The relationship between education and economic growth has been acknowledged at least since 1890, when neoclassical economist Alfred Marshall wrote that "knowledge is our most powerful engine of production."

Furthermore, innovation is increasingly tied to higher education because innovation requires more highly specialized learning and training than it did in the past. University-trained scientists have replaced the backyard mechanic and shop floor tinkerer as the primary sources of technical breakthroughs.

Yet to acknowledge the link between growth and higher education is not the same as saying that increased public support of higher education necessarily causes a healthier economy. Indeed, if the returns on investment in higher education were as great as many studies claim, then why would anything but exponential growth occur anywhere on the globe? Governments could throw every possible dollar into their university systems, then watch their societies flourish. Yet this is not happening.

But that fact has not stopped policymakers and scholars from proclaiming higher education as the main engine of economic development. And much of academia has adopted this redefinition of its purpose with relish and has eagerly engaged its two partners in the endeavor—the business community and government.

This cooperation is not new. The intent behind the state land-grant universities founded in the 19th century was to facilitate commerce. By 1912, many universities had patenting and licensing offices to smooth the transfer of technology from school laboratories to the production line. Yet World War II, with its urgent demands for sophisticated weaponry and rapid communications, really brought all three institutions into full cooperation. Collaboration subsequently grew more intense. Federal funding of research remained at high levels through the 1950s, fueled first by Cold War defense spending and then by the space race. The Department of Defense was joined by the National Institutes of Health, the National Science Foundation, and in the 1970s the Department of Energy as major funding sources for universities and industry.

Hence, a new model of the university emerged. It was dubbed the "multiversity" by former University of California president Clark Kerr in a seminal 1963 article in *Harper's*, "The Multiversity: Are Its Several Souls Worth Saving?" Departing from the long-standing conception of academia as an isolated community of scholars, Kerr's vision embraced society and accepted new roles of involvement.

A new business model emerged in the postwar era, too. It was based on knowledge, innovation, entrepreneurship, and the ability to make rapid adjustments. Government's participation in the economy exploded as well. According to the Bureau of Economic Analysis, government activity was 13 percent of the U.S. gross domestic product in 1930; in 1947, that number had grown to 24 percent; and in 2009 it was 46 percent.

The term *triple helix* was adopted by Henry Etzkowitz, Phil Cooke, and Loet Leydesdorff, among others, to describe the cooperation among government, private industry, and universities. As the name implies, it refers to three independent structures joined together to create one structure.

Higher education's new role kicked into high gear in 1980 with passage of the University and Small Business Patent Procedures Act, commonly called Bayh-Dole. This law gave universities much more ability to get exclusive patents and licenses from federally funded research in the hope that this change would give the sluggish economy of the 1970s a jolt.

THE RISE OF THE TRIPLE HELIX

The triple helix is considered generally to be a win-win-win situation. Universities use government and private industry funding for research, often in shared endeavors, and everyone benefits: professors can take their innovations private, schools get research money and patent and licensing fees, government gets a stimulated economy, and businesses use university research and university-trained workers.

Yet despite the triple helix's nearly universal acceptance in policy circles, whether the nation has benefited from this taxpayer-supported development is

> The relationship between education and economic growth has been acknowledged at least since 1890, when neoclassical economist Alfred Marshall wrote that "knowledge is our most powerful engine of production."

difficult to know. Neither government nor academia is known for efficient use of resources or ability to discern profitable endeavors. Confidence in government funding ignores an obvious problem. Risk is substantial in high-tech and especially biotech ventures, and if projects are deemed too risky by private venture capitalists, whose livelihoods are based on making wise decisions about risk, then it is likely that government support of these projects is doomed to fail.

And it may not be possible to create high-tech centers at will. In spite of his great enthusiasm for the triple helix, Etzkowitz contends that "a local region must have some scientific and technological institutions" before attempts to turn it into a scientific and technical hot spot will be successful. Similarly, Dan Berglund and Marianne Clarke state that "to build an R&D base requires a long-term, sustained, and significant investment." They add that government should make up for any venture capital "shortfalls."

And the final results may not justify all the effort. A 2003 Brookings Institution report, "Signs of Life," casts doubt on the impact of new biotech companies. According to *University, Inc.* author Jennifer Washburn, the report stated that "most biotech companies are small, so new job creation tends to be limited…. [M]ost biotech start-ups, even the successful ones, do not grow into large pharmaceutical firms. Instead, they tend to license their technologies to larger, established drug companies, to form joint ventures, or to sell off their entire companies, so that whatever commercial activity they generate locally may actually be short-lived."

A key trade-off caused by Bayh-Dole and other triple-helix mechanisms is between basic research, in which underlying scientific principles are sought, and applied research, which seeks to solve more immediate problems. According to Washburn, universities increasingly tend to forgo basic research while hoping for financial gain from applied research.

This reduces new knowledge for the common domain, to be used freely by all, thus "weakening the nation's capacity for innovation."

The focus on monetary rewards from research raises another critique. Innovation has a powerful random quality that can foil the best-laid plans. A state can invest many millions on university research without any return; in contrast, a lone professor with little or no grant money can make a discovery that leads to many millions in future tax revenues for the state.

In fact, most universities have failed to garner large profits from their research. A 2003 study by Cornell University economists Ronald Ehrenberg, Michael Rizzo, and George Jakubson found that for 138 major research institutions in 2000, the median of net revenues from patents and licenses was only $343,952.

CONCLUSION

In the final analysis, there is a definitive answer to this essay's central question: Does increased state spending on higher education promote economic growth? That answer is, sometimes it does, and sometimes it does not.

That statement is not meant to be facetious. State investment in education, like just about everything else under the sun, is subject to the law of diminishing marginal returns. We all can get too much of a good thing, and the answer to whether more of a good thing is beneficial usually depends on how much of it has already been used. Invest a little in higher education, and it yields great rewards; invest too much, and it chokes off other opportunities for growth.

So where are we now? Two economic models, one by Rich Vedder and Matthew Denhart and one by Bornali Bhandari and Bradley Curs, provide some insight. Both fit the classic Laffer curve model of diminishing returns, and they indicate that our society has already crossed the threshold at which more spending on

higher education no longer has a positive effect on the economy. The Bhandari-Curs model also suggests that some public investment may be simply replacing private money, rendering state subsidies ineffective at best.

However, much more research in this area needs to be conducted. But these economists are likely onto something. Some expenditures by colleges, such as high levels of nonfaculty staffing, obviously do not contribute to growth. Even more spending on education may no longer produce economic gains. Roughly half of all Americans go to college within a few years of turning 18, meaning that nearly all of the few gifted individuals with the ability to innovate and create economic growth are already attending.

But even if state money targets only practical research, it does not automatically translate into growth. Government and academic officials are usually ill equipped to make investment decisions based on the potential monetary returns from research. For example, Washburn cites Arthur Rolnick, a senior vice president at the Federal Reserve Bank of Minneapolis, who "strongly questioned the wisdom of asking the state's university system to drive economic development and productivity in the state. States weren't very good at picking 'winners and losers,' he said, and neither were universities."

Too often, policymakers hoping to create the next Research Triangle Park assume that the same conditions that existed in the North Carolina of the 1950s exist perpetually in every state in the union. But the Triangle is the creation of a particularly promising place at a particular point in time. According to Albert Link, a University of North Carolina at Greensboro economics professor who wrote the definitive history of the park, its founders took note of the nation's first high-tech clusters formed around colleges (in Boston and what is now Silicon Valley in California). They also realized the potential of having three world-class research universities in close proximity to one another and understood that the nation was ripe for a tremendous expansion of research after World War II. In so doing, they were far ahead of the rest of the country. Today, the landscape seems to be less promising, as every state is attempting to attract research development. When all is said and done, alternatives—including tax relief and regulatory reform—might grow the economy better.

But just as we should not expect that throwing money at higher education will produce vast economic benefits, we should be just as wary of dismantling our public university systems before we know more. We can be fairly sure of some things: Having large numbers of smart young people study difficult and important subjects is good for the world and the economy. And having extremely smart people explore the wonders of the universe leads to greater knowledge, which in turn leads to greater material comfort.

So the key word is *caution* until more is known. That caution must be practiced first and foremost by those demanding more funding for higher education on the basis that universities are the "engine" of economic growth. Higher education is much more likely to be one small component in a vast economic engine that is difficult to comprehend. After trying to cut through the confusion, it appears that current general levels of public spending on higher education are very likely too much of a good thing, limiting rather than promoting economic growth.

REFERENCES

Berglund, Dan, and Marianne Clarke. *Using Research and Development to Grow State Economies*. Washington, D.C.: NGA Center for Best Practices, 2000. http://www.nga.org/Files/pdf/2000RESEARCH.pdf.

Bhandari, Bornali, and Bradley R. Curs. "The Roles of Higher Education Expenditure and the Privatization of the Higher Education on U.S. States' Economic Growth." 2008. In possession of the author.

Chantrill, Christopher. *U.S. Government Spending as Percent of GDP*. 2009. www.usgovernmentspending.com/us_20th_century_chart.html#usgs303.

Cooke, Philip, and Loet Leydesdorff. "Regional Development in the Knowledge-Based Economy: The Construction of Advantage." *Journal of Technology Transfer* 31 (2005): 5–16.

Etzkowitz, Henry. *The Triple-Helix of University-Industry-Government: Implications for Policy and Evaluation*. Stockholm: Swedish Institute for Studies in Education and Research, 2002. www.sister.nu.

Link, Albert N. *A Generosity of Spirit: The Early History of the Research Triangle Park*. Research Triangle Park: Research Triangle Foundation of North Carolina, 1995.

Vedder, Richard, and Matthew Denhart. "North Carolina Higher Education: Facts and Fiction." 2007. In possession of the author.

Washburn, Jennifer. *University, Inc.: The Corporate Corruption of Higher Education*. New York: Basic Books, 2005.

UNIVERSITY AND COMMUNITY:
What Is the Role *for* Economic Development?

JESSE L. WHITE JR.

Halfway Home and a Long Way to Go set the goal: "Increase the economic development role of higher education by 1992." As far as I know, this statement was the first—and certainly the most important—acknowledgment of the critical relationship between two domains that had been historically placed in separate policy "smokestacks." This recommendation led to a greater focus on the role of postsecondary education in the development process. Between 2004 and 2011, I had the opportunity to act on this recommendation as director of the Office of Economic and Business Development.

The Commission on the Future of the South recognized that the economy was moving rapidly from one based on brawn to one based on brains, or human and intellectual capital. And since higher education had a substantial role in creating human capital, the report focused on ways to improve it and to include minority, disadvantaged, and rural students. The objective called for improvements in the structure of governance (arguing that the "systems" should be rationalized), for higher quality tied to funding formulas, for more and better remediation, for more scholarships to disadvantaged students, and for the building of bridges between the private sector and academia. Only the last recommendation dealt with specific economic development approaches for postsecondary education; the others dealt with quality and access.

The higher education objective was closely related to others of the ten recommendations, especially those dealing with producing a globally competitive workforce, increasing the region's capacity to develop and use technology, and developing pragmatic leaders with a global vision. Increasingly, higher education was seen to have a role in solving a variety of complex, often seemingly intractable, problems. Some universities were beginning to become centers of entrepreneurial development through spinoffs. Over the next few decades, college and university assets became part of the discussion of economic development.

There are three categories of postsecondary education institutions dealing with economic development. The first is the land-grant colleges created by the Morrill Act of 1862 and the system of historically black schools created in 1890. These colleges were the original technology transfer systems, producing applied research in agriculture and transferring it to farmers through the Co-Op Extension Service. These universities later began working in industrial extension and specific emerging sectors such as life science, aerospace, medical devices, and defense. Many, like North Carolina State University, created millennium campuses to promote company creation. It is noteworthy that all of the public universities cited in Innovation U (see below) are land-grants.

The second category is two-year community colleges. They began after World War II to retool from junior colleges preparing students for four-year colleges to a focus on vocational training and skill development. Led by North Carolina in the 1950s, community colleges began "customized training" programs to prepare workers for employment in specific industries. Community colleges also established sector-specific centers such as the Hosiery Technology Center at Catawba Community College. They supported entrepreneurship by creating small-business assistance centers connected to most colleges. As Cynthia Liston, Trent Williams, and Stuart Rosenfeld state, "By the 1990s, economic development had become a widely accepted part of the community-college mission, with many institutions providing a broader range of services."

Finally, regional four-year colleges also had an important niche to fill. Less burdened by the "publish or perish" imperative of research universities, their administrators and faculty often created programs to help with community economic development in their service areas. The legendary Cotton Robinson, president of Western Carolina University, created the Center for Improving Mountain Living in the 1970s. East Carolina University created a regional development institute, now called the Office of Engagement and Innovation. Outreach offices were also created by regional universities in states other than North Carolina, such as Mississippi's Delta State University and Alabama's Jacksonville State University.

An increasing focus on understanding and promoting the complex relationship between higher education and economic development emerged from the board's "Innovation U: New University Roles in a Knowledge Economy" report, which examined 10 areas in which these new roles were emerging:

- industry research partnerships;
- technology transfer;
- industrial extension and technical assistance;
- entrepreneurial development;
- industry education and training partnerships;
- career services and placement;
- formal partnerships with economic development organizations;
- industry/university advisory boards and councils;
- faculty culture and rewards; and
- leadership structures, policies, and institutionalization.

The authors examined 12 case studies of universities doing excellent work in these 10 areas. Three of the institutions were in the South: Georgia Tech, North Carolina State, and Virginia Tech. Georgia Tech was considered best in class.

Innovation U was followed by more research on these relationships, much of it from the board's Southern Technology Council and a nonprofit spinoff, Regional Technology

Strategies. Others followed up on these themes, including the Appalachian Regional Commission (where I served as federal cochair), MDC of Chapel Hill, the National Governors' Association, and the Corporation for Enterprise Development.

In addition, national associations of universities working in this domain blossomed. The National Association of Management and Technical Assistance Centers, begun as an association of the Economic Development Administration–funded centers, changed its name to the University Economic Development Association. Perhaps more significantly, the National Association of Universities and Land Grant Colleges (now called the Association of Public and Land Grant Colleges) created a very active committee, the Council on Innovation, Competitiveness, and Economic Prosperity, which is chaired by one of the university presidents.

One could argue that the South has made considerable progress toward connecting three categories of public colleges and universities to the economic development enterprise. A special challenge, however, has been the non-land-grant universities that are categorized by the Carnegie Foundation as doctoral/research extensive. In the South, these include the University of Virginia, UNC-Chapel Hill, and the Universities of South Carolina, Alabama, and Mississippi. (Most of the other flagships also are the land-grants.) The source of some of the most distinguished scholarship in the world, they are often not well connected to the states they serve. The "publish or perish" system of rewards discourages public service and applied research.

An example of the struggle unfolded at UNC-Chapel Hill, which, like most research universities, moved into more formal roles of economic development with the passage of the

1980 Bayh-Dole Act giving universities the property rights to federally funded research innovations and discovery. In 1994, UNC created its Office of Technology Development to promote and manage technology transfer to the private sector, including licensing agreements and company spinoffs. And, of course, engagement work had been going on for years in individual departments (City and Regional Planning and so forth), schools (Public Health, Government, and the like), and centers (such as the Kenan Institute and Odum Institute)

Beginning in the 2000s, the administration began to build a broad-ranging and senior administrative structure to help deploy UNC's assets for the good of the state, especially economic development. The following steps were taken:

- March 2002: Office of Associate Vice Chancellor for Economic Development and Technology Transfer created;
- April 2003: "Economic Development" added to the title of Vice Chancellor for Research and Economic Development;
- April 2004: Office of Economic and Business Development created; and
- November 2006: Office of Vice Chancellor for Public Service and Engagement created.

All of these units were designed to create a focal point for interdisciplinary work relating to economic development not just in the Research Triangle but across the state. Some of the many innovations were campuswide seminars on state economic development research, grant funds for research, corps of graduate students to assist local governments, multidisciplinary studies, and annual campus dialogues on engaged scholarship.

Unfortunately, all of these units have since been dismantled. This retrenchment occurred as the recession tightened its grip on North Carolina—exactly when the state most needed the help of its flagship research university. To some degree, the engagement infrastructure has been replaced by a focus on innovation and entrepreneurship. While this is a worthy emphasis for students, many of whom will become North Carolina's future leaders, the spatial impact of this initiative will redound almost entirely to the Research Triangle area. This region is already the most prosperous in the state and will likely renew the criticism that UNC-Chapel Hill's direct economic impact benefits mostly its immediate locale.

A remaining bright spot has been the UNC system's commitment to promoting economic development. This effort began under the presidency of Molly Broad (1997–2005), when staff was devoted to encouraging and promoting economic development outreach on all sixteen campuses. This focus increased under President Erskine Bowles (2005–10), who hired Leslie Boney as the associate vice president for economic development and engagement. The Economic Transformation Council consists of senior officials from each campus who meet once a quarter to discuss how their universities are undertaking the work of community economic development. Economic development was one of the central thrusts of Bowles's UNC Tomorrow report.

In sum, it would be fair to say that the states of the Southern Growth Policies Board have taken seriously the mandate "to increase the economic development role of higher education." The commitment has not been uniform, and the current budget crisis in every state has put enormous stress on this work. But with the prospects of global competitiveness becoming ever more acute, deploying UNC and its peer universities' intellectual capital into the communities of the South is more important than ever.

REFERENCES

Liston, Cynthia, Trent Williams, and Stuart Rosenfeld. "Reporting to Work: Postsecondary Institutions as Regional Economic Development Actors." *Popular Government*, Spring–Summer 2004, 23–30.

INCREASING THE SOUTH'S CAPACITY TO INNOVATE AND
IMPLEMENT NEW ECONOMIC DEVELOPMENT STRATEGIES

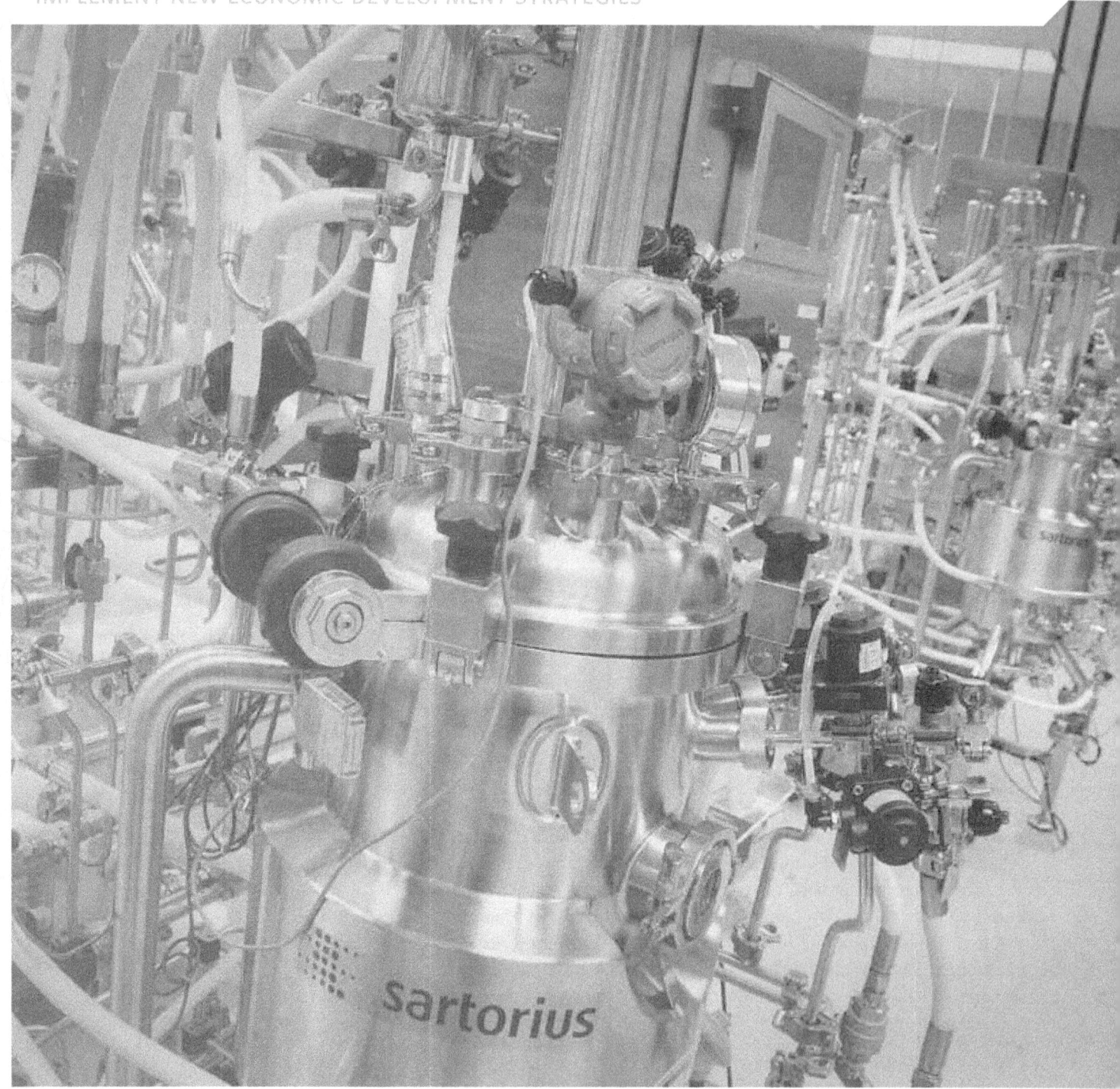

Southern Industrialization Revisited:
Industrial Recruitment as a Strategic Tool *for* Local Economic Development

NICHOLA LOWE

INTRODUCTION

Southern industrialization has long been associated with the practice of industrial recruitment: that is, an attempt by state and local governments to lure business establishments and investment to a region, often with the help of generous incentive offers or subsidies. As noted in MDC's *Shadows in the Sunbelt* report, "The Southern strategy for economic development has been simple: Recruit new industry. Industrial recruiters have been able to claim great success as thousands of new plants have located in the South, both in urban and rural areas." A similar message was echoed in *Halfway Home and a Long Way to Go*'s review of economic development practice. Still, while acknowledging economic and employment gains from recruitment, both reports recommended significant policy changes in an attempt to end the pernicious practice of recruiting firms on the basis of a cheap, complacent Southern workforce and minimally regulated business environment.

Twenty-five years later, industrial recruitment continues to dominate Southern — and for that matter, non-Southern — economic development. At first glance, this suggests that the calls for reform put forward by the Southern Growth Policies Board and MDC were largely ignored. Yet in pushing for change, the authors of these influential reports also were careful to reserve space for improvements to industrial recruitment. In this regard, they foreshadowed and likely helped inspire institutional changes currently under way in several areas of the South today.

This essay highlights some of these accomplished reforms through a case study of industrial recruitment involving North Carolina's biopharma manufacturing industry. In particular, it features innovative aspects of North Carolina's approach to recruitment and the specific steps that are taken by state and local practitioners to embed this strategy within a larger economic planning effort that centers on making high-quality jobs both accessible and long lasting in the state. The future challenge for this region is drawing policy inspiration and direction from this and related cases to reclaim industrial recruitment as a truly innovative, development-enhancing Southern tradition.

BACKGROUND AND CONTEXT

With the creation of the Balance Agriculture with Industry program in 1936, Mississippi became the first U.S. state officially to sanction and support industrial recruitment. The program was vetted and designed carefully, with nested layers of state and federal oversight and the added requirement that local decisions regarding the use of scarce public resources for incentivizing industry recruitment be put to a community-wide vote. Other Southern states quickly followed Mississippi's lead, thus enabling state and local agencies throughout the region to finance industrial recruitment and retention activities and incentives and hire dedicated staff to support these efforts.

Still, as these strategies diffused across the regional landscape, recruitment practices changed considerably, and in the process, many of the early standards achieved through the program were watered down. Furthermore, recruitment efforts were dramatically rescaled, shifting from smaller deals with manageable incentive amounts in the 1950s and 1960s to fiercely competitive megadeals involving hundreds of millions in corporate tax breaks and cash giveaways from the 1980s onward. It is not surprising, therefore, that strategy diffusion met with considerable criticism, especially from economic development scholars and historians who claimed that Southern recruitment efforts simply encouraged Northern businesses to relocate south to take advantage of lower production costs, mostly in the form of a less educated and nonunionized workforce. In addition to the ever-increasing size of incentive offers, concern about labor arbitrage and growing awareness that businesses could easily relocate to even cheaper, non-U.S. locations eventually led to calls for widespread reform both from within and outside the South.

Over the past few decades, economic development practice in the region has changed considerably. Like other states, those in the South have embraced alternative development strategies and goals designed to promote entrepreneurship, upgrade and innovate technologies, and deepen workforce skills, often through increased investments in university infrastructure. Furthermore, many Southern states have tackled pressing equity concerns head-on by expanding the reach of their vocational-tech and community college systems, with the goal of providing individuals with a "second-chance" educational system for securing quality job opportunities and transferring existing skills from declining to expanding industrial sectors. These efforts reflect insightful recommendations made by both MDC and the 1986 Commission on the Future of the South.

But this story of Southern strategy reform involves more than just a shift away from traditional recruitment activities. It also involves significant improvements to recruitment practice itself. Southern states continue to rely heavily on industrial recruitment. In fact, a national survey conducted in 2009 by the International City/County Management Association found that twice as many southern counties and municipalities had official plans for guiding industrial recruitment activities as had comparable plans for small-business development or industrial retention. As this finding suggests, recruitment remains a regional policy priority and continues to guide contemporary economic development activities in the South.

Still, it is important to recognize that not all industrial recruitment is the same. Some places in the South continue to recruit businesses in less than ideal ways and often rely on the use of excessive incentives that can undermine much-needed public services, including public education. But others use recruitment in a more strategic and targeted way and in the process embrace standards and performance controls that help to temper and moderate excessive incentive use. Furthermore, in some places, recruitment is not simply viewed as a development panacea but rather is situated within a larger portfolio of complementary development strategies, including those supporting workforce development and small-business assistance. In this context, recruitment may be used strategically to fill gaps in the local supply chain, to elevate the global status of or reposition a regional industry or cluster, or to expand career ladder opportunities for less educated individuals who might normally be excluded from processes of economic, industrial, and technological transformation. Furthermore, by linking recruitment to other economic development strategies, practitioners in these places not only influence firms' initial location decisions but also, and more important, help to anchor them to the region and thus help to buffer against future rounds of disinvestment. Turning to North Carolina, we see how strategic recruitment efforts have been institutionalized in the case of biomanufacturing, with job-access and skill-transference concerns in mind.

RECRUITING IN THE LIFE SCIENCES

In recent decades, North Carolina has established itself as a national leader in life science industry development. Ranked third in the nation after California and Massachusetts, North Carolina boasts an expanding population of entrepreneurial biotechnology and medical device companies as well as the nation's highest concentration of clinical trial research support firms, most of which are homegrown. In addition, North Carolina is home to a fast-expanding biopharma manufacturing subsector, with prominent global firms in the mix, including Merck, Pfizer, Novartis, Biogen-Idec, and NovoNordisk. As this suggests, life science employment opportunities are not only isolated to holders of advanced degrees but also expand across all segments of the industry and include everything from entry-level production operators and manufacturing quality-control specialists to pharma technicians and research scientists. And this employment diversity is by design.

State agencies continue to play a crucial role in building the institutional infrastructure needed to support life science innovation and entrepreneurship. This includes investing in institutions of higher education, research laboratories, technology-transfer systems, and venture financing. But industrial recruitment also plays a pivotal role in industry and employment expansion. This is especially true for biopharmaceutical manufacturing, whose development provides important job alternatives to both new labor-market entrants and manufacturing workers displaced from declining sectors in the state, such as textiles, furniture, and microelectronics. In contrast to other prominent life science states, few of North Carolina's biopharma manufacturers are homegrown. In fact, close to 85 percent are nonlocal, and many of them were actively recruited from Europe, Japan, and other U.S. locations.

In supporting the expansion of biopharma manufacturing, North Carolina's state government has long been praised for its innovative workforce development initiatives. But it is also a successful case of strategic industrial recruitment, which has been institutionalized through three interrelated practices. First, biopharma manufacturing recruitment efforts are best described as proactive and paced. State agencies try to avoid surprise deals, which can

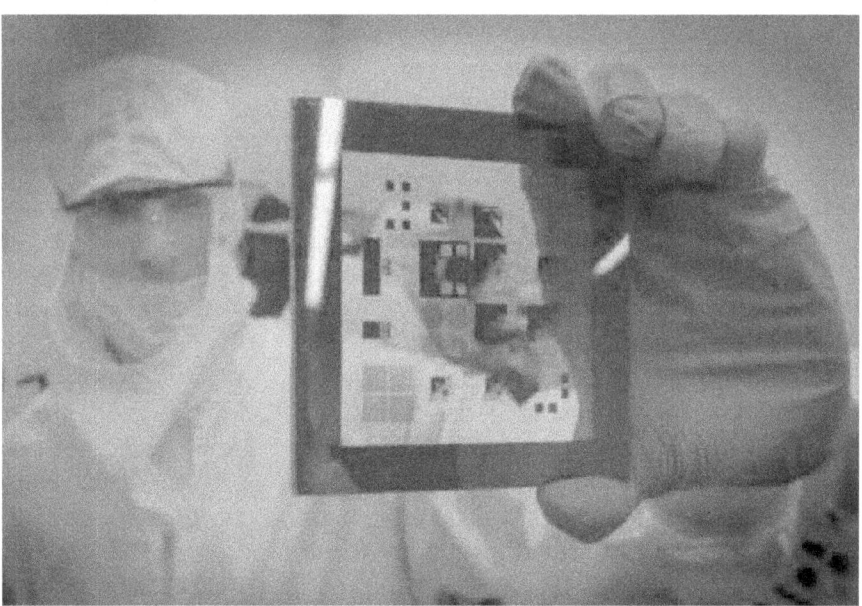

undermine both preparedness and North Carolina's relative bargaining power. Instead, state agencies spend considerable time and resources identifying prospective biopharma firms years in advance of when they need to establish new manufacturing facilities. Staff at these agencies focus almost exclusively on industry analysis and data gathering. They continuously update information on hundreds of international life sciences firms, much of it gathered through informal conversations at industry meetings, networking events, and conferences. This information is used to estimate the time frame — often several years out — when pharmaceutical or biotech firms might be ready to establish new production facilities and ultimately helps state and local recruiters prepare well in advance for discussions with these firms and their site-location representatives.

A second, related activity involves up-front community preparation. Other states also support community development, often by helping local practitioners catalog and market industrial buildings and available infrastructure. But North Carolina prioritizes local-practitioner education. Local practitioners are brought into a state-coordinated outreach system that enables them to learn about the nuances of the biopharma industry, including technology and skill demands of both large and small manufacturing firms. Practitioners also learn about existing institutional supports within the state and how to leverage them to make their community more attractive to these firms. Again, this is not something that happens in response to a call by an industrial prospect but rather involves an ongoing process of outreach and professional development support.

A third important step involves bringing workforce development agencies into the mix early in the negotiation process. In other states, training institutions typically function in the background and during the early phase of a recruitment deal may simply be asked to write letters of support outlining the

> State agencies continue to play a crucial role in building the institutional infrastructure needed to support life science innovation and entrepreneurship.

state's training commitment. In contrast, representatives from North Carolina's community college system are brought in early in the process and essentially sit at the head table during the first round of negotiations with prospective firms. In this regard, educators are treated as equals to state recruiters and thus receive an equal opportunity to learn about and influence prospective firms' thinking. This becomes essential for promoting the state's workforce development strengths and recruiting firms on the basis of worker skill and quality.

These practices are institutionalized through a complex division of labor involving three state-funded agencies. An essential actor in this partnership is the North Carolina Biotech Center (NCBC), which was established in 1981 as the nation's first state-funded economic development agency in the life sciences. The NCBC primarily focuses on information gathering and reaching out to life science firms at various phases of development. As the initial contact point for prospective firms, the NCBC also helps to reinforce long-range strategic thinking. In contrast to more traditional recruiters, NCBC staff are evaluated and rewarded not solely on the basis of successful recruitment deals but rather on the quality and depth of the relationships they develop with companies that may become future recruits. This practice encourages NCBC staff to stay well ahead of the recruitment process and to deepen their industry knowledge and networks.

The Department of Commerce, an agency often known as a more traditional recruiter in the state, also plays a key role. However, within this partnership, its primary responsibility is community preparation—that is, helping local practitioners connect to various resources, networks, and individuals that can move them up the steep learning curve. Once NCBC has identified an interested firm, Commerce staff work with eligible communities and help them respond to the company's request for information.

The third major player is BioNetwork, a consortium of community colleges in the state that provides specialized biopharma training. Its primary role is to promote the state's workforce development system and to work with recruited firms to identify and address skills gaps. This partnership, which essentially forms the core of North Carolina's biomanufacturing recruitment team, was formalized about five years ago but builds on strong institutional connections that date back 15 years or so.

This coordinated effort improves recruitment practice. First, this structure opens up the possibility for better community-company matchmaking. By working with communities and drawing on in-depth industry information, the biomanufacturing recruitment team is in a position to put forward select communities that offer the best combination of assets for a given firm. This approach can put team members in a potentially awkward situation where they might be accused of simply playing favorites among communities. To address this concern, recruiters also use their deep understanding of the industry to identify a subset of firms that recognize real advantages to locating in more remote or rural areas of the state. For example, a maker of poultry vaccines saw value in locating in a rural county, closer to its customer base. But team members also work together to develop and better market unique advantages of the state's different regions.

This team approach also encourages a shift in focus away from the incentive offer toward other regional assets and advantages, such as quality local labor and strong research and development supports. In fact, by staying in close communication with firms, team members can intervene when an incentive offer is initially requested and work to draw the focus toward other regional assets. Furthermore, by helping local practitioners recognize the importance of these locational advantages, the recruitment team helps to shift the bargaining power from the site-location consultant to the community while helping to reinforce performance standards for any local incentive that might be offered. This is not to say that the team's actions eliminate incentives altogether; rather, by carefully mediating this recruitment process, the team shifts the focus to other locational advantages, thereby helping to reduce the relative size and importance of the incentive. As one illustration, an executive from Novartis stated in the *Atlanta Journal-Constitution* that the "main reason for selecting" a site in Holly Springs, North Carolina, "was the availability of a highly trained workforce." Although Georgia offered Novartis a significantly larger incentive package, North Carolina was selected for the $1.2 billion vaccine-manufacturing plant because of the high quality of public education and workforce development.

HOPEFUL LESSONS FOR THE FUTURE

The wrong lesson for other states in the South is simply to follow North Carolina's lead in life sciences. This industry, after all, has specific institutional demands to support ongoing processes of innovation and applied research and development—institutions that North Carolina has spent decades building. Biomanufacturing firms are less dependent on these particular institutions because they are not research and development intensive. Nonetheless, they are attracted by North Carolina's rich institutional environment and in recent years have even turned to some of these support institutions for help in biomanufacturing innovations.

Rather, the transferable lesson involves the particular way that recruitment is institutionalized and embedded. As we see from this North Carolina example, low-wage advantages have given way to the active promotion of workforce skill and customized training supports, qualities that are relevant to a wide range of industries, not just life sciences. Similarly scattershot approaches to recruitment are being replaced by sectoral strategies that target specific groupings of firms, often with a goal of filling gaps in local supply chains or career ladders. Other states in the South likely will have a distinct set of regional advantages and industrial and institutional legacies from which to build a strategy of sector targeting. Still, by targeting particular sectors and using recruitment to address gaps, whether employment or supply chain related, state leaders will be in a better position to focus institutional resources and guide policy learning. Moreover, recruitment activities in North Carolina are highly coordinated, involving intensive collaboration among multiple agencies and nested levels of government. This structure helps to provide an important check against opportunism and hasty decision making on the part of potentially job-hungry communities. The ultimate result is a more tempered approach to industrial recruitment that not only helps to limit excessive incentive use but also ensures that recruitment activities are firmly anchored to strategic economic development goals. In this regard, recruitment complements rather than competes with other aspects of economic development and functions as one element of a coherent policy platform.

REFERENCES

Bartik, Timothy. "Solving the Problems of Economic Development Incentives." *Growth and Change* 36 (2005): 139–66.

Cobb, James C. *The Selling of the South*. 2nd ed. Urbana: University of Illinois Press, 1993.

Goetz, Stephan, Steven C. Deller, and Thomas R. Harris, eds. *Targeting Regional Economic Development*. New York: Routledge, 2009.

Lowe, Nichola. 2010. *Beyond the Deal: Integrating Industrial Recruitment into Economic Development Planning*. Lincoln Institute of Land Policy working paper. https://www.lincolninst.edu/pubs/dl/1782_1002_Lowe%20Final.pdf.

Markusen, Ann, ed. *Reining in the Competition for Capital*. Kalamazoo, Mich.: Upjohn Institute, 2007.

Weber, Rachel. "Do Better Contracts Make Better Economic Development Incentives?" *Journal of the American Planning Association* 68 (2002): 43–55.

SOUTHERN REGIONAL INNOVATION STRATEGIES

MARYANN FELDMAN AND STUART ROSENFELD

INTRODUCTION

The 1986 Commission on the Future of South gave significant credibility and legitimacy to ongoing Southern regional efforts to build capacity for science and technology as a driver of technology-based economic development. Stuart Rosenfeld served as deputy director of the Southern Growth Policies Board, where he founded and directed the Southern Technology Council. This advisory council on innovation and technology policy comprised professionals in the science, technology, and economic development fields and had as its principal mission strengthening the Southern economy through technology and innovation. Each state was responsible for setting its own priorities and designing its own programs.

As states in the South moved away from a historic dependence on agriculture and low-wage nondurable goods manufacturing to highly skilled high-tech industries and services, research and development activities became more prominent. This essay examines progress made to date in the South. North Carolina has arguably been the most successful state in realizing gains. Next, the essay turns to an examination of specific policies that were instrumental in crafting economic growth in North Carolina. We conclude by considering the path forward.

MEASURING PROGRESS

While we would prefer to report information on the rate of new product innovations introduced to the market, the implementation of productivity-enhancing technology, or the formation of new firm start-ups, our indicators are limited to research and development activities. Still, how research and development is performed is a good intermediate indicator of a state's capacity to generate the outcomes associated with economic growth. The South unfortunately still lags the nation. Table 7.1 examines research and development undertaken in each state along with gross domestic product, an indicator of state wealth. States are listed in the order of the amount of research and development conducted, with Virginia and North Carolina each accounting for more than $9 billion in research and development in 2007, the latest year for which data are available. Column 2 provides the overall size of the state economy, showing Georgia to be approximately equal to Virginia and North Carolina, with gross domestic product of $400 billion. Column 5 presents each state's rank in terms of the amount of research and development conducted, normalized by gross domestic product. This is considered a measure of how focused the state's economy is on knowledge-intensive activities. In the South, Virginia is the most highly ranked, at 17th in the nation, while North Carolina is 19th. Eight of the Southern states are in the bottom quartile nationally, and Louisiana is 50th.

It also is useful to examine who is performing research and development in each state. Table 7.2 considers how much research and development was undertaken at federal government labs and facilities, by industry, and by universities in each state. Nationally, federal labs account for about 7 percent of research and development; however, in four southern states—Alabama, Mississippi, West Virginia, and Virginia—government labs account for more than twice the national rate. Federal labs are working to translate their research into more commercial opportunities; however, doing so has proven challenging because of the specialized nature of the research conducted for government agencies.

To help the states with the weakest economies and least wealth (which nearly always also had the fewest technological resources), the federal government established the Experimental Program to Stimulate Competitive Research (EPSCoR) in 1979, which sought to compensate for selected states' uneven ability to compete for federal research and development funds. Its mission is to assist the National Science Foundation in its statutory function "to strengthen research and education in science and engineering throughout the United States and to avoid undue concentration of such research and education." All of the Southern states except for Virginia, North Carolina, and Georgia qualify for EPSCoR. The result is that the percentage of research and development undertaken at Southern universities is higher than that for the nation overall. As university research is typically far removed from the market, the direct benefits to the state have a long time horizon.

Private industry research and development is the best indicator of economic vibrancy: industry conducts research and development with the purpose of creating profits that have more immediate economic impact. Industry accounts for the largest share of U.S. research and development. The only Southern state that comes close to the national rate is North Carolina. Other Southern states still significantly lag behind.

THE NORTH CAROLINA STORY

In North Carolina, the hub of innovative activity is the Research Triangle Park, widely acknowledged as one of the world's most successful planned research parks. The park was conceived in 1955, when Governor Luther Hodges formed a committee of business leaders and university officials to investigate the strengths of the three top—though not yet nationally first-class—universities (Duke University, North Carolina State University, and the University of North Carolina at Chapel Hill) and design a strategy for economic development. At that time, the state ranked 49th in per capita income, and a large part of its employment was concentrated in tobacco, low-wage textiles, and furniture manufacturing. The committee argued that the three universities had sufficient strength in science and technology to attract the research and development facilities of large multinational firms.

In 1956, a group of citizens and corporations bought 6,700 acres of scrub pine in the middle of the triangle

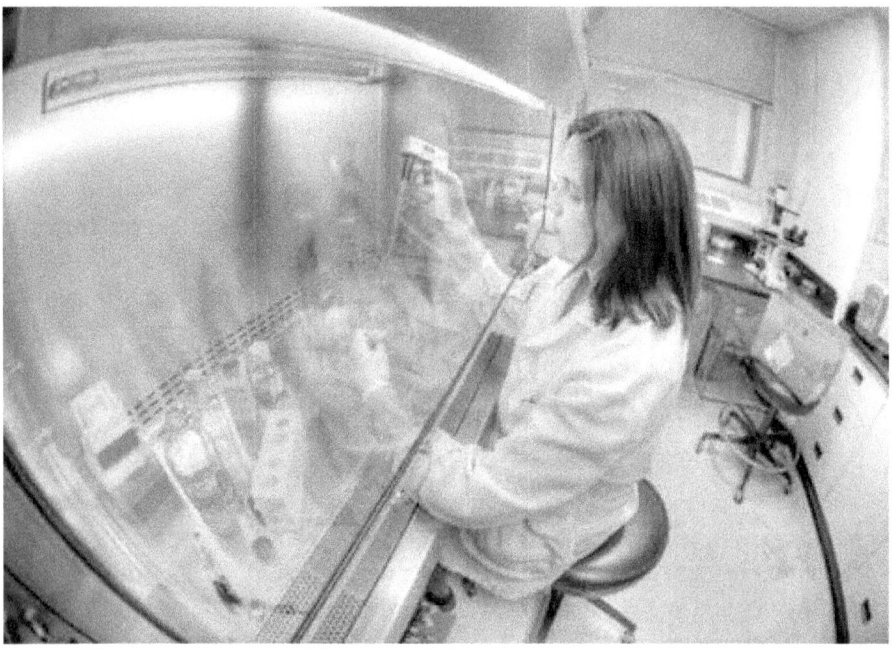

formed by the three universities. Established as a nonprofit entity, the Research Triangle Foundation received responsibility for oversight of the park. To provide research expertise to complement the universities, the foundation established the Research Triangle Institute, a nonprofit contract research company with interlocking boards drawn from the universities. Similar to the Stanford Research Institute in the Stanford Research Park, the idea was to provide what we would now term translational research. Through the foundation and the Research Triangle Institute, the interests of the universities were aligned to promote their common interest, and the park became more than just a real estate operation. Early inquiries to establish manufacturing operations in the park were turned away: The strategic vision was that the park would be a research and development center, and the commitment to that vision was and remains constant.

Science in North Carolina received another boost with the formation of the state Board of Science and Technology in 1963 under Governor Terry Sanford. Modeled after the National Science Foundation, the Board of Science and Technology provided research funding and served as a strategic policy adviser. Sanford also established a system of community colleges to spread the benefits of science education more broadly.

Research Triangle Park remained largely empty until 1966, when IBM and then the National Institute of Environmental Health Sciences located large facilities there. For those eight years, state officials and Research Triangle Institute board members had continued to promote their vision,

> Cuts to education, at all levels from elementary school to universities, endanger an economy's ability to innovate and the ability of individuals to participate fully in the global economy.

meeting with company executives throughout the United States and Europe. While many other states engaged in what is known as "buffalo hunting" for branch-manufacturing establishments, which had the immediate advantages of increased employment, North Carolina remained true to its commitment. With one large multinational technology company and a large government agency in place, other companies were enticed to locate research and development facilities in the park.

The next active phase of technology and innovation policy began in 1980, when newly elected governor Jim Hunt assembled a blue-ribbon panel of state, university, and industry leaders at the North Carolina Board of Science and Technology to strategize on the next phase of growth for the state. In the face of criticism that state policy should target low-wage jobs in manufacturing and tourism, Hunt promoted the vision that North Carolina could become a leader in technology industries, leveraging the strengths of the universities and the intention of Research Triangle Park to be a center for research and development. California's success in microelectronics served as a model, and North Carolina's policy identified the need to build a focal point for the industry and created the Microelectronics Center of North Carolina, the first quasi-public technology-based economic development agency in the United States (and a model subsequently copied by other states). General Electric quickly announced plans to build a semiconductor plant in the park, citing the newly established Microelectronics Center as a major factor in its decision. But North Carolina did not stop with this investment. Between 1980 and 1983, the General Assembly supported the establishment of the North Carolina Biotechnology Center to support the growing high-tech industry; the Technological Development Authority to help new high-tech business start-ups through incubators and risk capital; the North Carolina School of Science and Mathematics to produce a cadre of young scientists and raise the state's image in public education; and, with federal support, the North Carolina Small Business Technology and Development Center. The state already had strong research centers at its universities, an active Industrial Extension Service operating out of North Carolina State University, and a nationally renowned system of 58 vocationally oriented community and technical colleges. Thus, a fully integrated innovation system was established.

Over time, entrepreneurs have established new firms, creating a vibrant quilt of industrial activity. Innovation and entrepreneurship are two sides of the same coin: Entrepreneurs recognize opportunity and innovate. Location becomes important not only for recognizing opportunity but also for cultivating an environment dedicated to research and development activity, which in turn lowers the cost of innovating. While entrepreneurship is a private-sector activity, public policy can set the stage by establishing property rights, providing incentives to encourage experimentation and discovery, and determining how rewards will be allocated. Furthermore, policy is often needed to fill in elements of the ecosystem not provided by the private sector, supply information about opportunities, and offer incentives that lower the risk of engaging in innovative activity, making it easier for new firms to develop. In its efforts to encourage clusters and the entrepreneurial spirit, North Carolina offers an example of flexible and adaptive policy interventions that have spurred entrepreneurship in the Research Triangle region. Through consistent and persistent state policy coupled with a visionary consensus of what might be possible in the future, North Carolina has emerged as a vibrant innovative economy.

BUILDING ON OUR SUCCESS

In more recent years, North Carolina has focused on developing other regions within the state in an effort to spread wealth more generally. As the Research Triangle Park example demonstrates, this process requires a significant length of time, a sustained commitment of resources, and the sustaining of a vision across various political administrations. Too many times, we observe new governors take office, sweep away programs associated with their predecessors, and institute short-lived signature programs with political flourish and ceremony. The result is a waste of public resources and confidence.

State programs often are copied uncritically because they have been previously successful in a different place, at another time, and under a different set of economic circumstances. It is no surprise that such transplanted programs fail to achieve their desired results. The North Carolina approach demonstrates policy that was creative in its design and pragmatic in implementation. While technology-based economic development programs may be criticized as elitist given their focus on universities, the North Carolina example demonstrates that an inclusive, fully integrated system that incorporates community colleges, high school students, and business interests can provide a path to increased prosperity. Most critically, the North Carolina example demonstrates the role that government and public policy may play in creating an environment where private-sector activity thrives.

To conclude, we consider the path forward for the South. Having each state define its own path has been the strategy of the Southern Technology Council. Unfortunately, in times of fiscal austerity such as we now face, there is a tendency to cut the expenditures that would allow a state economy to grow out of unfavorable economic times. Cuts to education, at all levels from elementary school to universities, endanger an economy's ability to innovate and the ability of individuals to participate fully in the global economy. The danger is that the South becomes a place of low-wage employment where its citizens face a limited and uncertain future. Alternatively, recessionary times can be periods of reorganization and political commitment to guaranteeing the next generation's prosperity.

> While technology-based economic development programs may be criticized as elitist given their focus on universities, the North Carolina example demonstrates that an inclusive, fully integrated system that incorporates community colleges, high school students, and business interests can provide a path to increased prosperity.

TABLES AND FIGURES

table 7.1 TOTAL RESEARCH AND DEVELOPMENT (R&D) AND GROSS DOMESTIC PRODUCT (GDP) BY STATE, 2007

RANK/STATE	(1) R&D (CURRENT $MILLIONS)	(2) GDP (CURRENT $MILLIONS)	(3) R&D/GDP (%)	(4) U.S. RANK IN R&D/GDP	(5) U.S. R&D (%)
Virginia	9,473	384,132	2.47	17	2.6
North Carolina	9,204	390,467	2.36	19	2.6
Georgia	4,425	391,241	1.13	37	1.2
Tennessee	3,659	245,162	1.49	32	1.0
Alabama	3,289	164,524	2.00	27	0.9
South Carolina	2,291	151,703	1.51	31	0.6
Kentucky	1,406	152,099	0.92	44	0.4
Louisiana	1,073	207,407	0.52	50	0.3
Oklahoma	921	136,374	0.68	46	0.3
Mississippi	838	87,652	0.96	42	0.2
West Virginia	650	57,877	1.12	39	0.2
Arkansas	632	95,116	0.66	48	0.2

Source: National Science Board. 2010. Science and Engineering Indicators 2010. Arlington, Va.: National Science Foundation (NSB 10-01), Appendix Table 4-15.

table 7.2 R&D EXPENDITURES BY STATE AND PERFORMING STATE, 2007 (MILLIONS OF CURRENT DOLLARS)

STATE	(1) ALL R&D	R&D RANK	(2) FEDERAL R&D	%	(3) INDUSTRY R&D	%	(4) UNIVERSITY R&D	%
U.S. total	372,527		25,858	6.94	269,267	72.28	49,021	13.16
Alabama	3,289	27	823	25.02	1,771	53.85	655	19.91
Arkansas	632	44	42	6.65	339	53.64	240	37.97
Georgia	4,425	22	195	4.41	2,788	63.01	1,389	31.39
Kentucky	1,406	34	9	0.64	890	63.30	503	35.78
Louisiana	1,073	37	82	7.64	373	34.76	604	56.29
Mississippi	838	41	144	17.18	279	33.29	411	49.05
North Carolina	9,204	14	363	3.94	6,829	74.20	1,885	20.48
Oklahoma	921	38	65	7.06	527	57.22	299	32.46
South Carolina	2,291	29	114	4.98	1,426	62.24	569	24.84
Tennessee	3,659	26	89	2.43	1,638	44.77	761	20.80
Virginia	9,473	13	3,098	32.70	4,840	51.09	971	10.25
West Virginia	650	43	111	17.08	233	35.85	167	25.69

Source: National Science Board. 2010. Science and Engineering Indicators 2010. Arlington, Va.: National Science Foundation (NSB 10-01), Appendix Table 4-15.

NORTH CAROLINA's Board of Science and Technology: A Model *for* Guiding Technology-Based Economic Development *in the South*

JOHN HARDIN AND MARYANN FELDMAN

BACKGROUND

The idea for the North Carolina Board of Science and Technology originated at a December 1961 meeting to which Governor Terry Sanford invited 39 scientists from the three universities that form the points of the Research Triangle: Duke University, the University of North Carolina at Chapel Hill, and North Carolina State University. The scientists were charged with helping the state meet "the rapid pace of scientific and technological change" and enjoining the universities to help solve industry problems and help reposition the state as a scientific powerhouse. A two-page centerfold picture in *Time* magazine immortalized the meeting with the following caption: "Indicative of the State's pool of more than 2,000 leading scientists and engineers whose services are available to any industry within North Carolina."

The group of prominent scientists was designated the Governor's Science Advisory Committee, making North Carolina one of the first states to establish the primacy of science and its relationship to economic prosperity. This step followed on the heels of similar actions at the national and state levels. For example, the National Science Foundation, formed in 1950, had begun dispensing grants in 1952. The Research Triangle Institute, created in 1958 by Governor Luther Hodges, was charged with creating applied research facilities that would translate university research to applications useful to industry. And in 1959, a visionary group of the state's leaders from business, academia, and industry formed the Research Triangle Park, one of the world's largest public-private planned research parks. In 1961, President John F. Kennedy had created the Office of Science and Technology in recognition of the increased role of science in the economy as manifested in the space race with the Soviets.

Under the guidance of the Governor's Science Advisory Committee, several scientists were brought to North Carolina to consult and advise Sanford and the committee

on the possibilities for scientific and economic development. From these meetings, the idea of science-based economic development emerged as a strategy to move the state toward higher wages. The principal need identified was for additional financial support for scientific research.

THE EARLY SCIENCE AND TECHNOLOGY PERIOD

In 1963, the North Carolina General Assembly established the Board of Science and Technology "to encourage, promote, and support scientific, engineering, and industrial research applications in North Carolina." In response to this need, the board initially was established as a grant-dispensing agency patterned after the National Science Foundation. It operated the first competitive state grants program in the nation and the only explicit research grant program in North Carolina until 1984. The governor chaired the board, and its executive director reported directly to the governor.

The board was designated a state agency, and funding was appropriated by the General Assembly, which recognized its synergies with Research Triangle Institute. The board advanced its mission by awarding competitive funding to the best university ideas. In this way, North Carolina established a pipeline for the commercialization of academic discoveries.

From 1963 to 1969, the board reviewed 339 proposals, funding 110 (33.4 percent); 116 follow-on grants subsequently were obtained from other sources. The board's initial investment of $2.24 million yielded $9.42 million in additional research funding. Despite this strong track record, the General Assembly, under general fiscal pressure, cut funding for the board in 1969. Four years later, Governor James Holshouser transferred the board to the Department of Commerce and gathered all of the state's public universities into a consolidated system under a board of governors, which could then provide a focal point for science advice. For the next several years, the board played a more limited role, providing policy advice and supporting operations at the Commerce Department.

In the late 1970s, in the midst of a major recession, the need for additional investment in science and technology again was perceived as critical, particularly as a means for the state to grow the economy out of the recession and provide better jobs. In 1977, therefore, Governor Jim Hunt reelevated the board to a cabinet-level function to connect research institutions and organizations with the private sector. Hunt appointed his former professor and trusted adviser, Quentin Lindsey, to direct the board and design new science-based economic development policies.

The board's 1980 Lindsey Report provided a blueprint for growing the economy, proposing and advocating for many of the state's now core institutional infrastructure organizations, such as the North Carolina Biotechnology Center, the North Carolina School of Science and Mathematics, the First Flight Venture Center (formerly the North Carolina Technological Development Authority), and the Microelectronics Center of North Carolina (MCNC). Funding was also allocated for scientific equipment and increasing the public understanding of science. These innovative initiatives—all developed and executed during the 1980s—sought to build capacity in the state and helped position North Carolina as a serious location for technology-based economic development.

In 2001, the board staff was transferred from the governor's office to the Department of Commerce to more closely align the board's work in science and technology initiatives with economic development. The transfer also enabled the leveraging of the capabilities of the science and technology staff by providing the support of the Department of Commerce's policy and research, public affairs, marketing, legal, and administrative functions. This change mitigated the impact of contemporary recession-induced budget cuts.

MORE THAN HALFWAY HOME AND STILL GOING STRONG

In recent decades and particularly since the mid-1990s, the board has recommended and implemented various strategic initiatives and benchmarking efforts.

Vision 2030 (1998–99): a comprehensive "real options'" planning initiative undertaken to strengthen the competitiveness of North Carolina's workforce and industry by taking advantage of science- and technology-driven economic development opportunities in the areas of information technology, bioscience/biotechnology, and new materials sciences. *Vision 2030* yielded several outputs, including a series of benchmarking reports, policy recommendations, and draft legislation, along with recommendations that would assure North Carolina's potential to remain competitive in science- and technology-based economic development. The initiative also hosted science and technology roundtables in North Carolina cities, organized in conjunction with local authorities such as those in the chambers of commerce or regional economic development partnerships. Many of the initiative's recommendations have since been implemented, and the board's staff has continued to expand and refine the benchmarking efforts.

Tracking Innovation in North Carolina (2000; 2003): an "innovation index" assembling information from a wide variety of sources to document and benchmark technology-related activity in the state. Containing more than 50 measures (for example, research and development expenditures, venture capital, high-tech start-up activity, broadband access, educational attainment), the index compares North Carolina's innovation-related performance to that of other states. The index has served and continues to serve as the basis for many of the board's recommendations, including grant programs to provide early stage financial capital to small businesses, technology incubators and accelerators, and improved science, technology, engineering, and math (STEM) programs.

Roadmap for Nanotechnology in North Carolina's 21st-Century Economy (2006): a coordinated initiative to advance successful nanotechnology-based economic development and high-wage employment across the state. Produced by the Governor's Task Force on Nanotechnology and North Carolina's Economy and organized by the board's staff, the Roadmap issued a call to action to increase the state's ability to innovate, increase the levels of collaboration between the state's companies and R&D centers, develop a well-educated and -trained workforce, provide a supportive public and political policy environment, and diversify the state's technology cluster portfolio to include nanotechnology. The Roadmap laid the groundwork for numerous follow-on activities, including the Joint School of Nanoscience and Nanoengineering, administered by North Carolina A&T State University and the University of North Carolina at Greensboro.

Advancing Innovation in North Carolina (2008): a 76-page report that starkly defined the innovation challenges facing the state, extended and enhanced the metrics outlined in the board's previous *Tracking Innovation* reports, and recommended an innovation framework that leverages the state's unique strengths while addressing its specific challenges. Since its release in December 2008, the report has been accessed online 5,000 times from more than 40 countries and more than 40 states, and it served as a key impetus for Governor Beverly Perdue's establishment of the state's first-ever Innovation Council.

In the past decade, the board has enhanced its original mission of dispensing grants, primarily through two programs.

One North Carolina Small Business Program: Proposed by the board and established by the General Assembly in 2006, the program provides matching grants to North Carolina's small, early stage businesses that have received federal Phase I Small Business Innovation Research (SBIR) and Small Business Technology Transfer (STTR) grants designed to help them commercialize their innovative technologies. Since its founding, the program has awarded 244 matching grants totaling nearly $17 million to small businesses throughout the state. These investments, nearly half of which support active projects, have already helped create hundreds of jobs, with hundreds more to come as the remaining projects are completed. The grants also have leveraged more than $40 million in external capital investments, generated more than $51 million in follow-on Phase II federal SBIR/STTR funding, and project to produce hundreds of patents, licenses, and products.

North Carolina Green Business Fund: Proposed by Perdue when she was lieutenant governor and established by the General Assembly in 2008, the fund awards competitive grants to North Carolina organizations having innovative projects focused on developing and commercializing promising and innovative green technologies, such as biofuels, green

> Strategic planning, data-driven assessment, leadership, and programmatic implementation have yielded a productive record of technology-based economic development in North Carolina.

building, and environmentally conscious clean-technology and renewable-energy products. Funded projects are cross-cutting and capacity-building, spanning all facets of the economy and society. Since its founding, the program has awarded 85 grants totaling nearly $12 million to small businesses throughout the state. Because the majority of these projects are still active, their impacts cannot yet be assessed, but they are expected to resemble those for the One North Carolina Small Business Program.

This combination of strategic planning, data-driven assessment, leadership, and programmatic implementation has yielded a productive record of technology-based economic development in North Carolina.

LESSONS FOR THE FUTURE

In 1980, Governor Hunt noted that the center of gravity for technological innovation had shifted from the federal government to state governments. His knowledge came firsthand: North Carolina has been at the forefront of that movement for more than 50 years, developing and implementing innovative institutions, policies, and programs. The Board of

Science and Technology has played a central role. At least three notable lessons have been learned.

First, the board's strong analytic policymaking capabilities, coupled with its well-informed, nonpartisan leadership, the political willingness to invest in the state's future, and the resources needed to pursue its vision, produced the right mixture of smart, bold, effective action. Like any good recipe, absent any one of these core ingredients, the board and arguably the state would have been less successful.

Second, even with all the right ingredients, successful outputs were not guaranteed. More often than not, the board has had its greatest successes when a strong, committed leader, usually the governor supported by the board's executive director, was willing to champion a cause, take a risk, and remain persistent throughout the process, even in times of limited resources. While the importance of leadership should go without saying, it cannot be overemphasized. The board would not have existed or been as effective had it not benefited from the strong support of several committed state leaders.

And third, even with the right ingredients and leadership, the board would have outlived its usefulness had it not exhibited the flexibility and resourcefulness necessary to respond to changing circumstances. During times when the state budget was tight, the board turned its attention away from awarding grants and redirected its energies toward supporting operations at the Commerce Department and toward strategic visioning and planning. During these periods, the board produced its most innovative, enduring policy work. Conversely, during years in which the state budget was stronger, the board devoted a larger portion of its efforts toward allocating grant funds to innovative science- and technology-based projects likely to yield commercial value. Thus, faced with dynamic and often uncertain circumstances, the board has evolved to stay true to its mission to help the state meet the rapid pace of scientific and technological change.

INFRASTRUCTURE AND RURAL ECONOMIC DEVELOPMENT
The Case *of a* Rural Broadband Initiative

JOE FREDDOSO

INTRODUCTION

Investments in infrastructure feed economic development and economic prosperity. Business leaders, elected officials, and municipal, state, and county administrators fight heartily for infrastructure investments in their respective regions—for example, an improved road that feeds an industrial site, a railroad extension to a coal-processing facility, or a high-capacity electrical line that fulfills the power needs of a new financial-services processing center. For years, infrastructural investments in rural counties in North Carolina and elsewhere in the South have resulted in job growth, enhanced tax bases, and economic growth for businesses.

Investments in roads as well as in water, sewer, gas, and communications infrastructure have dominated over the past 75 years. The era of large centralized manufacturing and administrative workspaces has made it necessary to build these access and utility infrastructures for specific sites, where large offices and plants have been built. While this site-based infrastructure strategy still dominates the economic-prosperity landscape in 2011, a stark change has taken place in what is deemed "critical infrastructure" as a result of the onset of the Internet and Internet-based communications technologies.

The network of networks commonly referred to as the Internet has caused a sea change in the manner in which people communicate. A variety of "last mile" connectivity technologies (linkages that connect consumer homes or businesses to the Internet) have emerged through which users around the region and the world can connect to the Internet. Existing copper wire, power lines, wireless technologies such as WiFi, EVDO, LTE, and fiber-optic cable are all used for connectivity to the Internet. All produce varied results in terms of speed and accessibility, and all except fiber have top-end limits on broadband capacity that have been well tested and researched. Physicists continue to test fiber's capability and have reached speeds of more than 250 gigabytes per second.

ANYWHERE AT ANY TIME USING ANY DEVICE

The ability to connect to the Internet from anywhere at any time using any device has opened the world over the past two decades. This network of networks is leveraged in many ways:

- allowing everyone to "friend" folks around the world on commercial Internet-based social networking sites;
- enabling consumers to create competition among vendors wanting to provide goods or services;
- allowing participants on private research networks such as National Lambda Rail or Internet2 to collaborate with one another and control research equipment around the globe, speeding the pace of innovation; and
- allowing a single mother in a rural area to become a call center employee for national airline JetBlue, a company that uses remote employees for call center work.

Internet-based applications are becoming more complex, requiring more and more bandwidth. Those areas without high-capacity fiber infrastructure for the last mile to large and medium businesses, research institutions, universities, community colleges, K–12 schools, public and nonprofit hospitals, public safety facilities, museums—sites where many people gather and use Intranet and Internet simultaneously—will fall behind the rest of the globe. Those areas without fiber infrastructure for backhaul services and without Internet access that feeds the last-mile technologies that serve consumers and small businesses also will fall behind the wired world.

THE NORTH CAROLINA BROADBAND STORY

The number 1 recommendation of the 2000 North Carolina Rural Prosperity Task Force, a 28-member commission of state leaders led by Erskine Bowles, was to bring Internet-access infrastructure to rural North Carolina. This infrastructure was viewed as the key to added economic prosperity. From the commission's recommendations, several tangible actions took root:

1. North Carolina, through the Department of Commerce and the Rural Center, established one of the first rural broadband authorities. The organization, originally named the Rural Internet Access Authority and now known as eNC, was tasked with

    a. identifying areas of North Carolina that had little or no access to affordable broadband services;

    b. providing grants to serve these underserved areas from a $30 million fund donated by the nonprofit MCNC and from state appropriations; and

    c. educating rural North Carolinians on the basics of the use of the Internet and how it could be leveraged for education, health care, and economic development.

    eNC remains a leading rural broadband organization today, securing $6 million in federal funding to continue its dual missions of mapping broadband availability in the state and educating citizens about the use of the Internet.

2. Large private-sector service providers such as BellSouth (now AT&T) and Sprint (now CenturyLink) as well as small providers (Skyline, Yadkin Telephone, ATMC) matched eNC investments and built some modern infrastructure.

3. State leaders such as former lieutenant governor and now governor Beverly Perdue made

sure that North Carolina's large and medium-sized businesses, research institutions, universities, community colleges, K–12 schools, public and nonprofit hospitals, public safety facilities, and museums had adequate fiber infrastructure to fill their current and future broadband needs in a cost-effective manner.

Part of Perdue and other leaders' strategy involved creating a backbone network for public education from the existing North Carolina Research and Education Network, managed by the nonprofit MCNC. Today, NCREN serves

- all K–12 public schools;
- all of North Carolina's community colleges;
- all University of North Carolina system schools;
- 27 of the state's 36 independent colleges and universities;
- 20 K–12 charter schools; and
- numerous public libraries, nonprofit hospitals, public health agencies, and other public entities.

This backbone provides users at all these sites access to one another via a high-speed Intranet as well as deeply discounted Internet access, particularly in the case of rural institutions.

Through these and many other developments, North Carolina has become a leading state in the deployment and use of broadband technologies by its citizens. However, the state spent much of the decade after the Rural Prosperity Task Force Report relying on older telecommunications infrastructure to deliver services to consumers, citizens, and key public facilities. Thus, rural North Carolina faced a future in which the existing telecommunications infrastructure would not be adequate to meet the demands of our rural community institutions, businesses, and citizens.

> Bringing Internet-access infrastructure to rural North Carolina was the number 1 recommendation of the 2000 North Carolina Rural Prosperity Task Force. This infrastructure was viewed as the key to added economic prosperity.

THE BROADBAND TECHNOLOGY OPPORTUNITIES PROGRAM (BTOP)

The 2009 American Recovery and Reinvestment Act, commonly referred to as the stimulus program, included a $7.2 billion investment in broadband infrastructure in two competitive programs. The Department of Commerce's National Telecommunications and Information Administration managed one of these programs, the Broadband Technology Opportunities Program (BTOP), which offered MCNC the opportunity to address the paucity of fiber in rural North Carolina.

MCNC bid for and won two rounds of BTOP funding. The organization raised $40 million in matching funds, including $24 million from the Golden LEAF Foundation and $8 million from the MCNC endowment. These efforts attracted another $104 million in federal BTOP funds. The result is that MCNC is under contract to build 1,700 miles of new rural fiber-optic infrastructure and to acquire an additional 800 miles of existing infrastructure to serve 79 rural counties with a fiber-optic network that directly connects community institutions and, through private-sector service providers (should they choose to interconnect with NCREN or acquire fiber built by BTOP), consumers, and businesses. MCNC is making one of the largest investments in broadband infrastructure in North Carolina history. The project will create or save 2,000 jobs and will have an impact of approximately $1.4 billion—a $10 impact for every $1 spent on construction.

CONCLUSION

The goals of the 2000 Rural Prosperity Task Force report represented a journey, not a destination. As a result of the MCNC's BTOP awards, North Carolina has made progress on its journey toward bringing critical infrastructure to rural North Carolina.

North Carolina has clearly staked out a leadership role among its peers in the South and across the country in the deployment of broadband infrastructure. Through the BTOP-funded fiber build-up, the state has addressed the bandwidth needs of its community-based institutions in rural areas for the next couple of decades.

North Carolina also has positioned itself to address the availability of affordable broadband service in many currently underserved areas. To fully address these needs, private-sector companies and the public sector must work together to drive service deployment that makes sense for both consumers and private-sector providers. Advances in technology mean that this goal of meeting both deployment requirements and bottom-line profit needs is not far-fetched. As the BTOP construction is completed over the next three years, North Carolina will be a test case, illustrating whether productive public-private partnerships in broadband deployment can be achieved.

REFERENCES

Baller Herbst Law Group. Web site. http://www.baller.com/national_broadband.html.

INFRASTRUCTURE, *Southern Style*

There is little doubt that infrastructure investment has a positive effect on economic growth. Efficient transport, power, and communications systems are necessary for the functioning of any regional economy, and many studies relating to both developing and developed economies have established the link between infrastructure and development. Historical studies have pointed to the relevance of infrastructure in the rapid development of U.S. industry during the nineteenth century, and contemporary debate among policy-relevant researchers is centered not on whether there are positive effects but on the magnitude of the return and the trade-off of investing in infrastructure versus other investment options.

Despite its acknowledged importance, infrastructure in the United States is in a state of crisis, nowhere more so than in the South, as this North Carolina "report card"—the handiwork of the American Society of Civil Engineers—readily attests. Other state and local report cards can be viewed at http://www.infrastructurereportcard.org/state-and-local-report-cards.

Source: http://sections.asce.org/n_carolina/ReportCard.html

NORTH CAROLINA OVERALL GPA
C-

AIRPORTS
D+
An investment of $588 million is needed to bring all airports to good or excellent ratings in all categories

BRIDGES
C-
31% of bridges are considered structurally deficient or functionally obsolete

DAMS
D
23% of dams are classified as high-hazard

DRINKING WATER

B-

North Carolina must invest more than $2.5 billion in its drinking water infrastructure over the next five years to avoid reversing the public health and economic gains over the last 30 years

SCHOOLS

C-

More than 46% of schools will require some form of renovation in the next five years, one-third of them needed in the next two years

STORMWATER

C-

More than 75% of North Carolina's towns reported that their stormwater systems were in fair or poor condition

RAIL

C

Increasing ralroad capacity through track and signal improvements is critical in the efficient movement of passengers and goods

WASTEWATER

C+

North Carolina must invest more than $3.4 billion in its wastewater infrastructure over the next five years

ROADS

D-

Poor road conditions cost motorists approximately $1.7 billion per year in repairs and operating costs

SOUTHERN INFASTRUCTURE REPORT CARD

130

URBAN, RURAL, AND GREEN

A WAY FORWARD: BUILDING A GLOBALLY COMPETITIVE SOUTH

THE New Metro American South

FERREL GUILLORY

INTRODUCTION

A diverse array of "city-states" flourishes across the landscape of the American South. Among the many ways in which the South—once a land of small-farm, row-crop agriculture, small-town mills, and legalized racial segregation—has converged with the nation over the past quarter of a century, the burgeoning of megametropolitan regions stands out.

To call them city-states is not to suggest that they are independent political units of the classic Greek and Roman models. Rather, it is to signify their emergence as powerful economic and cultural organisms that sprawl across old city, county, and even state lines. The future of the South and the states of the region depends more than ever on the economic, social, and political vitality of these megaregions along with their smaller cousin metro areas.

The modern South contains one-third of the nation's 100 most populous metro areas as defined by the U.S. Census and 5 of the top 10. Since 1980, the South's metropolitan population has increased by more than 45 percent, so that three out of four Southerners now live in a metropolitan setting. From 1987 to the beginning of the deep 2007–9 recession, metropolitan areas accounted for 89 percent of the South's job growth, rural areas 11 percent.

In their *State of Metropolitan America* report, issued in 2010, the Brookings Institution's Metropolitan Policy Program scholars define seven categories of U.S. metros. It is significant that Southern metros fall into all seven categories. Some metro areas clearly fly higher than others or in different patterns. Brookings places Houston, Dallas–Fort Worth, and Austin among the "Next Frontier" metros, classifies Miami as a "Diverse Giant," and groups Atlanta, Raleigh-Durham, Charleston, and Nashville within the "New Heartland."

Brookings does not attach the *city-states* label or apply such terms as *global cities*, *ideopolises*, or *metropolitan magnets*, which other scholars and research organizations have used to describe metro areas in the South and elsewhere. But Houston, Dallas, Miami, and Atlanta surely rise to megametro dimensions, while Charlotte, the Research Triangle, Nashville, Tampa, Richmond, and the Hampton Roads region are emerging into substantial metropolitan prowess.

A telling indicator of the extent to which the South and its future have grown increasingly dependent on burgeoning metro areas as economic engines comes in the list of "next big boom towns" published in *Forbes* in early July 2011. To be sure, magazines have turned rankings and ratings into a cottage industry, but this one, developed in a collaboration between www.newgeography.com and the Praxis Strategy Group, used a relatively complex set of indicators, including job growth, educated migration, and family formation, to rank the 52 metros with populations above 1 million. The South accounted for 9 of the top 10, with Austin ranked first, Raleigh second, and Nashville third. Three more Texas metros—San Antonio, Houston and Dallas–Fort Worth—placed in the top 10, as did Charlotte, Orlando, and the Washington, D.C., area (which includes Northern Virginia and a section of West Virginia). This ranking, among many indicators, points to the reality that metropolitan areas increasingly define the look and feel of a once-agrarian region.

The presence of Raleigh and Charlotte high on this *Forbes* list as well as in other such rankings provides evidence of North Carolina's emergence as a metropolitan-oriented megastate. North Carolina contains all or portions of 15 Census-defined metro areas, 3 of them in the nation's 100 most populous. According to a Brookings calculation, North Carolina's three major metros—Charlotte-Gastonia, Raleigh-Cary, and Greensboro–High Point—account for 36 percent of the population and more than 40 percent of the state's economic output. Altogether, the state's 15 metros account for 70 percent of North Carolina's population and 75 percent of its economy.

THE RISE OF THE METRO REGION

Of course, Southern history is full of rivalry as well as mutual dependence between city and countryside. During the days of Jim Crow, Southern politics was defined not only by white officials' efforts to sustain segregation but also by the struggle of rural barons to maintain control of state governments. In *Baker v. Carr*, a case that originated in Tennessee, the Supreme Court issued its 1962 one-person, one-vote ruling that broke apart the malapportioned, rural-dominated legislatures of the South.

As the economy of the South began to diversify and grow stronger in the aftermath of World War II, the growth of its cities accelerated. In 1954, the University of North Carolina Press published *The Urban South*, a collection of essays edited by sociologists Rupert Vance and Nicholas J. Demerath. The editors observed that compared to the big industrial centers of the nation, Southern cities were small and relatively young. "Cities are growing more numerous and bigger," they wrote, "evidently *they are here to stay*." Still,

Sanford to the L. Q. C. Lamar Society, developed that theme in its 1980 Commission on the Future of the South. The commission called on legislatures to give cities annexation powers to prevent the fragmentation that plagued Northern metropolitan areas and proposed "state urban policy" developed through a cooperative effort of state governments, cities, and counties.

The 1986 Commission on the Future of the South identified "disparities in the economic progress of urban and rural areas" as one of its principal cross-cutting themes, though none of its 10 "regional objectives" outlined in *Halfway Home and a Long Way to Go* explicitly mentioned urban growth or metropolitan development.

Vance and Demerath found them mostly "unremarkable." That was then: Southern cities are unremarkable no more.

In the wake of the enactment of federal statutes and court rulings that struck down the South's racial segregation laws, combined with an era of expanded public and private investment, the region's growth accelerated further, and the South soon was leading the nation in both population and job growth. In *You Can't Eat Magnolias*, a 1972 volume of essays published by the L. Q. C. Lamar Society, Joel Fleishman proved prescient in writing, "If you want to know what Southern metropolitan areas will look like in 1990 or the year 2000, look at Los Angeles and not at New York or Chicago." Fleishman urged states and cities to develop an "urban growth policy."

The Southern Growth Policies Board, which grew out of a speech delivered by former North Carolina governor Terry

Still, the final objective called on the South to modernize its governmental structures, to consider "consolidating some local governments," and to have states offer incentives for regional planning.

The 1986 report by Chapel Hill–based MDC, *Shadows in the Sunbelt*, had as its driving purpose calling the region's attention to the people and places left behind amid the "impressive booms" of Southern cities. It urged state and rural officials to adopt broader economic development policies than the "buffalo hunt" of branch-plant recruitment. Though MDC would subsequently turn its attention to metropolitan issues in its *State of the South* reports, its 1986 focus was on preparing the rural South for economic change.

Over the past two decades, several Southern states have launched rural studies, rural task forces, and rural centers, resulting in rural development policies and programs.

Now the challenge is for the South—and the nation, for metro areas depend on federal action, too—to turn similar attention to metropolitan regional policies. The goal of such an effort is not to set city against countryside anew but rather to assure that the most powerful economic engines remain in tune and, well, powerful. A related issue is whether the South can figure out how to deploy metropolitan hubs as catalysts for regional economic advancement—that is, to connect rural people and communities to the metropolitan economies in ways that serve both city and countryside. To expand prosperity to more of its residents beyond the late-2000s recession will require the South to adopt not only rural-development but also metropolitan-focused policies to sustain both a thriving economy and a healthy democracy.

THE FUTURE OF THE METRO REGION

Indeed, metro areas present the South with challenging governance issues. Metro areas serve as more than simply economic drivers. They are repositories of entertainment, art, and culture. They are places where the "creative class" congregates. They bring together people with ideas and with money to invest in them. Simultaneously, metro areas serve as cauldrons in which boil some of the vexing and contentious issues of Southern and American life—issues of economic inequity, immigration, city-suburban fragmentation, access to jobs and upward mobility, energy consumption, and many others.

As Brookings demographer William Frey has documented, the burgeoning of Southern metropolitan areas has resulted from three streams of immigration and in-migration. Since 1990, the region's white population

> The modern South contains one-third of the nation's 100 most populous metro areas as defined by the U.S. Census and 5 of the top 10. Since 1980, the South's metropolitan population has increased by more than 45 percent, so that three out of four Southerners now live in a metropolitan setting.

has increased by more than a third as metro areas attracted affluent professionals, managers, and creative workers. By the late 1990s, black Americans were moving to the South more than to any other region, completely reversing the Great Migration out of the South during the mid-20th century. The South's black population also grew by more than a third, and more than half of black people in large metropolitan areas, in the South and elsewhere, now reside in suburbs, not the center of cities.

In search of work, Latinos have spread well beyond Texas and Florida, resulting in a regional shift from a biracial to a multiethnic society. The Latino population has mushroomed by more than 125 percent since 1990, with substantial increases in North Carolina, Georgia, and Tennessee. In metro areas, low-wage white, African American, and Latino workers have congregated to do gardening, to work on construction crews, to cook and serve restaurant meals, and to scrub office buildings—that is, to respond to the demand for goods and services by the well-paid, high-tech, knowledge workers drawn to the South's expanding metropolitan economies. In a 2006 study, the Economic Policy Institute ranked 7 Southern states in the top 10 in a measurement of income inequality.

In the South, metro dynamics foster income and wealth inequality. The South's penchant for sprawling metro areas, with job centers dispersed in multiple downtown-like pods, also put geographic distance between where people live and where they work, creating a dependence on the automobile and, where public transportation is scarce, erecting spatial barriers between people in need of jobs and the location of available work.

The economic recessions of the past decade hit the South hard, slowed its economic momentum, and elevated its poverty rates after a period of decline. Over the past decade, according to a Brookings analysis, the United States has experienced a "suburbanization of poverty." Aside from Midwestern industrial areas, said Brookings, "the South was the only other region in which both city and suburban poverty rates increased significantly between 2000 and 2008, though at a much slower rate."

In his recent book, *Triumph of the City*, Harvard economist Edward L. Glaeser writes that "all successful cities do have something in common." Synthesizing much scholarly analysis of metropolitan life, he argues that "to thrive, cities must attract smart people and enable them to work collaboratively. There is no such thing as a successful city without human capital."

In 1986, *Halfway Home and a Long Way to Go* spoke eloquently to the South's need to expand its human capital and to enhance its quality of life. A quarter of a century later, the South finds itself in a situation of mutual dependency between state governments and its metropolitan regions: The states need the economic engines provided by its city-states and smaller metro areas, and metro areas need state governments for public school financing, higher education, transportation, and social services.

It is a political nonstarter to suggest that states create metropolitan governments. But it is not too much to suggest that states set in motion the development of metropolitan policymaking for the 21st century: to sustain and strengthen metropolitan economic and civic vitality; to assure that midsize cities have sufficient amenities, capital, and educational opportunities to attract creative professionals; to connect more small towns to metro economic engines; to figure out how to govern in a democratic, participatory fashion city-states that sprawl across old jurisdictional boundaries. In a South that has grown so dependent on its major metropolitan areas, Southerners have to figure out how to align them to support a future of stronger competitiveness and expanded equity.

REFERENCES

Brookings Institution, Metropolitan Policy Program. *Blueprint for American Prosperity*. www.brookings.edu.

Brookings Institution, Metropolitan Policy Program. *The State of Metropolitan America*. www.brookings.edu.

Fleishman, Joel L. "The Southern City: Northern Mistakes in Southern Settings." In *You Can't Eat Magnolias*, ed. H. Brandt Ayers and Thomas H. Naylor. New York: McGraw-Hill, 1972.

Glaeser, Edward. *Triumph of the City: How Our Greatest Invention Makes Us Richer, Smarter, Greener, Healthier, and Happier*. New York: Penguin, 2011.

Kotkin, Joel. "The Next Big Boomtowns," *Forbes*, July 2011. http://www.forbes.com/sites/joelkotkin/2011/07/06/the-next-big-boom-towns-in-the-u-s.

MDC. *The State of the South*. Chapel Hill: MDC, 2010–11.

Vance, Rupert B., and Nicholas J. Demerath, eds. *The Urban South*. Chapel Hill: University of North Carolina Press, 1954.

Closing the Urban-Rural Gap: The Future of North Carolina and the South

MICHAEL L. WALDEN

INTRODUCTION

A quarter century ago, *Shadows in the Sunbelt* and *Halfway Home and a Long Way to Go* highlighted both the progress and peril of Southern economic development. The progress was the significant improvement in most broad economic measures of the South. But the peril was the uneven progress. The increase in living standards and economic conditions was most evident in urban areas, with gains in rural regions lagging behind. As a result, both reports recommended several policy initiatives for narrowing the urban-rural economic gap, including strengthening educational attainment, entrepreneurship, and infrastructure development in rural counties.

Since 1986, Southern economic progress has continued. For example, real (inflation-adjusted) per capita income increased 38 percent between 1986 and 2010. Also, Southern per capita income as a percentage of U.S. per capita income rose from 87.6 percent to 90.8 percent over the same period.

But has the progress been shared between urban and rural areas, or has the urban-rural development gap persisted or even widened? That is, in the terms of the seminal reports, has the South moved closer to home for all regions and brought lagging areas out of the shadows and into the sunlight? This essay examines these questions for one Southern state, North Carolina.

EXPECTATIONS

Technology is one of the leading factors in economic development. The major technological advance since the mid-1980s has been the development and spread of information technology. Broadly defined to be the rapid access to and transmission of information and data, information technology originally was thought to benefit rural regions. By moving information more rapidly, information technology theoretically would reduce the disadvantages of locating in more remote, less dense areas—that is, it would negate the cost of distance and help bring urban and rural areas closer together.

But the opposite seems to have occurred. Harvard economist Edward Glaeser has found that rather than reducing the desire for more face-to-face contacts (a benefit of urban areas), information technology expands our total number of contacts and thereby increases the number of contacts we want to pursue with personal meetings. So instead of sounding the death knell for large cities and dense environments, information technology has helped cities to thrive at the expense of small towns and rural regions.

If Glaeser's analysis is correct, then we would expect the urban-rural gap to have widened in the past two and a half decades. But perhaps public policies such as those recommended by the two reports have counteracted the geographic impact of information technology. In North Carolina, each of the three recommendations of the reports has been pursued. The 1994 *Leandro* ruling mandated that the state provide equal educational opportunities for students in all public schools. This ruling was buttressed by increased focus and funding of programs for disadvantaged pupils in the 1994 Improving America's Schools Act and the 2001 No Child Left

Behind Act. If rural schools typically have lagged behind urban schools, then these three changes could have improved funding and educational attainment of rural students relative to urban pupils.

In the past 25 years, the North Carolina General Assembly has been dominated by rural elected lawmakers who, urban leaders have complained, have directed road spending to rural counties. If these charges are accurate, then these investments would have upgraded the relative degree of highway infrastructure in rural areas compared to urban counties.

Finally, entrepreneurship programs also have expanded in the state in recent decades. For example, North Carolina's 58-campus community college system operates a Small Business Center Network, with access to resources and training available in every county.

THE EVIDENCE

An important issue in examining urban-rural economic differences is the definition of *rural*. Density (persons per square mile) is commonly used as the defining measure, and a single number is generally applied as the cutoff separating urban and rural. For example, the North Carolina Rural Center counts a county as rural if it has fewer than 250 persons per square mile.

While such a definition is understandable and easy to use, it has two drawbacks. First, any single numerical cutoff is arbitrary, and changes in the cutoff value will result in differing numbers of urban and rural counties. Second, if the distinctive feature of urban versus rural is density, then two categories based on one point in the density spectrum will lose considerable information for the policymaker. Therefore, rather than separating areas or counties into urban and rural groups and comparing economic trends since 1986, this essay looks at correlations between density and economic measures for 1986 and for the most recent year available (2008 or 2009). In this way, the direct impact of density and how that impact has changed can be ascertained. Correlation values are easy to understand. A positive value means that density and the other factor move in the same direction, increasing together or decreasing together. A negative value means they move in opposite directions—when density increases, the other factor decreases, and when density decreases, the other factor increases. Also, values (in absolute value) closer to 1.0 mean the relationship is stronger, while values closer to 0 mean it is weaker.

Table 8.1 reports density correlations for two key policy measures: per pupil K–12 spending from federal, state, and local sources and paved-road mileage per square mile in the county. For per-pupil spending there are two correlations, one for nominal spending and the second for per-pupil spending adjusted for differences in county prices.[1] In 1986, nominal per-pupil spending displayed a very small positive correlation with density. In 2008, the correlation was negative, indicating that spending rose as density fell. The correlation between spending adjusted for county prices was modestly negative in 1986 but more negative in 2008. The conclusion from both measures is that policy changes favored less dense counties for per-pupil spending between 1986 and 2008.

A similar conclusion is reached for highway infrastructure. Highway mileage per square mile in a county was strongly positively correlated with density in 1986. While the correlation remained positive in 2008, it was significantly less so. So highway construction in North Carolina moved in the direction of less dense counties between 1986 and 2008.

Therefore, based on these two key policy variables, it appears that North Carolina has worked to close economic gaps related to density. Has the state succeeded? Table 8.2 gives some answers. Both nominal per capita income and per capita income adjusted for county prices had strong positive correlations with density in 1986; in 2008, the correlations were still positive but much reduced. In contrast, the positive density correlations of both nominal average worker earnings and those earnings adjusted for county prices increased between 1986 and 2008. The Scholastic Aptitude Test (SAT) math score was positively related to density in both 1993, the earliest year of available data, and 2009, but the correlation was lower in the latter year. Similarly, business establishments per capita, a measure of entrepreneurship,

[1] Variation in national prices between years does not affect correlations since a constant factor (representing the change in national prices) is introduced for all counties.

has a positive density correlation, but the relationship was weaker in 2009.

The findings for per capita income, the SAT math score, and business establishments per capita all suggest a lessening role of density over time. The opposite conclusion is reached for worker earnings, which have become more correlated with density and therefore support Glaeser's hypothesis. The fact that per capita income showed the opposite trend suggests that nonearnings income, such as pensions and public transfers, has played an enhanced role in reducing economic differences resulting from density.

THE FUTURE

State-level economic development policy always faces a choice between focusing on people or places. North Carolina appears to have done both, with educational policy attempting to provide adequate training wherever a person lives, while highway infrastructure policy has bolstered transportation opportunities in less dense counties. But information technology appears to have improved job opportunities in more dense areas, so a brain drain from less dense to more dense counties will remain an issue.

Therefore, the future will likely continue to see economic differences based on density. Will future technology work to narrow or expand these differences? And will the state continue to use policy tools to lessen any adverse effects of low density? Answers to these questions are only speculative. However, technological advances in personal imaging and simulated meetings may ultimately reduce the advantages information technology has given to more dense areas and level the playing field for urban and rural regions. Furthermore, at least in educational policy, both the federal and state governments appear committed to providing equal educational opportunities to all students, regardless of their location. So although differences will remain, when the next assessment is taken in another 25 years, we could very well see that urban and rural areas have grown closer together rather than farther apart.

REFERENCES

Data are from the U.S. Department of Commerce. The department's geographic of definition of Southeast is used for the South.

Glaeser, Edward. *Triumph of the City: How Our Greatest Invention Makes Us Richer, Smarter, Greener, Healthier, and Happier.* New York: Penguin, 2011.

Siceloff, Bruce. "New Ways to Fund Roads Proposed." *Raleigh News and Observer*, April 19, 2006. http://www.newsobserver.com/news/story/430132.html.

Walden, Michael L. "How Much Income Variation Really Exists within a State?" *Review of Regional Studies* 27 (1997): 237–50.

TABLES AND FIGURES

table 8.1 NORTH CAROLINA COUNTY DENSITY CORRELATIONS WITH PUBLIC SCHOOL SPENDING AND HIGHWAY AVAILABILITY

MEASURE	1986	LATEST YEAR
Nominal per-pupil spending	0.023	−0.233 (2008)
Per-pupil spending adjusted for county prices	−0.128	−0.285 (2008)
Paved highway mileage per square mile	0.703	0.595 (2008)

Source: North Carolina State Data Center; author's calculations.

table 8.2 NORTH CAROLINA COUNTY DENSITY CORRELATIONS WITH KEY ECONOMIC MEASURES

MEASURE	1986	LATEST YEAR
Nominal per capita income	0.708	0.591 (2008)
Per capita income adjusted for county prices	0.707	0.531 (2008)
Nominal average worker earnings	0.265	0.436 (2008)
Average worker earnings adjusted for county prices	0.201	0.367 (2008)
SAT math score	0.381 (1993)	0.271 (2009)
Business establishments per capita	0.345	0.302 (2009)

Source: North Carolina State Data Center; author's calculations.

THE FUTURE *of* the Green South

JERRY WEITZ

INTRODUCTION

The 1986 Commission on the Future of the South set out a major objective: "Enhance the South's cultural and natural resources by 1992." *Halfway Home and a Long Way to Go* identified five target objectives for state action: (1) adopt systems of environmental management; (2) help local governments manage growth; (3) concentrate on water management; (4) improve waste management; and (5) preserve historic and cultural resources. The commission demonstrated some remarkable and impressive foresight in putting together these recommendations. One missing objective was air quality, which has since emerged as both a major issue for the South and an area of considerable innovation by some Southern states.[1] To what extent have these five target objectives been attained? This essay provides an overall assessment of environmental and natural resources protection efforts in the 13 states that are members of the Southern Growth Policies Board, plus Florida, which was at one time part of the board. The essay concludes that the South still lags behind in various environmental management efforts recommended in 1986 and has lagged behind in embracing objectives of the evolving green movement.

STATEWIDE GROWTH AND ENVIRONMENTAL MANAGEMENT

Georgia, for one, embraced many of these objectives and has made considerable progress in attaining them. In keeping with the spirit of the directive, Georgia adopted coordinated planning legislation (the 1989 Georgia Planning Act), which included environmental management, water management, and provisions to preserve historic and cultural resources. The following year, Georgia passed minimum environmental standards for water management and comprehensive planning as well as a law requiring local governments to prepare comprehensive solid-waste-management plans. Twenty-plus years later, virtually all local governments in Georgia have plans that address these considerations.

But Georgia is the exception with regard to state growth-management programs. Florida has remained a national leader in state growth management and substantially revamped its statewide growth-management laws in 1985. Some Southern states, including North Carolina and South Carolina, considered adopting laws to establish growth-management programs in the early 2000s or appointed commissions that further studied policy solutions similar to the *Halfway Home* suggestions. In 1998, Tennessee surprised the nation by adopting a requirement that urban growth boundaries be established. And several states have allowed local governments to adopt impact fees, as Georgia did in 1990. Georgia thus met yet another one of the benchmarks of the 1986 report.

Some growth-management initiatives have been undertaken in coastal regions. For example, North Carolina has been a strong pioneer in prohibiting hardening of the coast and thus of greener development along the ocean. North Carolina also passed a major reform of its coastal insurance "Beach Plan," which has provided a far more equitable balancing of risk and cost incentives for coastal development through the leverage of insurance premiums. North Carolina has long had more progressive policies regarding urban annexation of surrounding planning jurisdictions and service areas than has Georgia, where the city of Atlanta is substantially strangled by its suburbs' independent jurisdictions.

Other Southern states have done little to adopt growth management, initiate regional planning, or review large-scale developments as specifically recommended in 1986. In fact, in Florida and Georgia, which

---

[1] *Many Southern states cooperated on the 10-year Southern Appalachian Mountains Initiative in the 1990s, and North Carolina passed an exceptionally innovative 2002 law, the Clean Smokestacks Act, that forced cleanup or retirement of all the state's coal-fired power plants. Subsequent litigation extended those requirements to all of the Tennessee Valley Authority's plants. Several Southern states, including North Carolina, also have passed Renewable Energy and Efficiency Portfolio standards laws, raising major and important questions about the future of the South's old coal-fired economy; the potential for the transition to cleaner fuels such as natural gas, nuclear power, and renewable energy sources; and the long-neglected area of energy efficiency.*

established regional planning and systems for reviewing large-scale development impacts, those systems have come under attack, and their survival has been threatened during the past decade. The outlook that additional states will follow with adoption and implementation of statewide environmental- and growth-management programs appears bleak.

North Carolina has long had active regional-planning institutions, though not as effective as some observers might wish. It also has been home to a variety of "new urbanism" green development examples as well as to a statewide Clean Water Trust Fund, which finances the purchase and protection of environmentally valuable areas, and to numerous land conservancy organizations, which partner with state and local governments to protect areas of high natural value. A state natural heritage inventory identifies and prioritizes areas particularly deserving of protection, and several major high-value areas (among them Grandfather Mountain and Chimney Rock) have now passed from private ownership into permanent state protection.

GREEN INDICATORS

Brian Wingfield and Miriam Marcus ranked states according to various green indicators, including carbon footprint, air quality, water quality, hazardous-waste management, policy initiatives and energy consumption, and the number of buildings (on a per capita basis) that have received the U.S. Green Building Council's benchmark Leadership in Energy and Environmental Design (LEED) certification. Table 8.3 shows the rankings of Southern states in Wingfield and Marcus's evaluation as well as in a green/environmental rating by Greenopia USA.

Southern states occupy 8 of the 10 bottom spots in Wingfield and Marcus's rankings. Florida (20th) fared the best, followed by Virginia (23rd), North Carolina (26th), and Georgia (29th). The South fared only slightly better in Greenopia USA's assessment, taking 5 of the 10 worst slots. West Virginia ranked last in both rating systems.

WATER MANAGEMENT

Scorecard: The Pollution Information Site also provides environmental indicators and rankings for states. Table 8.4 shows the percentages of surface

waters with reported problems in each state and total number of water bodies with reported problems in 1998.

In both Mississippi and South Carolina, the vast majority of surface waters had reported problems, and most other states had very high numbers of problems. These statistics clearly signal a need for better water-quality management, in keeping with the 1986 recommendations. Hopeful examples include the North Carolina Neuse River Basin cleanup project and the Tar-Pamlico pollutant trading program.

AIR QUALITY AND WASTE MANAGEMENT

The *Scorecard* site also provides state rankings for various air-quality and waste-management indicators, as summarized in table 8.5. Only Florida, Arkansas, and Oklahoma ranked in the upper half of states with regard to total environmental releases per the Toxic Release Inventory (TRI). And only Arkansas, Oklahoma, and West Virginia ranked in the top half of states with regard to volatile organic compound (VOC) emissions. Tennessee, Georgia, and North Carolina ranked among the worst offenders in both categories.[2]

Table 8.5 also shows how the states ranked with regard to total animal waste. Only Missouri and Oklahoma ranked in the top 10 offenders in that regard. However, the total rank masks

[2] *The use of only TRI data and VOCs to represent air quality can be inadequate because toxic releases do not occur solely into the air. There is significant variation in state efforts to clean up "criteria" air pollutants (the dominant combustion emissions such as SO2, NOx, ozone, particulates, and so forth, which are not part of TRI). Moreover, these data are more than a decade old and miss some Southern states' major initiatives to improve air quality.*

some interesting observations. North Carolina ranked second in the nation in terms of tons of hog waste produced in 1997. Southern states occupied the top 5 positions in terms of poultry waste produced: Arkansas (1); North Carolina (2); Georgia (3); Alabama (4); and Mississippi (5). Clearly, animal-waste disposal remains a significant challenge for many of the Southern states. Also, as table 8.5 indicates, most of the states have a dozen or more Superfund sites that require attention, with North Carolina ranking third among the Southern states in this category.

OPEN-SPACE PROTECTION AND RENEWABLE ENERGY

In 1999, the Sierra Club produced an analysis of sprawl and published open-space-protection rankings for states based on eight criteria, including state open-space protection; agricultural-protection districts; agricultural-protection zoning; purchase of agricultural conservation easements; transfer of development rights; percentage of prime farmland destroyed between 1982 and 1992; floodplain sprawl; and field expert input. Table 8.6 indicates how the Southern states ranked nationally with regard to open-space protection.

With the exception of Florida, the Southern states did not fare well in these rankings. Other than Florida, only Kentucky ranked in the top half of states, and Southern states occupied 5 of the 10 lowest slots—West Virginia (50th), South Carolina (48th), Louisiana (47th), Missouri (44th), and Arkansas (41st). Two of these are coastal states, and the other three have some mountainous terrain. The South's coastal and mountainous environments are among the region's most prized resources, as the 1986 report noted. To fail in the protection of those critical natural resources is likely to result in harm to the region's long-term economic well-being. To more adequately assess protection of coastal and mountain areas, we need more specific data on these environments than the Sierra Club rankings provide, including information on North Carolina's Ridge Protection Law, which prohibits major structures visible in the mountain areas, and its Coastal Area Management Act, one of the nation's best.

Table 8.6 also shows the percentage of total electricity supplied by renewable energy sources (solar, wind, hydroelectric, geothermal, and biomass waste). While the Southern states are not well endowed compared with other states with regard to wind and geothermal energy, the percentages of total electricity supplied by renewable energy sources are still strikingly low. However, North Carolina has some of the best wind resources in the eastern United States, both in the mountains and off the coast. Significant resources also exist in other Southern states, even West Virginia, where renewable energy is beginning to be advocated as an alternative to coal. North Carolina now has a Renewable Energy and Energy Efficiency Portfolio Standard (REPS) law mandating increases in renewable energy to more than 12 percent of total generation by 2021 and is on track to meet those requirements.

In contrast, Oregon, often considered a national leader in terms of environmental policy, produces 66 percent of its electricity from renewable sources (especially hydroelectric

power). Oregon is heavily supplied by huge hydropower dams built in the 1940s, a resource to which Southeastern states—and indeed, most states—do not have access and that also has environmental impacts (for example, reducing salmon runs). While hydroelectric power is often not considered a substantial future supplier in the Southern states, biomass energy production from animal wastes appears to hold some promise.

HISTORIC RESOURCES

The Southern states certainly have a large number of preservation-worthy cultural and historic resources dating back to the Revolutionary War, antebellum, and Civil War periods as well as relating to Native American and African American heritage. It is difficult to provide comparative benchmarks to evaluate the extent to which the subject states have protected their historic and cultural resources. One such indicator, however, is the number of listings on the National Register of Historic Places. The U.S. Department of the Interior's National Park Service, which administers the National Register, keeps a database that shows Virginia leading the Southern states with 3,965 listings, followed by Kentucky with 3,391 and North Carolina with 2,799. West Virginia, Oklahoma, and Alabama have the fewest National Register listings among the Southern states.

There is reason to suggest that other indicators of cultural protection need to be developed, since the National Register is only a descriptive identifier that does not afford any protection to historic resources. Local historic districts, which typically authorize historic preservation commissions to prevent demolition of historic structures without of a certificate of appropriateness, would be a better indicator of cultural resource protection than the National Register of Historic Places.

CONCLUSIONS AND POLICY IMPLICATIONS

When the 1986 commission reported, Florida was taking notable actions in the area of statewide growth management, including significant efforts at environmental management. Today, *Halfway Home* is still relevant, though we are now in a green era that could not have been anticipated by the report's authors. The time has come to renew interest in and attention to improving the status of the environment in the South. The Southern states continue to lag substantially behind in terms of environmental indicators such as water quality, air quality, waste management, and open-space protection. However, active and effective forces in the South are pushing for innovations, including the Southern Association for Clean Energy, the Sierra Club, the Environmental Defense Fund, land conservancies, and many other more regional and indigenous groups.

The 1986 recommendations regarding statewide environmental management programs and significant aid to local governments to manage growth are certainly understandable, especially in the context of the decade in which they were written, and they remain valid today. However, the policy window of opportunity to initiate such programs as regional planning and large-scale development reviews has largely closed. Yet the fundamental concerns about the environment remain, and even greater concern about degradation of the environment is appropriate.

This essay cannot articulate all of the policy recommendations for protecting the region's environmental and cultural resources. However, one recommendation that merits serious consideration is a formalized benchmarking and environmental indicators project for Southern states. This essay identifies only a few of metrics that could be used to measure progress, and a multitude of more detailed measures could be added. For example, the quality of coastal environments should be maintained. Evaluation programs by the National Oceanic and Atmospheric Administration have been evolving during the past five years and should be integrated into a more formal, comprehensive evaluation framework for environmental quality attainment, such as a major federal study of North Carolina estuaries, the Albemarle-Pamlico Estuarine Study.

The environmental indicators and state rankings discussed here suggest that much more work needs to be done in the areas of water quality, air quality, and waste management even if we cannot expect new, major statewide initiatives regarding growth management. A careful analysis of a comprehensive set of environmental indicators could go a long way toward not only evaluating progress and performance but also pointing the way to new opportunities. As *Halfway Home*'s authors recognized 25 years ago, the region's future economic well-being depends on protecting its environmental and cultural resources. Urgency should prevail during the next decade. Southern states need to benchmark, evaluate, and improve the environment to ensure that the South advances appropriately in the evolving new era of green.

REFERENCES

Greenopia USA Environmental Rating. *Eco-Friendly Green State Guide.* http://www.greenopia.com/USA/state_search.aspx?ID=5&input=Name-or-product&Listpage=0.

"Renewable Energy Production by State." *Wall Street Journal*, March 31, 2011.

Scorecard: The Pollution Information Site. http://scorecard.goodguide.com/env-releases/land/rank-states.tcl.

Sierra Club. *Solving Sprawl: 1999 Sierra Club Solving Sprawl Report*. 1999. http://www.sierraclub.org/sprawl/report99/openspace.asp#ratings.

U.S. Department of the Interior, *National Park Service. National Register of Historic Places.* NPS Digital Library, search by state.

Weitz, Jerry. "The Next Wave in Growth Management." *Urban Lawyer* 42–43 (2010–11): 407–16.

Weitz, Jerry. *Sprawl Busting: State Programs to Guide Growth.* Chicago: Planners Press, 1999.

Wingfield, Brian, and Miriam Marcus. "America's Greenest States." Forbes.com. October 17, 2007.

TABLES AND FIGURES

table 8.3 RANKINGS OF SOUTHERN STATES WITH REGARD TO GREEN INDICATORS

Southern State	Wingfield and Marcus America's Greenest States Ranking (1 = best)	Greenopia USA Environmental Rating, Eco-Friendly Green State Guide (Rank) (1 = best)
Alabama	48	42
Arkansas	44	23
Florida	20	16
Georgia	29	21
Kentucky	45	46
Louisiana	47	49
Mississippi	46	41
Missouri	41	29
North Carolina	26	25
Oklahoma	38	33
South Carolina	36	34
Tennessee	43	35
Virginia	23	26
West Virginia	50	50

Source: Wingfield and Marcus 2007; Greenopia USA.

table 8.4 CLEAN WATER ACT INDICATORS BY SOUTHERN STATE, 1998

Southern State	1998 Clean Water Act Status: Percentage of Surface Waters with Reported Problems	1998 Clean Water Act Status: Number of Water Bodies with Reported Problems
Alabama	14	154
Arkansas	4	51
Florida	18	712
Georgia	12	584
Kentucky	10	231
Louisiana	22	196
Mississippi	71	729
Missouri	4	174
North Carolina	18	477
Oklahoma	10	531
South Carolina	63	658
Tennessee	22	352
Virginia	13	883
West Virginia	14	722

Source: Scorecard: The Pollution Information Site.

table 8.5 AIR QUALITY AND WASTE MANAGEMENT INDICATOR RANKINGS, SOUTHERN STATE

Southern State	Total Toxic Release Inventory Environmental Releases (1 = worst)	Rank, Volatile Organic Compound (VOC) Emissions (1 = worst)	Tons of Animal Waste Ranking (1 = worst)	Number of Superfund Sites
Alabama	13	15	23	15
Arkansas	28	30	13	11
Florida	7	*	*	52
Georgia	10	10	21	16
Kentucky	18	23	17	14
Louisiana	11	18	35	16
Mississippi	15	24	30	5
Missouri	15	21	8	27
North Carolina	12	8	10	29
Oklahoma	32	28	7	11
South Carolina	22	22	37	25
Tennessee	8	11	20	13
Virginia	19	13	26	30
West Virginia	17	36	41	9

Source: Scorecard: The Pollution Information Site.
* Data not available.

table 8.6 OPEN-SPACE PROTECTION STATE RANK (1999) AND RENEWABLE ENERGY SHARE

State	Open-Space-Protection Ranking, Sierra Club, 1999 (1 = best)	Renewable Energy as a Percentage of Total Electricity Generated
Alabama	37	11
Arkansas	41	10
Florida	14	2
Georgia	25	5
Kentucky	21	4
Louisiana	47	4
Mississippi	36	3
Missouri	44	3
North Carolina	28	6
Oklahoma	26	9
South Carolina	48	4
Tennessee	34	14
Virginia	32	5
West Virginia	50	3

Source: Sierra Club 1999; "Renewable Energy Production by State."

WORK, THE SAFETY NET, AND FAITH

Creating *"Good Jobs"* in North Carolina and the South

ARNE L. KALLEBERG AND JENNIFER E. SWANBERG

INTRODUCTION

Work in North Carolina and other Southern states has undergone a marked transformation in the past several decades, and social, political, and economic forces have made the quality of jobs problematic. The notion of job quality, or a "good job," communicates that workers are concerned about the nature of their work, not just whether they have a job. Concerns about job quality have been overshadowed in recent years by the fact that many Southerners have no jobs at all as a consequence of the Great Recession and its aftermath. Nevertheless, the quality of available jobs has been a continuing source of distress for some time. The importance of job quality stems from the centrality of work to human welfare and to the functioning of businesses and communities.

By *job quality* or *good job*, we mean the extent to which employment provides sufficient economic compensation (pay and benefits such as health insurance and retirement income) to satisfy a person's needs as well as the opportunity for people to exercise control over their schedules (to permit them to balance their work and nonwork lives) and over what they do at work.

Twenty-five years ago, *Halfway Home and a Long Way to Go* set out a number of goals related to the question of job quality. These goals included enhancing education for all students and education's role in economic development, preparing a globally competitive workforce, and increasing the South's capacity to use technology. Unfortunately, these goals have only partly been achieved.

HISTORICAL/EMPIRICAL TRENDS

Over the past few decades, North Carolina and other Southern states have changed from a manufacturing-dominated economy to one dominated by services. Accompanying this industrial change have been changes in the occupational structure, as shown in figure 9.1. The number of high-end service jobs, such as professionals and managers, has grown. These are generally regarded as good jobs and in North Carolina's case have resulted from high-wage, high-growth companies, especially in high-tech industries such as biotechnology, pharmaceuticals, health care, financial services, and education.

The decline in manufacturing industries such as tobacco, textiles/apparel, and furniture also has led to a

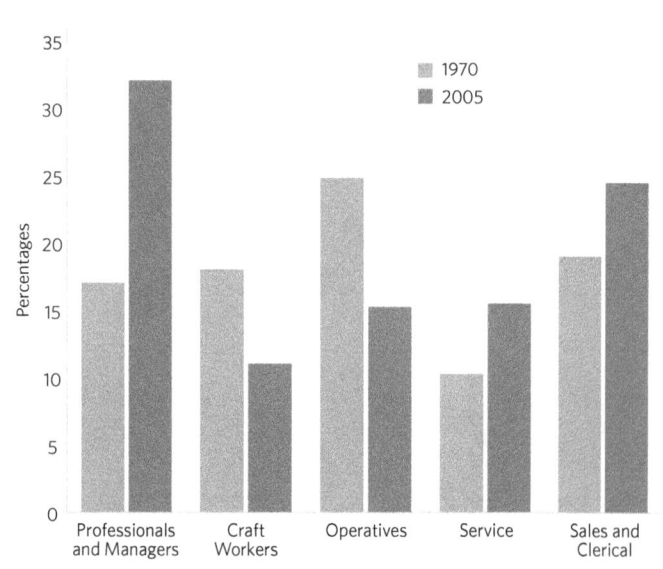

figure 9.1 POLARIZATION OF OCCUPATIONS IN NORTH CAROLINA, 1970 TO 2005

> The importance of job quality stems from the centrality of work to human welfare and to the functioning of businesses and communities.

decrease in middle-level blue-collar jobs such as those in crafts occupations and operatives. These manufacturing jobs were relatively well paid even if they did not require high levels of skill. At the same time, the shift from manufacturing to services also has led to an expansion of many bad jobs, especially sales and service jobs in very low-wage industries such as retail trade and temporary services. Sales occupations such as cashiers and service occupations such as nursing aides, hospital attendants, and wait staff illustrate the growth of low-wage jobs.

The expansion of job quality at the top and bottom of the occupational structure—combined with a decline or hollowing out of middle-quality jobs—has resulted in a polarization of job quality in North Carolina and in the South. This polarization in turn is intimately related to the growth in earnings inequality and poverty. The growth of low-wage jobs in sales and service occupations has contributed to the rise in poverty in North Carolina: The number of households living in poverty grew from about 12 percent of the population in 1999 to more than 16 percent in 2009. Median household income in the state (calculated in constant 2009 dollars) fell from $50,441 in 1999 to $43,674 in 2009, a 13.4 percent decline. Employment growth has been uneven geographically within North Carolina: It has been greater in places with more highly educated workforces, such as the metropolitan regions of Charlotte and the Triangle, and in resort and retirement areas, such as Boone and Asheville.

Hence, we have not really fulfilled the promise and hopes of 25 years ago in regard to job quality. North Carolina and the South still have too many bad jobs. We must create not just jobs but good jobs.

CHALLENGES FOR THE FUTURE: PROMISING PRACTICES FOR CREATING GOOD JOBS

Creating quality jobs in North Carolina's new economy requires us to address two specific problems associated with many current and future jobs. First, North Carolina has many low-wage, low-skill jobs: 60 percent of jobs require a high-school diploma or less and pay below the state's average earnings. Occupational projections indicate that this situation will not improve unless significant changes are made.

Second, unlike traditional middle-level jobs that provided decent wages and required limited education, new middle-level jobs entail advanced skills and often necessitate an associate's degree, postsecondary certificate, high school diploma, or general equivalency diploma. Gaps exist between many of the skills needed by employers and the skills training offered by community colleges and workforce-development entities.

To address local and national workforce and job-quality challenges, we need to establish innovative public-private partnerships among employers, workforce-development entities, and community colleges. The following examples illustrate strategies that have been successfully employed in North Carolina and Kentucky to train entry-level workers, provide career pathways, and reduce skill gaps and labor shortages.

REGIONAL LEARNING CENTERS AND PATHWAYS TO PHARMACY

CVS Caremark, one of the country's largest pharmacy benefits managers, has established two workforce initiatives,

Regional Learning Centers and Pathways to Pharmacy, that provide training to entry-level workers and development opportunities for workers desiring advancement. As a recruitment/retention strategy, CVS has teamed with state and federal workforce agencies in eight cities around the United States, including Baltimore; Washington, D.C.; and Atlanta, to establish regional learning centers that provide employment services and training to underserved populations. Six regional learning centers located in public labor department one-stop career centers deliver training to more than 1,500 entry-level and incumbent workers annually per site. Since 1996, more than 80,000 entry-level workers have been hired from the public assistance population. On average, 60 percent of employees referred from regional learning centers are retained, compared to 30 percent of regular employees.

CVS Career Path, created to support the company's growth, provides low-skilled workers with a guide for advancement within the organization. Advancement is accomplished through on-the-job training, customized training, mentoring, and continuing education at local community colleges and universities. One Career Path initiative, Pathways to Pharmacy, encourages youth and entry-level CVS employees to consider pharmacy careers.

In North Carolina, CVS has partnered with several high schools and community colleges. Sixteen youth from the Academy at Smith in Greensboro participated in a 10-hour summer Pathways to Pharmacy internship where they shadowed pharmacists. Several students subsequently applied to pharmacy school. CVS also partnered with Fuquay-Varina High School to offer a semester-long work-study program and with Cape Fear Community College in Wilmington and Craven Community College in New Bern to develop pharmacy technician programs in which students may apply for paid internships with CVS.

HEALTHCAREER PATHWAYS

HealthCareer Pathways, based in Louisville, Kentucky, is a collaborative initiative among schools, postsecondary institutions, and employers that was established to focus high school students' career aspirations, increase their likelihood of college enrollment and completion, provide professional development and advancement opportunities for current health care workers, and address a health care labor shortage. Jefferson Community and Technical College spearheaded this effort, securing participation from more than 10 local health care organizations. Based on the region's workforce needs, HealthCareer Pathways targets high-need allied health fields. Participating employers offer employees educational advancement linked with incentives such as financial aid, time off from work to attend classes, and career development. Employer investment in the workforce's educational advancement helps raise the quality of jobs and service delivery, per capita income, workforce capacity and quality, and area standards of living.

HOSIERY TECHNOLOGY CENTER

North Carolina's Catawba Valley Community College formed a similar collaboration to address the needs of the hosiery industry. The community college established the Hosiery Technology Center in 1990 in partnership with individual hosiery firms, suppliers, and the regional trade association as a means of tackling the local skilled and semiskilled labor shortage by creating an area training center available to all participating firms. The Hosiery Technology Center provides a variety of training to area hosiery firms and serves all aspects of a vibrant industry cluster, such as research and development, marketing, and streamlining manufacturing processes. This collaboration has kept semiskilled and skilled jobs that pay decent wages in North Carolina and has improved the quality and safety of hosiery jobs. Workers often receive better benefits, more varied and safer work, fewer variable schedule assignments, and higher wages. Weekly wages (in real dollars) for hosiery workers in North Carolina increased from $508 in 2001 to $620 in 2005. Moreover, the hosiery industry in North Carolina continues to offer higher wages than hosiery industries in other parts of the United States States ($620 versus $551 in 2005) as well as other service-producing industries in North Carolina ($620 versus $582 in 2005). These examples illustrate the potential for public-private partnerships not only to create good jobs in North Carolina and the South but also to benefit participating businesses.

IMPLEMENTING THE SOUTHERN "GOOD JOBS" AGENDA

Achieving economic prosperity in North Carolina and the South requires an integrated, multifaceted approach to creating quality jobs. Government support is essential to establish legislation that encourages the creation of jobs that pay living wages (for example, the Work Opportunity Tax Credit) and provide workers with the flexibility to manage their nonwork lives (such as right to request legislation and paid sick leave laws). Community colleges and workforce-development entities can complement these job-creation efforts by preparing workers who have the skills for these good jobs. Moreover, involvement of economic development agencies is necessary to ensure that regions attract and retain businesses that provide communities with quality jobs. Evidence indicates that businesses, communities, and working families thrive when employers take the high road to job creation, resulting in more high-skilled and better-quality jobs.

REFERENCES

Corporate Voices for Working Families. *Recruiting and Training through Public Workforce System Produces Strong ROI: CVS Caremark.* 2010. http://www.cvworkingfamilies.org/system/files/CVS+micro-case+Final.pdf.

Walden, Michael L. "Economic Change in North Carolina: Implications for Workforce Development." Paper prepared for the University of North Carolina Tomorrow Commission, August 2007.

Willis, R., and R. Connelly. *Keeping Good Job Opportunities in the Community: How and When to Use Public Training Resources to Revitalize Good Manufacturing Jobs in the United States.* Chapel Hill: Center on Poverty, Work and Opportunity, University of North Carolina Law School. http://www.law.unc.edu/centers/poverty/publications/policybrief/default.aspx.

Willis, R., R. Connelly, and D. DeGraff. "The Future of Jobs in the Hosiery Industry." In *Low-Wage America*, ed. E. Appelbaum, A. Bernhardt, and R. Murnane. New York: Sage, 2003.

Will the Government Strengthen at-Risk Families?

AMANDA SHEELY AND ANNIE JENKINS

INTRODUCTION

This essay assesses whether the public social safety net for poor families in the South offers more support than it did 25 years ago. In 1986, the Commission on the Future of the South expressed grave concerns about families living in poverty and about the inadequacy of government programs serving them. In 1989, 23.5 percent of Southern children were living below the federal poverty level. Since the late 1980s, childhood poverty has remained high. In only three years during this period were fewer than 20 percent of children living in poverty; the lowest level was 18.9 percent of children in 2000. In 2009, the percentage of children living in poverty in the South was 22.9 percent, only slightly less than the level 25 years ago. Childhood poverty is still concentrated among African American families: In 2009, 8 percent of white families with children in the South lived in poverty, compared to 23 percent of African American families.

Given the high levels of need, one might expect to see a robust social safety net system. However, Southern states have long been characterized as limiting access to means-tested public programs and as providing meager benefits to recipients. This characterization is evident in the 1986 report, in which the primary recommendation to strengthen at-risk families was to bring welfare benefits in the South more in line with those in the rest of the United States. Evaluating whether progress has been made in meeting this goal is complex given the significant changes to the social safety net for poor families. For example, the passage of welfare reform in 1996 fundamentally restructured the cash aid program for poor families by granting states broad flexibility to design and implement such programs. Under the Temporary Aid to Needy Families program, states have the ability to set eligibility and participation requirements, determine the amount of time families can receive cash assistance, and offer additional incentives to families who combine welfare with work. In addition, with federal support in the mid-1990s, states started creating programs to offer health insurance to more working-poor and moderate-income families than Medicaid covers. The federal Earned Income Tax Credit was expanded in 1993, and some states enacted similar credits to offer additional financial support to workers in low-wage jobs. To assess government support for poor families, one must consider the generosity of all of these programs.

ASSESSING THE SOUTHERN SAFETY NET

Temporary Assistance to Needy Families Benefit Levels

One of the simplest metrics used to assess the generosity of welfare programs is the amount of money that poor families receive under Temporary Assistance to Needy Families. In 1985, Southern states gave a family of three with one adult $219 a month in cash aid. In contrast, the average monthly benefit for a similar family was $342 in the United States as a whole and $398 per month in non-Southern states. The disparity between benefit levels in Southern and non-Southern states has persisted over time. In 2010, the average monthly benefit level in non-Southern states (in current dollars) was $508, compared to $292 in Southern states. In both 1985 and 2010, 9 of the 10 states with the lowest benefit levels were located in the South. Benefit levels, adjusted for inflation, have decreased throughout the United States since 1985, so regardless of where poor families reside, they cannot subsist on government cash benefits.

Temporary Aid to Needy Families Policy Provisions

With the passage of welfare reform, the federal government granted states discretion to create welfare programs. However, all state programs must include two provisions: reductions in cash aid for noncompliance (sanctions), and a five-year limit on the amount of time that families can receive aid. While all state programs must include these provisions, states can decide how large the reductions in cash aid will be. States also can opt to have shorter time limits than those required by federal law or can decide to use state funds to keep providing aid after the five-year limit. In general, Southern states have used their discretion to create more stringent cash assistance programs than non-Southern states. In all Southern states, families lose their entire grant if they do not comply with program requirements. In contrast, six Northern states decided to reduce cash benefits only partially for noncompliance. Thirty-seven states adopted the federal five-year lifetime limit on cash aid. However, Arkansas, Delaware, Florida,

and Georgia are four of the eight states that set the limit at under five years. Of the six states that decided to use their own funds to support families after they reached the federal time limit, none are in the South. Researchers have also found that policies adopted in the South after welfare reform's passage are more stringent than such policies in other regions.

Role of Other Safety-Net Programs

One of the primary goals of welfare reform was to promote work among poor mothers. The legislation explicitly included provisions to reward work as well as to discourage welfare dependency. After the passage of welfare reform, some states have expanded programs for working-poor families. Specifically, states have sought to increase enrollment in the food stamp program (now called the Supplemental Nutrition Assistance Program); expand health insurance coverage through Medicaid and children's health insurance programs; and increase income through tax credits for working families. Using this broader definition of the safety net, Southern states are keeping pace with the rest of the country in some programs but not others. In 2008, the participation rate in Supplemental Nutrition Assistance Program was 70 percent of those eligible in the South, compared with a 68 percent in the rest of the country. While higher participation rates are important, Southern recipients of the Supplemental Nutrition Assistance Program and Temporary Aid to Needy Families remain financially disadvantaged compared to families in Northern states. Combining the benefits of these programs in West Virginia, the most generous Southern state, brought a family of three only to 57 percent of the federal poverty level in 2010—an annual income of less than $10,000 a year. On average, the incomes of Southern families receiving both forms of assistance were only 53 percent of the federal poverty level, compared to 66 percent of the federal poverty level among families living in Northern states. Participation rates in the Medicaid/children's health insurance programs are slightly higher in the South (83.1 percent of eligible children) than in the United States overall (82.2 percent). However, the percentage of uninsured children is higher in the South (10.3 percent) than among non-Southern states (8.0 percent). To increase the incomes of working-poor families, 6 Southern states (Delaware, Louisiana, Maryland, North Carolina, Oklahoma, and Virginia) have instituted state tax-credit programs that supplement the federal Earned Income Tax Credit. However, only 37.5 percent of Southern states have adopted these programs, whereas 47 percent of non-Southern states have done so.

POLICY RECOMMENDATIONS AND CONCLUSIONS

Southern states still have a long way to go to offer an adequate public safety net for poor families. Childhood poverty remains a significant problem, especially

> Southern states must provide services that help families escape poverty instead of simply enduring it.

among African American families. Given the long-term educational, physical, and social impacts of childhood poverty, Southern states must provide services that help families escape poverty instead of simply enduring it. However, it does not appear that government programs in the South are even doing enough to help families endure poverty. Benefit levels for both the Temporary Aid to Needy Families and Supplemental Nutrition Assistance Program are still inadequate to help families meet their basic needs. The policy provisions of Southern Temporary Aid to Needy Families programs also are more stringent than those in the rest of the country, which may make it harder for families to stay in the program. Most Southern states also have not funded tax credit programs to increase the incomes of working families. However, participation rates for both Supplemental Nutrition Assistance Program and government health insurance programs are higher in the South than in the rest of the country.

When making recommendations to improve the social safety net 25 years ago, the commission could not foresee the fundamental shift in the goal of welfare provision from providing benefits to poor families to encouraging them to work. Indeed, since the passage of welfare reform, Temporary Aid to Needy Families caseloads have plummeted. At the same time, the number of families that are classified as working poor has increased dramatically. Over the next 25 years, the social safety system will need to adjust to support two types of families: those who work but remain in poverty, and those who face significant barriers to employment and must rely on government aid. Southern states can serve both of these groups by ensuring that families access federal programs for which they qualify, including the Supplemental Nutrition Assistance Program, the Earned Income Tax Credit, and social security insurance. However, as cash assistance is time-limited, Temporary Aid to Needy Families providers also must learn to work with other government agencies to improve the employment prospects of poor parents, including those related to education, training, and economic development.

REFERENCES

Cunnyngham, K., and L. Castner. *Reaching Those in Need: State Supplemental Assistance Participation Rates in 2008*. 2010. http://www.fns.usda.gov/ora/menu/Published/snap/FILES/Participation/Reaching2008.pdf.

McNichol, E., and J. Springer. *State Policies to Assist Working-Poor Families*. 2004. http://www.cbpp.org/cms/?fa=view&id=899.

Pavetti, L., and D. Bloom. "State Sanctions and Time Limits." In *The New World of Welfare*, ed. R. M. Blank and R. Haskins. Washington, D.C.: Brookings Institution Press, 2001.

Schott, L., and I. Finch. *TANF Benefits Are Low and Have Not Kept Pace with Inflation: Benefits Are Not Enough to Meet Families' Basic Needs*. http://www.cbpp.org/cms/index.cfm?fa=view&id=3306.

Urban Institute. *Maximum Monthly Benefit for a Family of Three with No Income*. http://anfdata.urban.org/wrd/maps.cfm.

U.S. House of Representatives, Ways and Means Committee. *Green Book, 2004: Background Material and Data on Programs within the Jurisdiction of the Committee on Ways and Means*. WMCP 108-6. Washington, D.C.: U.S. Government Printing Office, 2004. http://www.gpoaccess.gov/wmprints/green/2004.html.

Zedlewski, S. "States' New TANF Policies: Is the Emphasis on Carrots or Sticks?" *Policy and Practice* 56 (1998): 57–64.

Zimmerman, J. "Contextualizing Cash Assistance and the South." *Southern Rural Sociology* 18 (2002): 1–20.

Faith-Based Nonprofits *and the* Social Safety Net in the South

MAUREEN BERNER AND SHARON PAYNTER

The South's social safety net is rooted in small organizations in small towns with names such as Ministries of the Bread of Life, Shiloh Missionary Baptist Church, and Mother Hubbard's Cupboard as well as in larger organizations such as the Catholic Charities Center in Raleigh and Loaves and Fishes in Charlotte. These organizations cross religious lines, and some exist as part of senior centers, Head Start day cares, or AIDS services. More than likely, though, the source of strength for at-risk families comes from a local volunteer, and the bag of groceries includes a blessing and a prayer. In just one region of central and eastern North Carolina covering 34 counties, there are 984 pantries or related agencies providing free or cheap food to those who need it.

Due to ever-tightening constraints on government budgets, community-based support is often the best form of a social safety net. Faith-based organizations are now considered partners with government in meeting social needs, and such groups often do so more efficiently and effectively. Approximately 75 percent of food pantries in North Carolina work hand in hand with local departments of social services. To meet the needs of people in the wake of a disaster, food banks often partner with local government to process and deliver supplemental nutrition assistance. These local organizations and the people who volunteer with them seem to carry a sense of moral obligation and commitment missing from the private business and larger governmental sectors. As such, we embrace faith to save our social services—faith rises in troubled times.

Berner and Paynter analyzed several hundred random client files from 40 pantries in central North Carolina.

- most clients returned to pantries consistently for more than one year;
- the average client returned to pantries for five consecutive years;
- 24 percent of clients were married with no children;
- 15 percent were elderly and single;
- 42 percent were married with kids;
- many (but not a majority of) pantry clients received food stamps;
- in 2007, the median income of clients was 29 percent lower than that of other North Carolinians;
- only 7.8 percent of clients were living below the federal poverty line; and
- most pantries are helping more people.

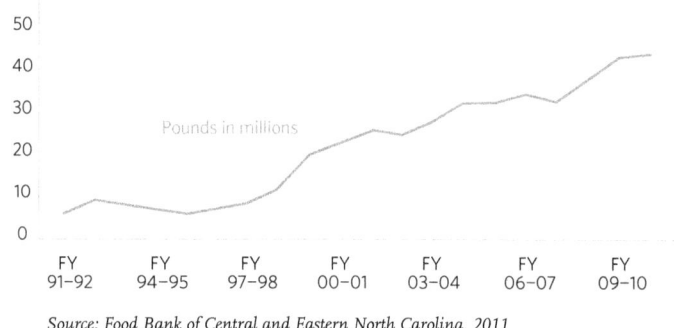

figure 9.2 POUNDS OF FOOD DISTRIBUTED BY FOOD BANK OF CENTRAL AND EASTERN NORTH CAROLINA

Source: *Food Bank of Central and Eastern North Carolina*, 2011

REFERENCES

Derewicz, Mark. "The Hands That Feed: A Portrait of Hunger in North Carolina." *Endeavors*, Winter 2010. http://endeavors.unc.edu/win2010/hands_that_feed.php.

figure 9.3 PERCENT OF POPULATION ON FOOD STAMPS

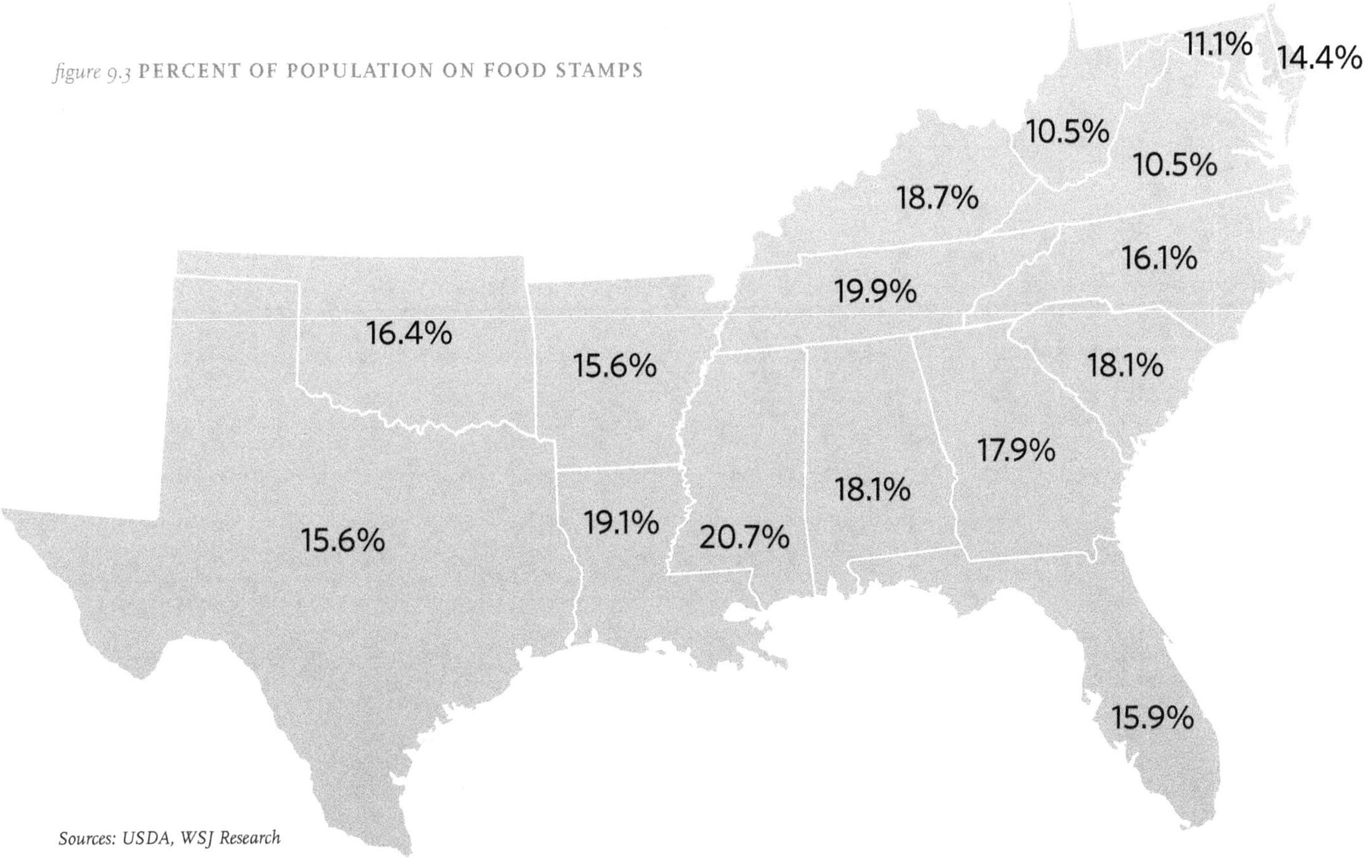

Sources: USDA, WSJ Research

A CHANGING SOUTHERN DEMOGRAPHY

A WAY FORWARD: BUILDING A GLOBALLY COMPETITIVE SOUTH

Disruptive Demographics *and the* AMERICAN SOUTH

JAMES H. JOHNSON JR.

The population of the American South[1] changed dramatically—in size, composition, and distribution—during the first decade of the new millennium. Some of the changes were a continuation or an acceleration of late-20th-century trends. Others were decade-specific, newly emergent trends. But irrespective of timing and periodicity, the observed population shifts drastically have altered the social, economic, and political fabric of the American South, leading me and my colleague, Jack Kasarda, to label them "disruptive" demographic trends.

This essay provides snapshots of two of the disruptive demographic trends that are transforming the American South—the browning and graying of the region's population. I draw on data from a diverse array of sources, including the 2010 Census, the American Community Survey, and the Current Population Survey, to describe the nature and magnitude of these two disruptive trends as well as to assess the underlying opportunities and challenges.

THE SOUTH RISES—AGAIN

Between 2000 and 2010, according to the 2010 Census, the U.S. population grew by 27.2 million. More than half of this growth (52.3 percent) was concentrated in the South. In absolute numbers, the South's population increased by 13 million during the first decade of the new millennium, continuing for the fourth consecutive decade the South's dominance as the nation's primary population growth magnet (table 10.1).

Over the past several decades, interregional population shifts and international migration have played pivotal roles in the South's rapid growth. That trend continued during the first decade of the new millennium. As table 10.2 shows, 7.8 million newcomers settled in the South between 2000 and 2010, up from 6.6 million during the 1990s and 6.4 million during the 1980s.

Movers from abroad accounted for 62 percent of the net migration. Domestic migrants moving into the South from other regions of the United States accounted for the balance. Continuing a trend dating back to the early 1970s, for example, the South was a net importer of white, black, Hispanic, Asian, and elderly migrants from the Northeast (+237,415), the Midwest (+143,479), and the West (+83,662) between 2005 and 2009. No other region of the United States experienced this type of net in-migration.

---

[1] I use the U.S. Census Bureau's definition of the South, which includes the states of Texas, Florida, Georgia, North Carolina, Virginia, Tennessee, South Carolina, Maryland, Alabama, Oklahoma, Kentucky, Arkansas, Mississippi, Delaware, Louisiana, and West Virginia plus Washington, D.C.

figure 10.1 NET MIGRATION FLOWS IN THE UNITED STATES, 2005 TO 2009

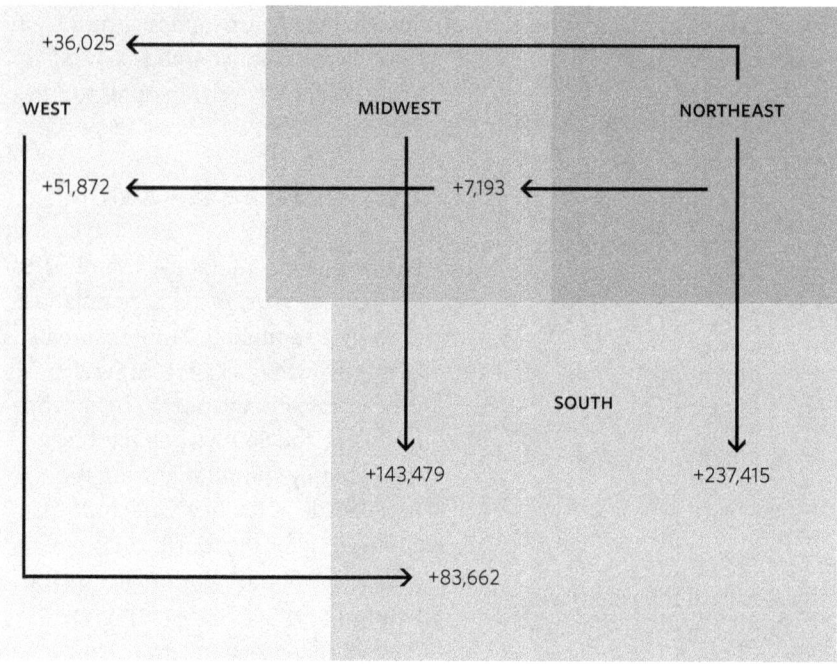

Source: American Community Survey (2009)

THE REGION'S CHANGING COMPLEXION

As figure 10.1 illustrates, two colorful demographic processes undergird the South's aggregate growth over the past three decades: the browning and graying of the region's population.

The term *browning* is used to refer to shifts in the sources of the region's growth—from native-born and non-Hispanic whites to foreign-born (that is, immigrants) and nonwhite ethnic minority groups—which in turn are changing the South's racial and ethnic complexion. Non-Hispanic whites were responsible for only 36 percent of the region's net growth of 35 million between 1980 and 2009, down from 45 percent in the 1970s and from well over half in earlier decades (see table 10.3).

Emblematic of the browning of the American South, nonwhite minority groups—Hispanics (32.7 percent), Asians (6.6 percent), and blacks (18.9 percent)—together have accounted for 58 percent of the region's net growth since 1980.

Again, immigration was the primary driver for these shifts in the sources of the region's growth. Between 1980 and 2009, as figure 10.2 illustrates, foreign-born (296.5 percent) and nonwhite immigrant groups, especially Hispanics (256.6 percent) and Asians (496.5 percent), were the fastest-growing segments of the region's population. The native-born (36.5 percent) and non-Hispanic whites (22.5 percent) were the slowest-growing segments.

The term *graying* is used to refer to the South's two most rapidly growing population cohorts: those born prior to 1945 (pre-boomers), who have for the most part already exited the labor market, and those born between 1946 and 1964 (popularly referred to as the boomer generation), who will be aging out of the labor force over the next 20 years. As table 10.4 shows, pre-boomers and boomers combined accounted for 57 percent of the South's net population growth between 1980 and 2009. The younger generations grew much more slowly and accounted for a smaller share of net population growth during this period.

CHALLENGES AND OPPORTUNITIES

The simultaneous browning and graying of the American South will likely continue well into the future. On the browning side, continued growth is likely largely due to differential age and fertility rates between native-born and foreign-born women and between nonwhite ethnic minority women and non-Hispanic white women. As table 10.3 shows, foreign-born and nonwhite women are much younger and have significantly higher fertility rates than native-born and non-Hispanic white women. Even if migration were to slow considerably, the South's population would continue to grow and diversify as a consequence of these enormous age and fertility gaps.

On the graying side, the South's aging population will expand in the years ahead, in part because of the region's continued attractiveness for retirees, and in part because both pre-boomers and boomers are not only living healthier and more active lives but also benefiting from major medical advances that extend life. Today's average 65-year-old can expect to live another 18.7 years.

At the same time, these demographic shifts pose major challenges for the region's future viability and prosperity. Here, I highlight two specific challenges rooted in the pattern of population growth and how the various race/ethnic and age groups have sorted themselves out within the region.

As in the recent past, the South's rapid population growth during the first decade of the new millennium was not evenly distributed throughout the region. Rather, 70.6 percent of the growth occurred in four states: Texas (30 percent), Florida (19.7 percent), Georgia (10.5 percent), and North Carolina (10.4 percent). None of the South's other 12 states captured more than 10 percent of net growth between 2000 and 2009 (table 10.4).

In part as a consequence of the interregional shift of population to the South and this uneven pattern of population growth within the region, America's nonwhite youth, especially those living in the South and the West regions, increasingly find themselves growing up in three radically different demographic and geopolitical contexts that place them at a substantial risk of falling through the cracks of our nation's public education system and reduce their odds of qualifying for admission to college and, by extension, acquiring the skills needed to compete in the unsparing global economy of the 21st century. Figure 10.2 highlights the nature and geographical extent of the problem.

The counties colored red in this map are "racial generation gap" communities. In these counties, the youth population (< 15) is predominantly nonwhite, while the adult, voting-age population (> 15) is predominantly white, with many aging empty-nesters. In fiscal matters, whites are more likely to advocate property tax cuts and retirement amenities than to lobby for additional resources for public education and other child-development activities. Because whites make up a majority of the voters, only limited local financial support exists for the education of the predominantly minority youth in these communities.

The counties highlighted in yellow are "minority-majority" communities. In contrast to the racial generation gap communities, in these communities both the adult population (62 percent) and the youth population (75 percent) are predominantly nonwhite. As the voting-age majority, nonwhite adults are more likely than resident whites to lobby for greater support for public education. But these are mostly low-wealth communities, and therefore the local tax base is probably too small to ensure the predominantly nonwhite school-age population a high-quality education.

The uncolored counties in figure 10.2 are "majority-majority" communities, where both the adult population (83 percent) and the youth population (75 percent) are predominantly white. But roughly one-quarter of the youth in these counties are nonwhite. What distinguishes these communities from the other two types of communities is the level of support for education; it is much stronger, especially among whites, than in the other two types of communities. But most of the minority youth in these communities, not unlike their counterparts in the racial generation gap and minority-majority communities, attend schools that are undergoing resegregation

> Irrespective of timing and periodicity, the observed population shifts drastically have altered the social, economic, and political fabric of the American South

and thus do not fully benefit from the rich educational resources—financial and otherwise—that exist in these majority-majority communities.

THE FUTURE OF THE SOUTH

In other words, no matter where they live and through no fault of their own, the majority of America's nonwhite children, especially those living in the South, are caught between a rock and a hard place. Simply put, they are not receiving the type of high-quality public education they will need to propel the region and the nation forward in the years ahead.

Assuming that the political will can be mobilized, one might think the region could be able to generate sufficient tax revenues to provide nonwhite youth with a world-class education as well as sustain other health and social safety net programs. After all, two of the region's three dependency ratios, which measure the proportion of the population that is either too young or too old to work and thus do

figure 10.2 RACIAL / ETHNIC TYPOLOGY OF U.S. COUNTIES, 2005

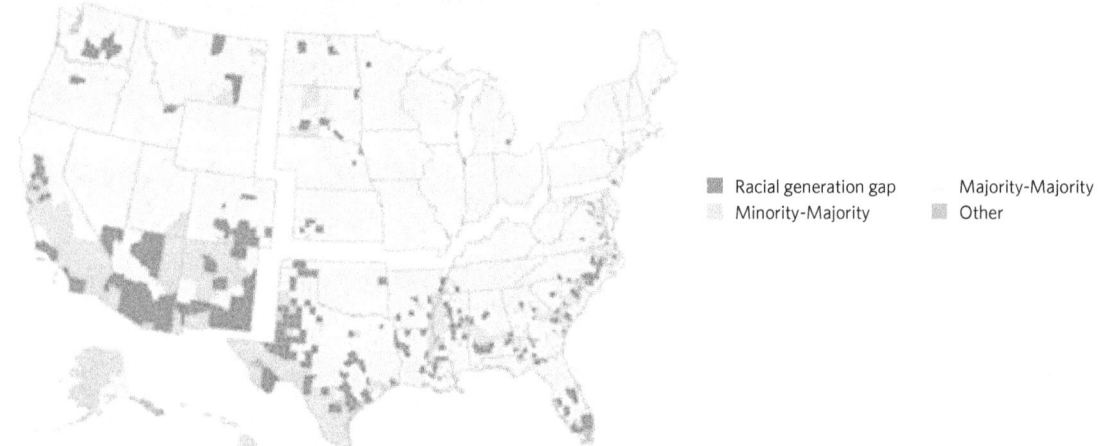

Source: Urban Investment Strategies Center, Frank Hawkins Kenan Institute of Private Enterprise, UNC-Chapel Hill

not contribute to region's fiscal health and financial well-being, have become slightly more favorable since 1980.

Between 1980 and 2009, the South's youth population grew more slowly (24.6 percent) and senior population grew more rapidly (63.9 percent) than the working-age population (55.8 percent). As a consequence of this pattern of growth, it is not surprising that the old-age-dependency ratio worsened slightly between 1980 and 2009, moving from 5.1 to 4.7 workers for every senior citizen (> 65) in the region. But given the difficult educational circumstances minority youth face, it is especially noteworthy that the youth-dependency ratio improved from 1.7 to 2.2 workers for every young person (< 20) in the region during this period. Similarly, the South's total dependency ratio improved from 1.2 to 1.5 workers for every nonworking young (< 20) and old (> 65) person in the South between 1980 and 2009 (table 10.5).

But a word of caution is in order about these dependency ratios: They probably understate the burden a rapidly increasing senior population imposes on the working-age population and overstate the working-age population's ability through tax contributions to sustain programs that benefit the total and youth-dependent populations. The ratios either under- or overstate the problem because the 20–64-year-old working-age population (that is, the denominator of the dependency ratio) includes people who are not contributing to the tax base (such as the disabled, the unemployed, and non-labor-force participants). It also includes individuals who are high school dropouts, a population whose lifetime fiscal contributions amount to -$5,200.

Among the 20–64-year-olds, the well-educated (those with at least some college) will be expected to financially sustain the South and our nation more generally in the years ahead. In the last three recessions, however, both long-term joblessness (defined as being unemployed for six months or longer) and poverty have increased more rapidly among people with some college, a bachelor's degree, or higher than among people with a high school diploma or less (table 10.6). Thus, even the well-educated may not be reliable sources of tax revenue in the years ahead.

Further clouding the picture, college students not only are taking longer to complete their degrees but also are having difficulty securing employment after they graduate. And graduates are saddled with an average $20,000 of college debt.

To avoid the fiscal train wreck in the making, the South must aggressively embrace newcomers, especially immigrants, who tend to be far more entrepreneurial than the native-born, and recognize the potential value added of leveraging immigrants' presence to develop export markets in their home countries for locally produced goods and services. The region also must recognize the business-development and job-creation potential of both the emergent elder-care economy and the diverse ethnic markets that undergird the South's amazing browning and graying demographic growth and change over the last quarter century.

REFERENCES

Center for Labor Market Studies. *Left behind in America: The Nation's Dropout Crisis*. Boston: Center for Labor Market Studies at Northeastern University; Chicago: Alternative Schools Network, 2009.

Fairbanks, Amanda. "2011 College Graduates Moving Home In Record Numbers, Saddled with Historic Levels of Student Loan Debt." *Huffington Post*, May 13, 2011. http://www.huffingtonpost.com/2011/05/13/college-graduates-moving-home-debt_n_861849.html.

Johnson, James H., Jr. "Immigration Driven Population Change in North Carolina: Opportunities for the Banking Industry." *Carolina Banker*, Fall 2004, 13–14.

Johnson, James H., Jr. "People on the Move: Implications for U.S. Higher Education." *College Board Review* 209 (2006): 4–9, 48.

Johnson, James H., Jr., Walter C. Farrell, and Chandra Guinn. "Immigration Reform and the Browning of America: Tensions, Conflict, and Community Instability." In *The Handbook of International Migration*, ed. C. Hirschman, P. Kasnitz, and J. DeWind. New York: Sage, 1999.

Johnson, James H., Jr., Karen D. Johnson-Webb, and Walter C. Farrell Jr. "Newly Emerging Hispanic Communities in the United States: A Spatial Analysis of Settlement Patterns, In-Migration Fields, and Social Receptivity." In *Immigration and Opportunity: Race, Ethnicity, and Employment in the United States*, edited by F. Bean and S. Bell-Rose. New York: Sage, 2000.

Johnson, James H., Jr., and John D. Kasarda. "Hispanic Newcomers to North Carolina: Demographic Characteristics and Economic Impact." In *Latino Immigrants and the Transformation of the U.S. South*, ed. M. Odem and E. Lacy. Athens: University of Georgia Press, 2009.

Johnson, James H., Jr., and John D. Kasarda. *Six Disruptive Demographic Trends: What Census 2010 Will Reveal*. Chapel Hill: Frank Hawkins Kenan Institute of Private Enterprise, Kenan-Flagler Business School, University of North Carolina at Chapel Hill, 2011.

Kasarda, John D., and James H. Johnson Jr. *The Economic Impact of the Hispanic Population on the State of North Carolina*. Chapel Hill: Frank Hawkins Kenan Institute of Private Enterprise, Kenan-Flagler Business School, University of North Carolina at Chapel Hill, 2006.

Kasarda, John D., James H. Johnson Jr., Stephen J. Appold, and Derrek Croney. *A Profile of Immigrants in Arkansas*. Vol. 2, *Impacts on the Arkansas Economy*. Little Rock, Ark.: Winthrop Rockefeller Foundation, 2007.

TABLES AND FIGURES

table 10.1 SOUTH'S SHARE OF U.S. NET POPULATION GROWTH, SELECTED YEARS, 1910 TO 2010

YEARS	U.S. ABSOLUTE CHANGE	SOUTH'S ABSOLUTE CHANGE	SOUTH'S SHARE OF CHANGE (%)
1910-30	30,974,129	8,468,303	27
1930-50	28,123,138	9,339,455	33
1950-70	51,886,128	15,598,279	30
1970-80	23,333,879	12,576,995	54
1980-90	22,164,068	10,073,568	46
1990-2000	32,712,033	14,790,890	45
2000-2010	27,323,632	14,318,924	52

Source: 2010 Census

table 10.2 IN-MIGRATION, OUT-MIGRATION, NET MIGRATION, AND MOVERS FROM ABROAD FOR THE SOUTH, 1980 TO 2010 (NUMBERS IN THOUSANDS)

YEARS	IN-MIGRATION	OUT-MIGRATION	NET INTERNAL MIGRATION	MOVERS FROM ABROAD	NET MIGRATION
2000-2010	10,563	7,935	2,588	4,867	7,808
1990-2000	11,761	9,357	2,403	4,185	6,588
1980-90	13,661	10,587	3,024	3,959	6,372

Source: Current Population Survey

table 10.3 MEDIAN AGE AND FERTILITY FOR FEMALES IN THE SOUTH, 2009

DEMOGRAPHIC GROUP	MEDIAN AGE	FERTILITY/ 1,000 WOMEN*
All Females	37.6	58
White, Not Hispanic	42.1	51
Black	33.2	62
American Indian and Alaskan Native	34.3	68
Native Hawaiian and Pacific Islander	28.4	72
Some Other Race	26.2	88
Two or More Races	19.8	62
Hispanic	28.0	81
Native-Born	36.2	55
Foreign-Born	39.0	79
Asian	34.8	64

Source: American Community Survey
*Women 15–50 with births in past 12 months.

table 10.4 STATE SHARES OF SOUTH'S NET GROWTH, 2000 TO 2010

REGION/STATE	ABSOLUTE CHANGE	STATE'S SHARE (%)
The South	14,318,924	100.0
Texas	4,293,741	30.0
Florida	2,818,932	19.7
Georgia	1,501,200	10.5
North Carolina	1,486,170	10.4
Virginia	922,509	6.4
Tennessee	656,822	4.6
South Carolina	613,352	4.3
Maryland	477,066	3.3
Alabama	332,636	2.3
Oklahoma	300,697	2.1
Kentucky	297,598	2.1
Arkansas	242,518	1.7
Mississippi	122,639	0.9
Delaware	114,333	0.8
Louisiana	64,296	0.4
West Virginia	44,650	0.3
Washington, D.C.	29,664	0.2

Source: Census 2010

table 10.5 INVERSE DEPENDENCY RATIOS FOR THE SOUTH, 1980 AND 2009

RATIO	1980	2009
Total	1.2:1	1.5:1
Youth	1.7:1	2.2:1
Old Age	5.0:1	4.7:1

Source: 1980 Census and American Community Survey

table 10.6 POVERTY RATES BY EDUCATIONAL ATTAINMENT IN THE SOUTH, 2007 TO 2009

EDUCATIONAL ATTAINMENT	2005-2007	2007-2009	PERCENTAGE CHANGE
Less Than High School	3,187,545	3,161,626	−0.8
High School Graduate	2,677,189	2,755,133	2.9
Some College, Associate's Degree	1,496,186	1,717,350	14.8
Bachelor's Degree or Higher	624,196	681,330	9.2

Source: American Community Survey

GENERATION Z and North Carolina's Future

PATRICK CRONIN

> The first decade of the 21st century ended with considerable pessimism regarding the future of the South and fears that the coming "new normal" will mean lower living standards and higher levels of inequality.

Given these real concerns, it is important to point to one source of hope for the future: a new generation of workers and citizens coming of age in the region and bringing with them optimism, talent, and a desire to do things that matter. To engage this group in ways that maximize its contributions to the state and region's economic and social health, today's leaders would do well to study its character—that is, its composition, motivation, and skills. Understanding what this new generation has to offer provides important guideposts for involving today's youth in tackling our pressing challenges.

PROFILING GENERATION Z

This essay focuses on what some refer to as Generation Z, individuals born between 1990 and the early 2000s.[1] In North Carolina, as in the country as a whole, this generation is the most racially and ethnically diverse in history. This trend has been driven by a rapid influx of Latinos into the state (and South more generally) over the past 20 years.

From 2000 to 2010, North Carolina's Latino population increased 111.1 percent, a much higher rate than for what the Census defines as non-Hispanic whites (10.3 percent) or blacks (17.9 percent). As a result, Latinos increased from less than 1 percent of the state's population in 1990 to 8.4 percent in 2010, while the percentage of non-Hispanic whites fell to 65 percent and the African American population held steady at about 22 percent.

Given that the median age of the Latino population is significantly younger (25 years in 2008) than for whites (40) and blacks (33), it is not surprising that North Carolina's primary and secondary school population is becoming more diverse. In 2009, 41 percent of the state's children were minorities, a number that is expected to rise in the coming decade. North Carolina is not alone in this projection. The Census Bureau announced in 2011 that for the first time in the country's history, white children were no longer a majority among the country's three-year-olds.

Generation Z (or Gen Z for short) also is noteworthy for other differences with earlier generations. In particular, researchers point to the impact of technology. While all age groups are adopting new communications technologies, none are doing so more than members of Gen Z. Rapid communication, advanced technology, and social networking are integral parts of this cohort's lives. Its members have never known a world without the Internet. Like fish to water, the newest generation takes to new technologies, particularly those that facilitate connecting with others, locally and around the world. Three-quarters of "Millennials"—a larger generational cohort of 9- to 30-year-olds that includes Gen Z—use social networking sites. More than half of teens in this group check their sites more than once a day, and 22 percent do so more than 10 times a day. The Millennial generation enjoys stronger connections to family and friends than any previous generation.

Millennials, including their Gen Z cohort, are strong multitaskers, able and even preferring to work in environments that would distract older generations. In contrast to earlier generations that grew up sitting around the television, Gen Z members read and write constantly. Of course, their preference for texting (because e-mail is too slow!), with its own shorthand and language, is creating fears that this form of communication will erode traditional

---

[1] While there is an inherent risk in making generalizations about a whole generation, there is no doubt that cohorts of individuals acquire commonly held traits as a result of shared experiences that affect their lives and society. It is also difficult to talk about generational values in this case because some members of Generation Z are younger than 10 years old. Some observers prefer to include this cohort within a larger group of individuals born between the early 1980s and early 2000s, referred to variously as the Millennials, Echo Boom, Generation Y, or Net Generation. This essay's definition of Generation Z provides a focus on those who will be our state and region's youngest workers, roughly those aged 18–30 in the year 2020. At present, they are between 9 and 21 years old.

reading, writing, and speaking skills. Similarly, a preference for building and maintaining relationships through virtual means is giving rise to concerns that Gen Z members may not develop the same socialization and relationship-building skills as their predecessors.

Finally, research on the Millennial generation suggests that members are motivated not by money and the long hours that may be needed to earn it but by working at activities that they feel give value and meaning. The older members of this generation, those aged 21–30, are less interested in following earlier generations' path to success than in moving around, trying different jobs and locations before settling down. There is every reason to expect Gen Z workers, as they enter the workforce in larger numbers in the coming decade, to follow this same path.

Overall, generation researchers have concluded that Millennials are sociable, talented, open-minded, and optimistic. While they appear to lack some of the basic skills of the older generations, they possess considerable talents and advanced skills in other areas, particularly those involving technology and networking.

GEN Z AND NORTH CAROLINA'S ECONOMIC DEVELOPMENT FUTURE

North Carolina—and the South more generally—face formidable economic development challenges. Generation Z and the Millennials more broadly constitute the core of the state's future workforce and leadership. If the state is to prosper in the coming decades, it is incumbent on today's leaders in all areas of the economy and society to figure out how best to involve this emerging young adult cohort in the issues that affect our state's long-term competitiveness. Here are a few key areas.

Education

North Carolina must have a more educated workforce with the right skills and knowledge if it is to maintain, much less increase, its economic competitiveness. As others have noted, current rates of K–12 educational attainment are dismal, especially for minority students. High school graduation rates are increasing, but they must go higher, and the significant performance gap between different

racial and ethnic groups must be closed. Doing so requires an assault on the most important factors—classroom and societal—that impact performance. Given Gen Z's affinity for technology and connectivity, one area receiving deserved attention is how to teach—or promote learning—in ways that fit Gen Z's learning style. Doing so effectively will require redoubled efforts to deal with an existing "digital divide," the unequal access to computers and high-speed Internet service that often separates members of Gen Z and their families according to income, education, and geography.

Workforce Development

Millennial workers have different aspirations and motivations than do older generations with regard to work. They are less interested in roles and titles and more in values and skills. They are family- and lifestyle-focused and seek out opportunities that allow for flexibility for family-related activities and that recognize that personal and professional lives have become more blended. At the same time, younger workers want opportunities to grow, develop new skills, and apply themselves to work they feel has a larger social impact.

To secure the best work product from this generation, managers in the public, private, and nonprofit sectors must understand their workers' motivations and take advantage of their affinity for networking and using new communication technologies. As social media evolve, organizations are discovering new, effective ways to understand and meet the needs of their customers and clients. We are in the very early stages of understanding how virtual connectivity can help create and distribute needed products and services, solve problems, and raise living standards. Those who use this technology the most are well positioned to help us understand how best to use it.

Civic Engagement and Leadership

Successful efforts to deal with the forces buffeting our economy and communities will require effective leadership at all levels of government and in all sectors of society. Healthy communities depend on a critical mass of residents who are engaged and participatory, willing to volunteer, vote, and lead. Research suggests that like similar cohorts across the United States, North Carolina's youth and young adults aged 16 to 24 participate less in civic life than older residents. If participation rates were to rise significantly with age, this finding would be less worrisome. Discouragingly, however, rates of participation across all age groups in the state are low: No more than one-third of respondents in any age group reported engaging in nonelectoral political activities, such as attending a meeting where political issues were discussed, buying or boycotting a product or service, taking part in a rally, or donating to a candidate, in the preceding year. For 18- to 24-year-olds, the figure was 13 percent. Only 2 percent of respondents in this age group reported working with neighbors in the preceding year to solve a community problem. Nevertheless, substantial percentages of youth report an interest in civic engagement—if they are given a chance to do so.

Generation Z's affinity for networking and virtual engagement, along with a stated desire to do meaningful work, suggests that important and untapped opportunities exist for drawing youth into activities designed to find solutions to larger social and economic problems at the community and state levels. Figuring out the best way to do so effectively is the challenge facing today's policy and education leaders. With connectivity facilitating the spread of information and conversation, the hope is that we can collectively develop quicker and more effective ways to solve our problems.

REFERENCES

Manning, Terri M. *The Art of Communication and Networking for the "Under-30" Generation: The Impact Felt and Heard around the World.* Raleigh: Institute for Emerging Issues, North Carolina State University, 2011.

Manning, Terri M. *What the Under-30 Generation Wants in the Workforce: What Employers Need to Know to Retain Them.* Raleigh: Institute for Emerging Issues, North Carolina State University, 2011.

North Carolina Civic Education Consortium. *North Carolina Civic Health Index 2010.* October 23, 2010. http://www.ncoc.net/ncchi2010.

O'Brien, Kelly. *Engaging North Carolina's Net Generation in Civic Life.* Raleigh: Institute for Emerging Issues, North Carolina State University, 2011.

THE Old *in the* New Economy: CHALLENGES AND OPPORTUNITIES *for the* South *and* North Carolina

JOHN C. SCOTT

INTRODUCTION

While 2011 marks the 25th anniversary of *Halfway Home and a Long Way to Go*, this year also is significant because the first cohort of baby boomers turns 65. The 1986 Commission on the Future of the South did not focus specifically on aging, but many of its recommendations intersect with aging issues. The increase in the number of older people in the South and in North Carolina presents both challenges and opportunities. In terms of challenges, an aging population increases fiscal strains, heightens demand for certain services, and may lead to increased inequality. But at the same time, older adults can be a source of entrepreneurship, human capital, civic engagement, consumer spending, and labor in industries that struggle to find talent. As this state's population largely reflects national demographic trends, how should North Carolina and the South respond to the aging of their population?

This essay reflects on the effects of an aging population on economic growth, emphasizing three areas of economic life: labor force participation, entrepreneurship, and consumption and services. The essay concludes by considering some policy proposals.

AGING POPULATION TRENDS

The state has experienced rapid growth in its older population. In 1980, just over 1 million North Carolinians were age 55 or older, and about 600,000 residents were 65 or older. Today, North Carolina has more than 2 million adults over the age of 55 and 1.2 million over 65, placing the state 10th in the nation in terms of the size of its older population. The number of persons aged 65 and older in North Carolina increased by more than 25 percent in the past decade alone.

But absolute numbers may not adequately reflect a state's age structure, which is better evidenced by the state's median age and the percentage of older persons. Today, the median age of the North Carolina population is 36.6, close to the national median age of 36.5. North Carolinians age 55 and older make up 24 percent of the population (up from 19.6 percent in 1980), while those age 65 and older are 13 percent of the population (an increase from 10 percent in 1980). These numbers put North Carolina 32nd and 35th in the nation, respectively. North Carolina is a little older than Georgia and Virginia but younger than Tennessee and South Carolina.

Aging in North Carolina varies across several dimensions, including gender, race, and geography. For example, older women significantly outnumber older men in North Carolina; women represent 58.7 percent of the 65-and-older population and 70.9 percent of the 85-and-older population.

Whites constitute 81 percent of the 55-and-older population, 10 percentage points higher than their representation in the general population. The lower representation of African Americans in the aging population is likely based on higher mortality rates at younger ages than whites experience. The higher numbers of Latinos and Asian Americans in the general population than in the aging population likely results from the influx of younger immigrants. By 2005, life expectancy at birth in North Carolina had increased to 75.8 years. In general, women live 2.5 years longer than men within racial and ethnic groups, and whites live longer on average than minorities, depending on location. For example, white women in Wake County have an average life expectancy of 82 years, but African American men in Robeson County have an average life expectancy of 68.7 years.

Raw aging trends reflect population totals. In terms of numbers, the three counties (Mecklenburg,

Guilford, and Wake) with the three biggest cities (Charlotte, Greensboro, and Raleigh) have the most adults ages 55 and older. But a look at the median age of each county paints a different picture. In 2006, 57 percent of North Carolina's older adults lived in rural counties. For example, Clay County, in the far western corner of the state, has the state's highest median age, nearly 50. This east/west-versus-Piedmont dichotomy is bolstered further by looking at the percentage of the aging population for each county, with the middle of the state generally having a lower proportion of persons over age 55 and the aging population more concentrated in the east and west.

WHAT DOES FUTURE GROWTH LOOK LIKE?

Between 2010 and 2030, North Carolina's 65-and-older older population is projected to increase by more than 400,000 adults per decade, reaching 2.14 million, or about 18 percent of the state total, by 2030. North Carolina is projected to rank 19th among states in the growth of the 65-and-older population from 2000 to 2030. The oldest group of the over-65 population has grown by more than 50,000 people in the past five years alone and has doubled in the past seven years. Statewide, estimates show that the number of persons aged 55 and older will increase 37 percent, from 2,074,232 in 2007 to 2,839,469 by 2018. The median age will change from 36.9 in 2009 to an estimated 37.8 in 2030. Several counties will see large growth in their older populations, but their age structure (as reflected by the median age) will remain relatively unchanged as their overall populations increase. Examples of these age-stable counties include Wake (77 percent growth in the 55-and-older group), Mecklenburg (58.7 percent), Durham (40.7 percent), Union (82.8 percent), and Iredell (50.1 percent).

However, 20 counties will see higher-than-average growth in both their 55-and-older population and in the median age. Fourteen of these quickly aging counties are located in the rural eastern part of the state. For example, Brunswick County will experience both a 58 percent increase in the 55-and-over population and a 5 percent rise in its median age. This aging increase results from older people migrating to this part of North Carolina in search of more affordable living (that is, in-migration) and younger people leaving in search of better jobs (that is, aging in place).

AGING AND THE NEW ECONOMY

Labor Force Participation

For North Carolina to compete effectively and generate high-wage jobs, it must foster innovation and develop a highly skilled, highly productive labor force. Aging has two main workforce-related effects: an aging of certain economic sectors, and low workforce participation by older persons. The first effect matters because as older workers retire, they take their human capital— their education, training, experience— with them, and the number of younger workers may not be enough to offset this brain drain.

During the 10-year period from 2008 to 2018, North Carolina will lose an estimated 61,000 workers per year to retirement. Moreover, different sectors of the economy are seeing different rates of workforce aging. For example, state government is experiencing significant workforce aging: North Carolina is the seventh-oldest state in terms of its public-sector workforce. In another example, in 2006, 60 percent of all University of North Carolina system faculty members were between the ages of 42 and 60, while another 16 percent were 61 or older. If enrollments expand, faculty ranks may be insufficient to handle the load. In economic sectors that are heavily tilted toward older persons, there may be insufficient postsecondary-education graduates to replace retirees and generate productive output. Nationally, shortages of U.S. workers with college-level skills are estimated to top 14 million by 2020.

Many older adults who could be productive remain outside of the workforce. Labor-force participation in North Carolina declines from about 80 percent for those between the ages of 20 and 54 to 60 percent for those aged 55 to 64. In 2008, 15.5 percent of North Carolinians aged 65 and older were employed. This decline is, at least in part, a function of Social Security and Medicare incentives rather than any in productivity.

Entrepreneurship

According to the Bureau of Labor Statistics, 42 percent of the self-employed in the United States are 55 years of age or older, and nearly a third of them are incorporated self-employed. In North Carolina, workers in the 55–64 age group constitute more than 19 percent of the self-employed, and nearly 8 percent of the self-employed come from the 65–74 age group.

A variety of individual and environmental factors may encourage

entrepreneurship at older ages. Individual factors include household debt and the presence of dependents in the household. In addition, age, risk perceptions, and positive views on work in general also may encourage new forays into self-employment and away from wage-based employment. Older persons also may have more human, financial, and social capital than younger people. Environmental factors might include job loss or the loss of health or pension benefits so that a retiree would be compelled to reenter the labor market or start a new business.

Consumption and Personal Services
Population aging also has demand-side effects on the economy. For example, North Carolina is a destination for older persons nearing or in retirement, a fact illustrated by the high proportion of older persons in the golf communities of Moore County. Such consumption of tourism or leisure services represents an opportunity for the state in terms of increased tax revenues and demand for services.

But challenges also are present if an older population demands services that the state is not well prepared to provide. Older persons are high-volume users of the health care system, and their health needs are complex, involving chronic, geriatric, and mental health conditions. North Carolina, along with the rest of the nation, faces an impending health care crisis as the number of older patients outpaces the number of health professionals with the knowledge and skills to care adequately for them. For example, at the national level, older adults consume a large share of the services provided by nurses, pharmacists, and physician assistants, but fewer than 1 percent of these health professionals specialize in geriatrics. North Carolina will have to find workers across a range of professions to deal with the wave of aging that will crash over the state.

Policy Recommendations
These trends may have important implications in other areas of social, political, and economic life.

These and other effects and their interrelationships introduce policy challenges that affect economic development. How can we encourage continued productive work at older ages? How can North Carolina facilitate entrepreneurship among its older residents? How should our economy adjust for the aging that is taking place?

Encouraging Continued Work at Older Ages

North Carolina should play an active role in facilitating increased labor-force participation by older North Carolinians. Cost-effective actions include:

- A state-level review of barriers to hiring and retaining older workers in both the private and public sectors and models of aging-friendly workplace practices. Examples of such practices include workplace assessment; workplace adaptations to accommodate normal aging and ergonomic design of office and home workstations; training and professional development; job sharing; phased retirement; work-family assistance; and flexible employment. Any review should incorporate the perspectives of employers, managers, and older workers, among others.

- Based on the identification of successful models, states should implement aging-friendly workplace policies for the states' benefit and to illustrate best practices.

- Education and training are important components in encouraging continued work. Older persons, whether in or out of the workforce, need flexible access to education and training, which requires investing in education, training, and counseling.

- North Carolina should advocate for increases in federal funding of workforce training and development. Poverty among the elderly is highly correlated with low levels of education. Federally funded workforce-development programs could be helpful to all older workers and particularly to those with little educational attainment, but such programs are woefully underfunded and reach few people.

Encouraging Entrepreneurship

Many programs that encourage and facilitate entrepreneurship exist throughout the state, and these programs could, to the extent they do not do so already, incorporate an emphasis on entrepreneurship at older ages. Our colleges and universities should target older persons for entrepreneurial programs with traditional and nontraditional learning methods.

In addition, state government can serve as a facilitator in the way it offers licenses by matching producers and suppliers and by providing seed grants to promising start-ups. North Carolina can foster this activity by highlighting the importance of older workers as a source of entrepreneurship.

Identifying and Addressing Potential Growth Areas and Blank Spots

Encouraging work and entrepreneurship at older ages does not make sense if sectors of the economy are underdeveloped or in need of additional resources. Moreover, some portions of the economy are likely to be more affected by aging than others. North Carolina needs to inventory its economy in terms of the strengths, weaknesses, threats, and opportunities posed by population aging.

In 2005, nearly half of North Carolina's native-born population was either aging baby boomers or pre-boomers, meaning that key parts of the economy may see increased reliance on immigrants. North Carolina policymakers need to study the state's economy through the interaction of aging and potential growth. Do some areas of the economy have potential for growth but worker demographics that are weighted toward older ages? In such cases, worker shortages could be identified and addressed through older-work initiatives, education for younger persons, or attracting immigrants.

Some sectors may need additional resources as a consequence of the demands of an aging population. There will be shortages in long-term care facilities, and rural communities are seeing a decline in pharmacy services. Understanding where we will fall short of anticipated demand across a range of age-related services is critical to adapting to an aging population.

Despite the recent economic downturn, the state can encourage continued employment, entrepreneurship, and productivity in a variety of cost-effective ways. Such efforts will likely provide important payoffs for workers, for employers, and for North Carolina over the long term.

REFERENCES

Bosley, Deborah S., Keith G. Debbage, James H. Johnson Jr., Beryl C. McEwen, and Michael L. Walden. "Workforce, Demographic, and Global Readiness Trends." In *Major Trends Facing North Carolina: Implications for Our state and the University of North Carolina.* 2007. http://www.northcarolina.edu/nctomorrow/reports/scholars/Workforce_Demographic_and_Global_Readiness_Trends_-_Executiv.pdf.

U.S. Bureau of Labor Statistics. "Demographics of the Self-Employed." *TED: The Editor's Desk.* October 22, 2010. http://www.bls.gov/opub/ted/2010/ted_20101022.htm.

Clark, R. A. and O. S. Mitchell. The Changing Retirement Paradigm. In *Reinventing the Retirement Paradigm*, ed. R.Clark and O.Mitchell.. New York: Oxford University Press, 2005.

Institute of Medicine. *Retooling for an Aging America: Building the Health Care Workforce.* Washington, D.C.: National Academies Press, 2008.

North Carolina Data Center. County/State Population Projections. 2009. http://www.osbm.state.nc.us/ncosbm/facts_and_figures/socioeconomic_data/population_estimates/county_projections.shtm.

Quinterno, John. The Demographics of Aging in North Carolina. *North Carolina Insight* 23(2009): 2–47. http://www.nccppr.org/drupal/content/insightarticle/81/demographics-of-aging-in-north-carolina.

Shackleford, Roger. *Future Workforce Needs in North Carolina.* Raleigh: North Carolina: Department of Commerce. 2008. http://www.aging.unc.edu/groups/work/forum2008/presentations/ShacklefordRoger.pdf.

Stein, Peter J. (ed.) *Report of the Forum on North Carolina's Aging Workforce.* Chapel Hill: http://www.aging.unc.edu/groups/work/forum2008/Report.of.the.Forum.on.North.Carolinas.Aging.Workforce.2009.pdf.

U.S. Census Bureau. 2011. Various tables. http://www.census.gov/.

University of North Carolina Institute on Aging. Quick Facts about Aging in North Carolina. 2011. http://www.aging.unc.edu/infocenter/data/quickfacts.html#1.

Wong, Michelle. "North Carolina Indicators: Aging and Work." March 2008. http://agingandwork.bc.edu/documents/states/NorthCarolina.pdf.

ADAPTING to a Plural Culture and the Future of the South

HANNAH GILL AND DEBORAH WEISSMAN

INTRODUCTION AND BACKGROUND

The Southeast has led the nation in the growth rate of immigrant populations since the 1970s. North Carolina in particular has become a favored destination as an expanding labor market and employer recruitment have attracted new migrants to the state. The majority of newcomers are Latin American in origin: North Carolina had the nation's fastest-growing Latino population from 1990 to 2000. While Latinos make up a diverse group of people with ancestry in 22 different countries in the Caribbean, Central America, and South America, more than 80 percent of Latinos in the state have Mexican roots. The rate of increase of the number of Latinos coming to North Carolina has recently slowed as a consequence of the economic downturn, more aggressive immigration enforcement at the border, increased hostility toward immigrants throughout the nation, and improving economic conditions in Mexico. Nevertheless, the 2010 Census revealed a 110 percent growth in the Latino population since 2000, and Latinos now make up 8.4 percent of the state's total population. From 2000 to 2010, of the nine states where the Latino population had doubled, seven were in the South: Alabama, Arkansas, Kentucky, Mississippi, North Carolina, Tennessee, and South Carolina. Demographic markers suggest that the Latino population will continue to grow.

This essay considers the larger historical, political, legal, and institutional contexts that have shaped demographic change and the increasingly permanent settlement of Latinos in North Carolina. We provide an overview of policy responses to immigration on national, state, and local levels and consider the role of public policy in facilitating social and economic integration measures.

HISTORICAL TRENDS

The arrival of Latino immigrants has connected North Carolina to centuries-old networks of trade, human travel, and labor recruitment that have facilitated migration between the United States and Mexico. In past centuries, most of the Latino immigrant population was located in traditional gateway regions—the Southwest, New Jersey, New York, and Florida. These migrant networks began to shift in the 1970s and 1980s, however, as southeastern states experienced economic growth and restructuring in traditional industries such as textiles, tobacco, furniture, and agriculture. Latino migrants were recruited from their countries of origin as well as from other parts of the United States to work in expanding construction, service, and manufacturing industries. By 2000, Latinos made up more than a quarter of all construction, manufacturing, and service workers in the state of North Carolina, with concentrations of up to 90 percent of all construction workers in locales such as Charlotte and the Triangle. Other factors, including poverty, war, and environmental disaster in countries of immigrant origin provided incentives for Latin Americans to move to the Southeast from the 1980s to the early 2000s, although by 2011, improving economic conditions in Mexico had slowed migrant streams to the United States.

SOCIOECONOMIC PROFILES

Thirty years after Latin Americans arrived to work in North Carolina, immigrants have become part of more settled Latino communities as native-born (and therefore U.S. citizen) children and grandchildren of immigrants grow up in the state. The increasing permanence of this population raises questions of how Latinos are integrating into North Carolina communities, a multigenerational process influenced by many factors, including policies, attitudes, and economic opportunities in receiving-society contexts. A number of indicators show that Latino communities are struggling to achieve socioeconomic parity with their more established native counterparts, an important measure of successful integration. According to 2010 Census figures, Latinos experience higher poverty and school drop-out rates than any other race or ethnic group in the state. Twenty-seven percent of Latinos live at or below the poverty rate, compared with 10.3 percent of whites, 25.1 percent of African Americans, and 24.2 percent of Native Americans.

RETROSPECTIVE AND PROSPECTIVE ANALYSIS

When *Halfway Home and a Long Way to Go* was released, the issue of immigration was absent from concerns about the development of the region. Not until the 1990s, as the numbers of Latin Americans coming to North Carolina increased, did the change in demographics begin to affect a wide range of state institutions, civic organizations, and popular attitudes. Some were positive developments. In 1998, Governor Jim Hunt created the Advisory Council on Hispanic/Latino Affairs to promote awareness of issues affecting North Carolina's Latino population. Although it has been less active over time, the council has advocated on behalf of resources for the growing Latino population and issued reports about newcomers' well-being. North Carolina public schools have developed strategies for students lacking English proficiency. Teachers have partnered with the University of North Carolina–Duke Consortium on Latin American Studies to find ways to improve learning opportunities for Latino students. Social workers and public health advocates have established bilingual networks to offer counseling, health care, and other social services. Lawyers have created bar association committees to address immigrants' legal needs.

Notwithstanding these salutary developments, it is not difficult to discern nativist sentiments expressed particularly about language issues, access to higher education and health care, and employment issues. Latinos are a growing target of housing discrimination and are vulnerable to crime and racial profiling.

Much of North Carolina's response to immigration can be best understood in the context of the federal immigration system, which has failed to achieve its complex and sometimes contradictory goals of border control and an efficient legalization program that unites families, protects workers, and improves the economy. In the past two decades, the absence of overarching legal reforms has failed to accommodate the changing nature of the globalized labor force that has contributed to the growing number of immigrants in the state. Moreover, since 1996, the expansion of immigration enforcement laws has eliminated many forms of humanitarian relief, enhanced penalties, and

A WAY FORWARD: BUILDING A GLOBALLY COMPETITIVE SOUTH

curtailed the processes for obtaining lawful immigration status. More recently, federal-state programs authorizing local immigration enforcement have increased dramatically. North Carolina, which has embraced such programs, has the country's third-highest number of municipalities that have signed 287(g) local immigration enforcement agreements with the federal government, including the sheriff's offices of Alamance, Cabarrus, Gaston, Henderson, Mecklenburg, and Wake Counties and the Durham city police. Among southern states, which account for 43 of the 68 agreements nationwide, North Carolina ranks second, behind Virginia. North Carolina also was one of two pilot "secured communities" states to target undocumented immigrants for deportation and is now one of eleven states to have implemented the program statewide. These programs have increased fear of police among immigrants and have contributed to their reluctance to report crimes.

In addition to local law enforcement programs, an increase in subnational restrictions on immigration throughout the South has adversely affected immigrants' access to health care, employment, housing, and education. In the 2011 North Carolina legislative session, no fewer than 13 immigration-related bills were introduced. One of these bills would improve housing standards for migrant farm workers; however, the overwhelming majority of the proposed laws are likely to make life more difficult, if not impossible, for many immigrants. Two such bills were enacted into law. North Carolina now requires counties, cities, and private employers with 25 or more employees to use the federal e-Verify Program to confirm the work authorization of newly hired employees despite the fact that the government databases are known to be inaccurate and contribute to the real possibility of exacerbating the exploitation of undocumented immigrants while reducing labor standards that will impact all workers. North Carolina also passed the Safe Students Act, which requires parents to submit certified copies of children's birth certificates when registering them for schools, a requirement that may run afoul of constitutional protections and will foster fear among undocumented parents that the act of enrolling their children will bring them to the attention of immigration authorities. This requirement also will impose a difficult burden for immigrant parents and their children who are here lawfully who, for a variety of reasons (for example, refugee status or lack of issuance of formal birth certificates in countries of origin) will not be able to obtain birth documentation. Other legislative measures under consideration include limiting secondary education opportunities for certain categories of immigrants; prohibiting the use of consular documents as acceptable forms of identification; criminalizing immigrants who fail to carry their alien registration documents; and allowing local law enforcement to stop an individual on "reasonable suspicion" that such person does not have the legal right to be present in the United States.

> Limiting access to affordable higher education for our state's growing Latino population raises serious concerns about our state's ability to remain competitive in the years ahead.

These policies seem to ignore the reality of the permanence of the Latino population. As the 2007 *University of North Carolina Tomorrow Commission Final Report* warned, "Limiting access to affordable higher education for our state's growing Latino population raises serious concerns about our state's ability to remain competitive in the years ahead." Such policies fail to recognize the importance of immigrants, who are often valuable contributors to the economic vitality of North Carolina and the increasingly multiracial society that characterizes the South and the rest of the nation. Just as important, these policies may promote the resegregation of the South, perhaps along different color and ethnic lines than those identified in *Halfway Home* but nevertheless contributing to the obstacles that arise from the "two-Souths" phenomenon that has historically arrested the region's development.

RECOMMENDATIONS

North Carolina's responses are indicative of the need to enact comprehensive immigration reform at the national level. According to the U.S. Constitution, decisions pertaining to immigration status are made at the federal level and cannot be subject to local preferences or local prejudices. Rather than participating in programs that undermine trust between immigrant communities and local law enforcement or enacting restrictionist laws, North Carolina should resist laws that diminish the civil and due process rights of immigrants. History demonstrates that a very thin line divides anti-immigrant laws from those that diminish the civil rights and due process protections of citizens.

Most studies demonstrate that immigrants enhance the economic and cultural viability of the communities in which they live. Municipalities can create community integration plans to increase access to services and participation in political, social, and cultural affairs to enable immigrants to become productive and self-sufficient members of the community. Research reports undertaken by states hoping to provide meaningful integration strategies have identified the need for improved access in areas including civil rights, citizenship status, education, employment/workforce training, fair housing, health care, and language proficiency. Providing for some type of identification documentation is also key to integrating undocumented immigrants.

North Carolina should expand affordable educational opportunities for all immigrant students, including the undocumented. Access to higher education promotes workforce development and contributes to the competitive status of the state and region. Such initiatives, known as tuition equity laws, allow motivated immigrant students who meet certain requirements to pay in-state tuition rates at state universities and colleges. Tuition equity laws have been advanced in state legislatures nationwide and have been upheld in the nation's courts. In June 2011, the U.S. Supreme Court refused to consider a challenge to California's tuition equity law, considered the nation's strongest.

North Carolina's universities can play an important role through research, teaching, and service strategies to identify and eliminate the barriers to community integration for the growing newcomer population. Universities can partner with municipalities and community groups to respond to the needs of immigrants and promote and encourage their contributions to our communities.

Initiatives that integrate immigrants will not only help to achieve economic growth and prosperity but also will strengthen the cultural and social fabric of North Carolina's communities. The state and its localities must engage in endeavors designed to assure the dignity of all of its residents and to promote policies that unite people regardless of immigrant status. ➨

REFERENCES

Cave, Damien. "Better Lives for Mexicans Cut Allure of Going North." *New York Times*, July 6, 2011. http://www.nytimes.com/interactive/2011/07/06/world/americas/immigration.html?hp.

Gill, Hannah. *The Latino Migration Experience in North Carolina: New Roots in the Old North State*. Chapel Hill: University of North Carolina Press, 2010.

Gill, Hannah, and M. Nguyen. *The 287(g) Program: The Costs and Consequences of Local Immigration Enforcement in North Carolina Communities*. Chapel Hill: Center for Global Initiatives 2010.

Hirschman, Charles. *The Impact of Immigration on American Society: Looking Backward to the Future*. New York: Social Science Research Council, 2006. http://borderbattles.ssrc.org/Hirschman/.

Kasarda, John, and James H. Johnson Jr. *The Economic Impact of the Hispanic Population on the State of North Carolina*. Chapel Hill: Frank Hawkins Kenan Institute of Private Enterprise, Kenan-Flagler Business School, University of North Carolina at Chapel Hill, 2006. http://www.ime.gob.mx/investigaciones/2006/estudios/migracion/economic_impact_hispanic_population_north_carolina.pdf.

Mock, Brentin. "Immigration Backlash: Hate Crimes against Latinos Flourish." *Intelligence Report*, Winter 2007. http://www.splcenter.org/get-informed/intelligence-report/browse-all-issues/2007/winter/immigration-backlash.

New Jersey. *Report, Governor's Blue Ribbon Advisory Panel on Immigrant Policy*. 2009.

North Carolina Governor's Office, Office of Hispanic/Latino Affairs. 2002 Study.

Peri, Giovanni. *The Effect of Immigrants on U.S. Employment and Productivity*. San Francisco: Federal Reserve Bank of San Francisco, 2010. http://www.frbsf.org/publications/economics/letter/2010/el2010-26.html.

Portes, Alejandro, and Rubén G. Rumbaut. *Legacies: The Story of the Immigrant Second Generation*. Berkeley: University of California Press, 2001.

Preston, Julia. "Births Outpace Immigration for Mexican-Americans, Report Says." *New York Times*, July 15, 2011.

Tewari, Meenu. "Nonlocal Forces in the Historical Evolution and Current Transformation of North Carolina's Furniture Industry." In *The American South in a Global World*, ed. James L. Peacock, Harry L. Watson, and Carrie R. Matthews. Chapel Hill: University of North Carolina Press, 2005.

University of North Carolina Tomorrow Commission. *UNC Tomorrow Commission Final Report*. http://www.northcarolina.edu/nctomorrow/UNCT_Final_Report.pdf.

U.S. Immigration Customs and Enforcement. *Fact Sheet: Delegation of Immigration Authority Section 287(g) Immigration and Nationality Act*. http://www.ice.gov/news/library/factsheets/287g.htm#signed-moa.

U.S. Immigration Customs and Enforcement. *Secure Communities, Activated Jurisdictions*. http://www.ice.gov/doclib/secure-communities/pdf/sc-activated.pdf.

SOUTHERN POLITICS AND POLICY: THEN, NOW, AND TOMORROW

On Terry Sanford's Legacy for Southern Progressives Today

MAC McCORKLE

Editors' Note: In a 1971 speech, Terry Sanford provided the founding inspiration for the Southern Growth Policies Board. Sanford was the 65th governor of North Carolina (1961–65), a two-time presidential candidate in the 1970s, and a U.S. senator (1986–93). From 1969 to 1985, Sanford served as Duke University's president.

An important book on Terry Sanford's 1960 campaign for governor is *Triumph of Good Will: How Terry Sanford Beat a Champion of Segregation and Reshaped the South*, by John Drescher. It tells the story of a candidate who bucked the reactionary tide blanketing the South in the aftermath of the Supreme Court's *Brown v. Board of Education* school desegregation case, gave an endorsement speech at the Democratic National Convention for Massachusetts Catholic John Kennedy, and once in office pushed through a tax increase that overnight boosted North Carolina's teacher salaries from 39th to 32nd and per-pupil expenditures from 48th to 38th in the nation.

In one sense, the last part of the title about reshaping the South may seem like a misnomer because the Sanford progressive way usually has been the road not taken in other Southern states. But among Southern candidates and their key supporters whom I came to know, Sanford's success meant that the progressive road might be possible in their states as well. Sanford reinforced that hope 22 years after his gubernatorial term, when he won a U.S. Senate seat. After his victory, every other Southern state experienced at least one progressive moment in a governor or Senate race. So the Sanford example did play a major role in "reshaping" Southern politics by keeping progressive electoral hopes alive and kicking.

I had the fortunate timing to retire as a political consultant after the 2008 election, when North Carolina shockingly went for Barack Obama and Beverly Perdue became our first female governor. My new position at Duke's Sanford School of Public Policy felt like shelter from the political storm during the crucible of the 2010 Tea Party elections. The enormous gains of conservative Republicans throughout the region have in short order raised again the dread prospect of a new solid nonprogressive South. Seeing Sanford's pictures in the school's hallways every day has inspired me to think about how his legacy can help today's Southern progressives. Yet I strive here to engage the legacy of the historical Sanford rather than to conjure some mythic, all-purpose hero.

As the title of one biography puts it, Sanford had "outrageous ambitions" for himself, the South, and the nation. He was not just an electoral politician focused on winning for the sake of winning. When a conservative legislature was blocking any new initiatives late in his term as governor, Sanford went around it and gained foundation monies for the North Carolina Fund. A forerunner of today's nongovernmental organizations, the fund involved young college students in community action programs that became models for Lyndon B. Johnson's War on Poverty. And after his governorship,

Sanford led the effort to establish the Southern Growth Policies Board as an economic development think tank for the region.

Without apology, however, Sanford saw himself as an electoral politician intent on winning. And while the shape of political campaigns in the South and nationally have changed, his philosophical attitude toward politics and progress remains vital for Southern progressives today.

Sanford was not a standard optimist about the course of Southern political progress. Coming from relatively humble origins in small-town eastern North Carolina, he certainly understood how much the South was gradually changing for the better. To him, North Carolina was a special state with more progressive spirit than any other in the region. But he was acutely aware that even his beloved state could stop going forward and even head backward. When asked in 1976 about North Carolina's progressive reputation, Sanford bluntly responded in electoral terms that the state was often within "just a few percentage points of going" in the other direction.

Sanford's experience as a Bronze Star–decorated paratrooper in World War II shaped his view that progress was a possibility to be achieved, not an inevitability to be assumed. His combat service provided a very practical demonstration of the paradoxical truth about humanity's capacity for justice but inclination toward injustice. Sanford came home, as his longtime aide and friend Tom Lambeth has put it, "committed to making North Carolina a better place." Yet Sanford always knew that the other side could win.

Sanford often contrasted his political attitude with that of his intellectual mentor, Frank Porter Graham. Sanford was one of the many students whom Graham inspired while impressively expanding the University of North Carolina's national reputation as the bastion of Southern scholarly progressivism. In interviews over the years, Sanford depicted Graham as "representing the ideals that I thought were proper and I would like to have as my ideals." But Sanford made clear that he did not share Graham's Olympian certitude about how progressive ideas would triumph.

Graham was no starry-eyed utopian pacifist. He served (but did not see combat) in the Marine Corps during World War I, and he was a firm supporter of not only FDR's domestic New Deal but also his interventionist tilt toward the Allies leading up to World War II. Yet at the same time, Graham insisted that "the Sermon on the Mount was sound social and economic doctrine."

In the wake of his own and Harry Truman's upset victories in 1948, North Carolina's populist governor, Kerr Scott, made Graham a surprise appointment to fill a 1949 Senate vacancy. "You haven't got a better liberal in America than the Senator you got," Scott declared about Graham to a supportive audience. But in 1950, Graham lost a bitter primary runoff to Raleigh lawyer Willis Smith.

Smith's side relied heavily on raw racial appeals that screamed out, in the words of one pamphlet, "WHITE PEOPLE WAKE UP BEFORE IT'S TOO LATE." By all accounts, Graham's response during the runoff was belated and ineffective. At least one major campaign message took a haughty stance that insulted voters. "Are you ignorant or prejudiced?" asked a Graham newspaper ad widely circulated among white workers in the state's textile towns. "If so, you are the person at whom the phony race issue is aimed."

As president of the state Young Democrats, Sanford worked overtime for Graham. He held Raleigh broadcaster Jesse Helms covertly responsible for engineering the racist runoff strategy against Graham. Many supporters went on to praise Graham as the "master of defeat" as a result of his serenity and magnanimity throughout the campaign. Sanford shared this view of Graham as not stooping to conquer but distanced himself from praise for it.

Insisting that "you had to counterattack," Sanford squarely disputed the

Grahamian view that the Sermon on the Mount's turn-the-other-cheek philosophy was sound political doctrine. Even more basically, Sanford expressed frustration that Graham was not prepared to contend with the pushing of hot-button issues. In contrast, Sanford emphasized that his 1960 campaign for governor was "geared" to respond to "dirty politics."

However, rather than acting like an ideological lion, Sanford won in 1960 by being an organizational fox, playing all the political angles throughout a multicandidate primary in a one-party Democratic state. Sanford avoided endorsing the Supreme Court's *Brown* decision and embraced the state's Pearsall Plan designed to delay desegregation. One of the other primary candidates (Attorney General Malcolm Seawell) defended *Brown* while directly challenging the views of segregationist candidate Beverly Lake. And in the primary runoff, Sanford insisted that Lake lied in calling him a liberal "integrationist." Sanford made sure to position himself as a moderate compared to Lake's massive resistance stance in defense of segregation. Sanford later acknowledged that his positioning involved some hypocrisy but firmly held that "it was not a time to be a purist." He never thought that he could have won by being more of a profile in courage (and no serious analyst has ever said he was wrong).

When in office, moreover, Sanford found that his education tax initiative fell short in many progressive eyes, including those of some of the state's major newspapers. They were lukewarm to his $100 million tax package for the public schools because they believed that his chosen means, reimposing the sales tax on food, had a "regressive" impact on the poor. Sanford countered that poor and black families understood that their children were the prime beneficiaries of the educational improvements in his package.

Most North Carolinians ultimately understood the overall progressive impact of what Sanford was doing, but the only demographic groups who really liked it and stayed with him were indeed the poor and black populations and the liberal-minded. His courage earned him an abysmally low job performance rating as he left office in 1964 after his constitutionally limited one term.

Nevertheless, Sanford proved his continuing political skills more than two decades later by winning a U.S. Senate seat in 1986. A popular Republican governor had appointed his opponent, Jim Broyhill, a capable congressman for more than 20 years, to the Senate seat earlier in the year, and he initially looked like a strong bet to confirm the GOP's expanding muscle in the state. Yet Broyhill was from the old school of moderately conservative mountain Republicanism. He stayed well within the confines of what historian William Chafe has identified as a sporadically observed and now almost extinct North Carolina tradition of political civility. Sanford was a master at knowing how to operate with those slow-pitch rules. Bluntly put, Sanford won a boring affair with very low turnout: He took the seat with 52 percent of the vote but received only 823,652 votes, fewer than the 824,287 Walter Mondale had garnered when he won only 38 percent of the state's presidential voters two years earlier.

I believe that Sanford privately questioned whether he could handle the kind of two-party ideological warfare pioneered by Jesse Helms in outright defiance of the North Carolina tradition of political civility. I share the common Sanfordite belief that he would have won reelection to the Senate in 1992 against Lauch Faircloth, Sanford's friend turned Helms ally, but for the well-publicized heart surgery Sanford needed toward the end of the campaign. And he might have been able to summon bottomless reservoirs of political gumption to win any titanic grudge match against his bête noire, Helms.

But the truth is that Sanford was uncomfortable with the media-driven ideological competition changing Southern and national politics. A particularly searing

moment before his 1986 comeback was a 13-point (50 to 37 percent) loss to George Wallace in North Carolina's 1972 Democratic presidential primary. Sanford was not simply thrown off by the effectiveness of Wallace's new coded racial appeals. Fundamentally, he was unsettled by the plebiscitary turn in electoral politics. In 1981, he even wrote *A Danger of Democracy*, a book on the presidential nomination process.

The conclusion should be obvious that Sanford's path does not provide a playbook with detailed instructions for how progressive politicians can win Southern elections today. Nor do his long-ago rhetorical compromises on race need to be embraced. Sanfordites like me prefer to emphasize that at the famous 1963 March on Washington, the head of the National Association for the Advancement of Colored People, Roy Wilkins, singled Sanford out as a Southern governor who was "forthright in support of the civil rights progress."

Yet reviewing the historical Sanford on race should underline the electoral dilemmas that Southern progressives always have confronted. And it should undermine nostalgic talk that progressive candidates today need to summon up the "courage" that their predecessors supposedly displayed. After initially enjoying such flattery, Sanford would ultimately call for the shedding of all dime-store Nietzschean naïveté about the possibility of Superman candidates who can defy political gravity.

We Sanfordites are more stubborn about defending the step that he took on the food tax to make education progress. We are not impressed by assertions that such a conventionally progressive means as an income tax hike would have somehow succeeded in the 1961 North Carolina legislature. But in my view, the larger lesson is the fallacy in the progressive sentiment that some necessary harmonic convergence exists—especially in the South and when it comes to taxes—between "visionary" policy and popular support.

The underlying problem with progressive invocations of political courage and vision is the kind of optimistic philosophy whose manifestations in Graham's politics proved so disconcerting to Sanford. I've never met a Southern progressive who thought significant advancement anywhere in our region was automatic or just around the corner. But to this day, too many of us seem to believe that the problem simply amounts to some kind of cultural lag, that history is ultimately on our side, and catching up with the more enlightened parts of the country and the world is still only a matter of time.

On the one hand, this kind of progressive optimism can generate the attitude of benevolent acceptance toward unprogressive waywardness that Graham exhibited in defeat. On the other hand, as in the Graham ad asking white workers whether they were ignorant or prejudiced, it can serve as an excuse for elitism rather than engagement.

This problem of philosophical attitude was on display even in such a justly praised policy report as *Halfway Home and a Long Way to Go*. By that time, the report's progressive authors were obviously concerned about the "long way" that the South still had to travel. Yet as its introduction displayed, *Halfway Home* was still struggling to hold onto the progressive assumption of a cultural lag. "Why are we taking so long to become fully at home in the modern global village?" asked the report. "What has delayed the New South's transformation into the Promised Land it always seemed?"

By now, however, it is long past time for Southern progressives to jettison the belief that any manifest destiny is ultimately at work in favor of the cause. Sanford would agree that we need to take on the mantle of insurgent underdogs rather than continuing to act like we are the rightful heirs to the region's halls of governance. No manifest destiny is working against us either, and continued metropolitanization as well as growing demographic diversification in the South may soon combine to enhance our cause. But in the Sanford vein and even more so, Southern progressives need to be hungry for victory and make rather than expect a political realignment to happen.

Sanford would certainly be very concerned about the rise of the Tea Party movement and its opposition to virtually any manifestation of progressivism. Yet I doubt that he would care much about gathering together councils of elders so that they could reenvision progress once again and accelerate the production of policy papers on Southern problems. Instead, my bet is that he would be shaming these elders into paying for (among other things) a new North Carolina Fund to empower young people of all backgrounds.

Understandably in the context of the 1960s, the North Carolina Fund had a rather exclusive emphasis on the poor and poverty. Today, a new fund would need to be more broadly gauged to capture public imagination. For example, the environment and the need for green business growth would appear to be among new areas for focus.

Any effective grassroots work would no doubt experience at least some of the controversy that the North Carolina Fund encountered in the 1960s and could thereby complicate the short-term electoral picture further for Southern progressives. But the Sanfordian response is that progressives have to engage in grassroots work to ultimately change the political equation rather than relying on increasingly hollow calls for electoral politicians to have "courage" and "vision."

In a very helpful political way, the example of the North Carolina Fund also reinforces the distinctiveness of Sanford's progressivism. In their recent book, historians Robert Korstad and James Leloudis rightly attribute the creation of the fund to Sanford's growing "willingness to attend to dissenting voices, a capacity to learn life's lessons from outside his own circle of experience, and the courage to reconsider the moral foundations of his actions."

On the one hand, the fund involved a moderate Southern politician trying to incorporate (sometimes awkwardly and fitfully) radical notions about participatory democracy into his political portfolio. On the other hand, its status as an experiment at the state and local level tapped into his strong interest in getting away from the command and control of national welfare-state bureaucracy and transforming the conservative call for "states' rights" into a new progressive federalism. A few years later, he gave book-length treatment to this topic in *Storm over the States*.

Sanford's mixing of cross-cutting ideological appeals indicates that his progressivism was open, evolving, always unfinished. And to address the nation's current economic crisis, I would bet on Sanford confounding ideological boundaries and devising a cross-cutting progressive strategy that uses both conservative and radical elements. For example, especially based on Sanford's gubernatorial experience in nurturing the growth of the Research Triangle Park, I could see him campaigning in favor of abolishing the capital gains tax for real entrepreneurs who take the risk of founding new companies and create a significant number of good-paying jobs. In tandem, I could see him campaigning on establishing an environmental job corps, a 21st-century Civilian Conservation Corps, for the low-skilled unemployed.

I believe that my views are based on the historical Sanford, but I readily grant that my attempted channeling of him here is my own personal interpretation. And in true Sanfordian fashion, I understand that interpretation as open to criticism and better reflection from others. Yet I hope that at the very least, my effort has served the Sanfordian goal of stirring things up in Southern progressive circles.

> It is long past time for Southern progressives to jettison the belief that any manifest destiny is ultimately at work in favor of the cause.

REFERENCES

Covington, Howard E., and Marion A. Ellis. *Terry Sanford: Politics, Progress, and Outrageous Ambitions*. Durham: Duke University Press, 1999.

Drescher, John. *Triumph of Good Will: How Terry Sanford Beat a Champion of Segregation and Reshaped the South*. Jackson: University Press of Mississippi, 2000.

Korstad, Robert R., and James L. Leloudis. *To Right These Wrongs: The North Carolina Fund and the Battle to End Poverty and Inequality in 1960s America*. Chapel Hill: University of North Carolina Press, 2010.

Pleasants, Julian M., and Augustus M. Burns. *Frank Porter Graham and the 1950 Senate Race in North Carolina*. Chapel Hill: University of North Carolina Press, 1990.

Sanford, Terry. *A Danger of Democracy: The Presidential Nominating Process*. Boulder, Colo.: Westview, 1981.

Sanford, Terry. *Storm over the States*. New York: McGraw-Hill, 1967.

Southern Poverty, Southern Politics

GENE NICHOL

OUR POVERTY

The South, as it has been said, is the native home of American poverty. We have more poor people and more leaders who are untroubled by that fact than the rest of the nation. Seemingly, it has ever been so. Ever it remains. In this essay, I explore this disconcerting if long-lived anomaly.

Newly released Census data from 2009 reveal once again that the South has the lowest median income in the United States by a good margin. The Northeast and the West have median household income levels of more than $53,000; the South's is just above $45,000. Almost 16 percent of Southerners live in poverty, compared to 12 percent in the Northeast, 13 percent in the Midwest, and 14 percent in the West. About 20 percent of Southerners had no health care coverage of any kind, far outpacing the figure for the rest of the nation. And particularly in the South, all these disconcerting figures are markedly worse for African Americans, Latinos, and Native Americans. About 40 percent of Southern children of color live in stark, unrelenting poverty. And as the recession lingers, the gaps only widen.

Almost six million American children live in extreme poverty, surviving on seven or eight dollars a day. They are disproportionately concentrated in 15 Southern states. Ten of the 11 states where at least 1 in 10 children suffers from extreme poverty are Southern. Mississippi has the largest proportion at 14 percent; Louisiana, West Virginia, Kentucky, and Alabama follow close behind at about 12 percent; and Arkansas, South Carolina, Tennessee, Oklahoma, and Texas see at least 10 percent of their children struggle with extreme poverty. New Mexico is the only non-Southern state to haunt these debilitating frontiers.

OUR POLITICS

Then there is our politics.

During the fevered national debate over health care reform, I reviewed speeches by two U.S. senators from the South in which they decried, with intensity, the various reform proposals being debated in Congress. Both senators emphasized that we presently enjoy the greatest health care system in the world and that it should not be molested. Intrigued, I looked to see how many of their constituents were at that moment uninsured. To my at least partial surprise, I discovered that their state had more uninsured citizens than any other state in the union—almost a

quarter of the population. I wondered if these marginalized and threatened cohorts agreed with their distinguished senators about what is the "best health care system in the world."

In that light, I informally generalized the query. First, I compiled a list of the 10 states with the highest percentages of uninsured citizens. Unsurprisingly, the roster was very, very disproportionately comprised of Southern states. Then I examined the voting pattern of these states' senators on the health care reform proposals. Nearly all had cast votes and spoken vigorously against the measures. In other words, through their representatives, the states whose citizens had the most to gain under the proposed health care reform initiative opposed it.

I then determined which states had the smallest percentages of uninsured residents. These jurisdictions were located disproportionately in the Northeast. Their senators voted overwhelmingly in favor of the reforms. The states whose citizens had less to gain by the federal reform effort supported it almost unanimously. This finding turned most if not all of the premises of representative, factional democracy neatly on their heads. I wondered how this seeming rejection of interest could be explained to James Madison.

The answer, I surmised, had to do with who was, under existing circumstances, being left in the shadows. The 20 percent or more of citizens of these (mostly) Southern states without insurance, without recourse, were likely the poor, the threatened, the marginalized, often citizens of color, rarely (or never) the ready colleagues, funders, and confidants of the Southern political class. In fact, I would guess that the uninsured and excluded residents of Texas, Alabama, Mississippi, North and South Carolina, Tennessee, Oklahoma, Arkansas, and the like are as foreign, as alien, to their representatives in the U.S. Senate as if they lived in Indonesia or El Salvador. They are beyond the purview, outside the field of vision. A senator fails to register and even recognize the needs and interests of a quarter of his constituents only when deploying a politics in which large numbers simply do not count. They are, in practical terms, the disappeared.

This seeming invisibility was subsequently echoed in the repeated threats and occasional actual rejections of large troves of federal stimulus funding by various Southern governors in 2008–9, even as their states suffered under the intense and disproportionate exigencies of the Great Recession. In so doing, these governors acted directly against the interests of huge numbers of their constituents, apparently merely for political and ideological gain. Kicking back unemployment and educational benefits, massive public-employment projects, transportation projects, and the like even as growing and tragic numbers of their fellow citizens endured crushing economic hardship is, thankfully, a rarity in American political life. It is odd to flatly cast aside proffered resources to be distributed to those suffering from hunger, joblessness, homeless, and despair. Doing so is made more tenable, perhaps, when the purported beneficiaries do not actually count in the deliberative political calculus.

A quick survey of the new Tea Party caucus in the present U.S. Congress again reveals a strong Southern dominance. The four states with the largest contingents in the official caucus are all former members of the Confederacy—Texas (12), Florida (7), Louisiana (5), and Georgia (5). South Carolina and Tennessee register close behind. Conversely, the Tea Party caucus claims not a single member from New England, leading at least one pundit to note that the Tea Party movement would be more accurately named after Fort Sumter—it reflects merely the latest attempt of a white Southern minority to demand its way in American democracy. Whether or not this is so, the Southern enthusiasm for the Tea Party again reflects a governing premise that the states with the highest levels of poverty tend to be the most powerfully committed to the notion that government should not do anything about it.

Of course it is far easier to describe and identify this Southern political-economic disconnect than it is explain it. Bob Dylan had a go at it in singing of the assassination of Medgar Evers:

> The Southern politician preaches to the poor white man,
>
> "You got more than the blacks, don't complain.
>
> You're better than them, you been born with white skin," they explain.
>
> . . . .
>
> And the poor white remains
>
> On the caboose of the train
>
> But it ain't him to blame
>
> He's only a pawn in their game.

It is rarely safe to flatly disagree with the early Dylan. But it is my guess that by the second decade of the new millennium, Southern political strains are at least modestly more complex than the pawn analogy would suggest. My historian friend Sheldon Hackney explains, "The South lived in the nineteenth century more thoroughly and longer than did the non-South. The result is the persistence of the sort of self-reliant individualism that acts to protect the community from non-conformity. Add to that the notion that the Southern white identity is the product of a series of perceived threats, and one can understand why confrontations with the 'cultural other' will revivify the sense of crisis and reinforce parochial conformity. Parochial white Southerners experience a loss of liberty when the [dominance] of their group is threatened, whether the threat comes from the civil rights movement, the counterculture, the federal government, or some phantasmagoric combination of the three."

Regardless of the particulars of causation, for those of us who choose unreservedly to live in the American South, our politics continue to make it more difficult to face and resolve our problems. The silent marriage of privilege and privation mocks the American commitment to egalitarian constitutional democracy. We ignore it at the cost of our best selves.

> Almost six million American children live in extreme poverty, surviving on seven or eight dollars a day. They are disproportionately concentrated in 15 Southern states.

REFERENCES

Hackney, Sheldon. "Identity Politics, Southern Style." In *Where We Stand: Voices of Southern Dissent*, ed. Anthony Dunbar. Montgomery, Ala.: NewSouth, 2004.

Lind, Michael. "The Tea Party, the Debt Ceiling, and White Southern Extremism." *Salon*, August 2, 2011. http://www.salon.com/news/politics/war_room/2011/08/02/lind_tea_party.

Getting Past Our Civil War Hangover and
Moving toward Real Southern Progress

ANDY BRACK

My grandmother's old-style Southern dinner was a thing of legend: crispy fried chicken cooked in lard with butter-soaked mashed potatoes and green beans the color of army fatigues. It sure tasted good. But it wasn't heart smart. A comparable dinner for today's health-conscious Southerner might be chicken sautéed in olive oil (or, even better, grilled), potatoes laced with yogurt or fat-free sour cream, and beans steamed a bright green.

There is a lesson for the future of the South in these two ways of cooking Grandma's chicken. Doing things the way they have always been done has left the region mired in a Civil War hangover fraught with persistently high rankings for violence, poverty, educational torpor, and other impediments to progress. After years of doing things the old ways, maybe it is time for governments, churches, and nonprofits to reflect on new ways of collaborating and pulling together to get the South out of the nation's cellar.

Since the end of the Civil War, Southerners often have been cautious about big change, reluctant to take on a culture primed by years of fear, independence of spirit, and dependence on a ruling elite. Periodic flirtations with moving the region forward to a better quality of life—from progressive populism at the turn of the 20th century that pushed public education and social justice through Huey Long's "chicken in every pot" campaign speeches—quickly fizzled, and many things remained the same.

But Southerners coming home from World War II had seen more of the world than their hometowns. Some wondered why they fought for freedom when their states were segregated. Slowly shrugging

A WAY FORWARD: BUILDING A GLOBALLY COMPETITIVE SOUTH

off decades of economic stagnation, the South began modernizing. The civil rights movement soon blossomed. In the place of Jim Crow laws and segregation were enfranchised voters, integrated schools, and a long-overdue transformation of the region's multilayered culture.

Through organizations like the short-lived L. Q. C. Lamar Society and its offspring at the Southern Growth Policies Board, leading politicians, academics, and business executives started pushing for economic and educational progress. Enlightened, pragmatic leaders in the 1970s and 1980s offered agendas that set a future tone for the South to create a business environment based on more than cheap land, labor, and infrastructure. Southern states invested more in public schools, technical colleges, and higher education. The results? Dynamic hubs of innovation at places like Research Triangle Park in North Carolina and increases in foreign investment that diversified the region, albeit mostly in its urban areas.

Hand in hand with the development of additional economic muscle, outsiders started moving to the South's sunshine in record numbers—so much so that today's population is up a third compared to 20 years ago. A further testament to the changes and opportunities in the South is the number of African Americans returning from distressed Northeastern and Midwestern cities for opportunities in Dixie. By 2010, Census figures showed that the percentage of the nation's African American population living in the South was the highest in a half century.

In many ways, life is better today for the many Southern residents of yuppie-packed exurbs that offer every chain store imaginable—the same stores found in New York, Los Angeles, Seattle, Chicago, and Kansas City. Most Southerners today have the accoutrements of a better life—telephones, TVs, mobile phones, cars, and air-conditioning, the technology that made the region livable.

But while Dixie's population is up significantly and its quality of life

Periodic flirtations with moving the region forward to a better quality of life—from progressive populism at the turn of the 20th century that pushed public education and social justice through Huey Long's "chicken in every pot" campaign speeches—quickly fizzled, and many things remained the same.

is generally better than when John F. Kennedy was president, a statistical look at the American South shows that it has not achieved parity with the rest of the country. As Southern states tried to push from the bottom, states in other regions invested as much or more, thereby maintaining their superior positions.

As such, the numbers tell a chilling story rooted in tough places such as urban Memphis and Atlanta or the rural Delta. Throughout the South, poverty remains high. The Mississippi of 2008 ranked first in poverty in the nation, just as it did 20 years earlier. Tied for second were Louisiana, Arkansas, and Kentucky, all top 10 in poverty in the late 1980s.

More numbers: A third of Southerners are obese. Eight of the South's states have among the nation's highest infant-mortality rates. High school graduation rates are below the national average in 8 of 11 Southern states. Half of Southern states have among the highest violent crime rates in the nation. This list goes on and on in subject after subject, evidence perhaps of the notion that the more things seem to change in the South, the more they really remain the same.

Over the past 25 years, political progress to move away from these chilling parts of statistical lists has been thwarted by politicians frightened of taxes and of new solutions for old problems. These days in statehouses across the region, legislators often do little or nothing instead of making meaningful changes to reform unbalanced tax structures, generate zealous learning, or break the unhealthy cycle of poverty. Or worse, they jealously hunt for and use issue wedges like abortion, immigration, and voting to inject fear into the electorate, shore up their base, and thwart real leadership.

There is, however, some good news for people who want the South to stop bringing up the rear. Pockets of progressivism are alive and well in the area's cities and states. Demographics show that the ruling elites face changes as Southern whites are likely to become the minority in the next 25 years. Georgia and Mississippi already have 60 percent or fewer white residents, and their numbers are growing only in the single digits. In contrast, population growth among African Americans and Latinos is dramatic; the number of Latinos is growing at triple-digit rates in Alabama, Arkansas, Kentucky, Mississippi, North Carolina, South Carolina, and Tennessee. As the South becomes more diverse, progressives have the opportunity to attract these new minority voters, who tend to be more ideologically similar. If such a shift occurs, elections in two decades will be far different from those of today.

A dozen years ago, University of North Carolina at Chapel Hill sociologist John Shelton Reed reminded us that what the South really needed was the collective will to do something about its problems. "Mobilizing public opinion—building a consensus about who is to act, who is to benefit, who is to pay—that's the business of our politicians, and of people like yourselves," he told a 1998 audience of journalists.

Leaders interested in building a better South may want to consider five strategies:

Better education. If tomorrow's South is to change to reflect the diverse values of more people, universities and think tanks must better educate leaders and the public about implications of policy alternatives.

Better communications. Future leaders need to use the full array of public relations and communication tools to highlight why particular positions are important and smart. Instead, for example, of being tarred as liberals who want to raise taxes, progressives need to embrace meaningful tax reforms that update tax codes, dump special-interest tax exemptions, and modernize how Southerners are taxed. They must change their perception from being "tax and spend" leaders to responsible, effective representatives who use tax money efficiently to achieve positive outcomes through government.

Build coalitions. Successful future policymakers will cobble together coalitions of like-minded individuals based on issues instead of political party. There is no reason, for example, that a conservative Christian organization cannot support progressive environmental ideas if those alternatives are highlighted as ways to leave the Earth a better place than the current generation found it.

Better organizing. Tomorrow's leaders need to organize where people are, much as Barack Obama did when he visited barber shops and beauty parlors in South Carolina in 2007 and 2008 to spread his message.

Better use of issues. A key way to shift the South toward new solutions to old problems is for pragmatic leaders to focus on "agreeable issues"—a mainstream policy platform that seeks to bring people together on things on which they can agree. Why? Because if leaders can start agreeing more than they do these days, they likely will build trust and be able to work more closely on tougher issues.

Examples of "agreeable issues" include

- state structural **tax reform** to boost fairness and balance to provide more stability;
- improving **energy efficiency** efforts across the region, such as policies that promote renewable energy standards;
- reducing violence and improving **safety** to allow the 7 Southern states that rank among the 10 most violent to crawl out of that gutter;
- nurturing the **economy** by dramatically improving the number of Southerners with postsecondary degrees; and
- boosting **wellness** by improving life-expectancy levels to those of Canada.

The American South will evolve as more people move to the region and as technology helps to erase educational barriers. But for the region to get over its festering emotional and statistical Civil War hangover, its leaders have to work better together and be smarter about the policy choices they make so that tomorrow's South will be more than the stepchild of these United States.

REFERENCES

For a deeper look at some of the statistics mentioned in this piece, see the Center for a Better South's *2011 Briefing Book on the South*, a collection of demographic and statistical data on more than 50 indicators ranging from population and diversity to obesity and crime, and the *Agenda for a Better South*, both available at www.bettersouth.org.

VISIONS FOR THE FUTURE OF THE SOUTH

A WAY FORWARD: BUILDING A GLOBALLY COMPETITIVE SOUTH

Southern-Style Creativity: NEW METHODS for Tackling Nagging Challenges in the Next 25 Years

ANITA BROWN-GRAHAM

INTRODUCTION

"Today, the will to work must be matched with the skill to work." This warning was truthful and trending in 1986 when issued by the *Halfway Home* report. In 2011, it signals deepened pain and pessimism. Twenty-five years after *Halfway Home*, many in the South remain wedged at the halfway mark with no obvious road map for traveling ahead together.

For communities to be competitive in today's economy, they must develop a workforce capable of thinking and working creatively. While the South as a region must further develop its creativity quotient if it is to reach national averages in education, income, and wealth, this essay focuses on the stubborn cycle of poverty that pervades many communities in the South, sometimes for decades. What will a creativity-based economy mean for these places?

A focus on places left behind is not new. The same year the Southern Growth Policy Board emphasized the connection between education and the economy in *Halfway Home*, MDC's report, *Shadows in the Sunbelt*, highlighted the plight of rural places untouched by the successes of the South's 20th-century economic development strategies. MDC called for broadened "efforts to economic development—cultivating local entrepreneurship and harvesting from untapped local resources and markets

which provide fertile ground for development activities." MDC renewed this call and extended its focus to include persistent-poverty urban neighborhoods in *The State of the South 2002: Shadows in the Sunbelt Revisited*. The three reports altered the regional conversation about economic development by drawing the connection between education and the economy and insisting that the region needed a diverse set of "homegrown" economic development strategies for distressed communities.

The collective calls did not go unheeded, although one might argue that the challenges continued to dwarf the responses. The public sector, particularly the federal government, developed and funded myriad programs aimed at restoring economic vigor to distressed communities through job-creation and workforce-preparedness programs. National foundations, community funders, and civic-minded businesses also poured significant resources into the apparatuses set up to serve low-income communities. Simultaneously, private, not-for-profit community-based development organizations initiated and participated in employment efforts.

This essay focuses on the experiences of community-based development organizations in North Carolina to illustrate the challenges facing persistent, high-poverty communities and the important responsive role these organizations have played in the past 25 years; the remarkably changed current context for development of distressed neighborhoods; and the critical role for creativity in the work of community-based development organizations in the next 25 years. This essay's primary premise is that creative thinking—the kind that fuels innovation—is now a community's most valuable commodity.

COMMUNITY DEVELOPMENT AT THE HALFWAY HOME MARK

In many states, community economic development responsibility in high-poverty areas has been shared by the public sector and community-based development organizations. In North Carolina, these organizations often take the legal form of community development corporations chartered under Chapter 55A of the North Carolina General Statutes and recognized by the Internal Revenue Service as 501(c)(3) not-for-profit organizations. As such, their receipts are tax exempt and contributions to them are tax deductible.

Community development corporations have a relatively recent history in the South. They began in the 1960s as part of the federal government's War on Poverty. A few of these corporations in North Carolina date back to that period, but the majority were formed in the late 1980s. In 1985, shortly before the publication of *Halfway Home*, Legal Services of North Carolina and the Local Initiatives Support Corporation launched a pilot program for community economic development in eastern North Carolina to build the capacity of local organizations to engage in community economic development.

This demonstration effort was buoyed by a growing understanding of the possibilities created by the federal Community Reinvestment Act of 1976, which required banks to make investments in the communities from which they had deposits. In October 1985, the Legal Services Resource Center filed the state's first challenge under the act against First Union National Bank (later merged with Wachovia and then purchased by Wells Fargo). Subsequent challenges were filed against additional North Carolina banks, but the focus transitioned quickly to partnering with banks. By the time *Halfway Home* was released, Community Reinvestment Act agreements had been signed with several banks, and new financial capital was available to support community development corporation efforts in North Carolina.

Not far behind the support from private banks came support from the state. During its 1988 short session, the North Carolina General Assembly made its first appropriation to support these corporations' efforts to improve the lives of residents of underdeveloped minority communities through business, commercial revitalization, and housing development activities. Today, community development corporations continue to receive state appropriations.

A MAJOR STRATEGY: THE PHYSICAL DEVELOPMENT OF DISTRESSED COMMUNITIES

Community development corporations are diverse in size, composition, and scope of services, but they reflect some commonalities. Because they are community-based (meaning founded by and grounded in the communities they serve), they are considered more likely to understand and be responsive to the unique needs of their particular communities. Their comprehensive approach to community development is based on the belief that the problems of distressed neighborhoods are interrelated. The corporations believe in balancing bricks-and-mortar projects with economic and social development activities that improve the overall quality of life for the community's residents. Some corporations tackle many challenges, others address a single issue, but all understand that their agenda is part of a larger framework.

A 1996 study revealed that almost all of North Carolina's community development organizations claimed a connection to comprehensive initiatives and an emphasis on community building but were involved in housing development and related housing activities. The disproportionate focus on housing was no coincidence. Homeownership has long been viewed as a primary strategy for wealth creation for all families and as standing at the center of the American Dream. Also, high rent burdens or owner costs are significant issues for low-income families. In rapidly growing North Carolina, low-cost dwellings were disappearing from the housing stock during the 1990s.

Other community development corporation activities included commercial real estate development and management, business enterprise development, job training and placement services, crime prevention activity, and other human services delivery. Irrespective of the activity, the corporations claimed that their work also resulted in "community building" that could solve collective problems and improve or maintain that community's well-being. As a group, therefore, the community development corporations have a robust set of experiences in direct service provision through their various programmatic activities; in social activism through their negotiations with the private and public sectors; and in community diagnosis and capacity building through their understanding of comprehensive initiatives and their community engagement and collaboration activities.

COMMUNITY ECONOMIC DEVELOPMENT TODAY:

THE EMERGENCE OF A CREATIVITY ECONOMY

The South and its high-poverty areas face old and new challenges. Global forces have undermined the agriculture, textiles, electronics, and manufacturing industries; the nation's housing market has collapsed, with record foreclosures and significant depreciation of home values; and the region's jobless rates are in some places unprecedented in recent times. This crisis exists despite the fact that leading states in the region deserve credit for working hard to usher in the knowledge economy, expecting it to last forever, and playing to emerging strengths: good universities, an available and cheap labor force, research parks and cheap land for similar public-private initiatives, and a hardy entrepreneurial spirit. Some observers are surprised by the fact that the ability to compete on price, quality, and much of the left-brain digitized work associated with knowledge, once central to America's businesses, is now being reproduced by highly trained and lower-paid workers elsewhere around the world. The nation's knowledge economy is being replaced by a creativity economy, and the South is struggling to hold on to the relative gains made in the past 25 years.

Thoughtful New South leaders understand that workforce creativity will be key to expanding the number of high-skill, high-income jobs and to developing the communities in which such jobs predominate. The Institute for Emerging Issues and the North Carolina Department of Commerce measured North Carolina's creative workforce to identify "creative workers"— those holding the top 10 percent of jobs that routinely require creative thinking at high levels. The industries represented were as diverse as internet publishing and broadcasting, specialized design, personal care services, and independent artists, writers, and performers. The results offer five key ideas for community economic development.

1. Creative Jobs Pay above State Averages

In 2009, workers in creative occupations, including technologists, health professionals, artists, managers, and analysts, earned an average of $59,200 per year, compared to $36,697 for all state workers. Above-average salaries for creative work exist in metropolitan counties as well as more rural ones.

2. Faster Job Growth and Slower Job Loss

The growth of creative jobs in North Carolina outpaced total employment increases for the state as a whole from 2002 through 2008 (21.1 percent versus 13.3 percent), our most recent period of economic growth. Furthermore, creative work increased faster in North Carolina than it did in the United States as a whole (21.1 percent versus 15.5 percent). Within the state, creative employment increased more than the state average in all areas and often at substantially higher rates.

Given the recent hemorrhaging of jobs in North Carolina, the best news may be that North Carolina's creative occupations shed jobs at a much slower rate than all jobs during the current recession (a 2.4 percent loss compared to 4.4 percent from 2008 to 2009). This finding mirrors national trends.

3. Diverse Occupations and Industries

Creative workers are located in 69 occupations spread among many sectors of the economy. The diversity of industries is mirrored in the distribution of workers found in the 15 industries with the heaviest concentration of creative workers. This finding implies that creativity cannot be reduced to particular categories, but its implications must be considered across the breadth of North Carolina's economy.

4. Occupations Distributed across the State

Creative occupations are located across the state but are more heavily concentrated in North Carolina's 40 metropolitan counties (5.9 percent of total jobs) than in other areas (4.0 percent). However, they continue to outpace other employment in rural areas.

5. Higher Education Achievement Is Important

Creative occupations generally require some amount of postsecondary education. However, there are many occupations for which only a bachelor's degree or less is required, while others require no advanced training.

Some critics argue that the shift to a creativity economy is inconsequential to those places already left behind by the knowledge economy boom of the 1990s. In this era of a creativity economy—one that author Daniel Pink calls "The Conceptual Age" and *New York Times* columnist David Brooks calls "The Cognitive Age"—more and more jobs are beginning to depend on a complex and creative set of "right-brain" skills, including problem solving, communications, entrepreneurship, and collaboration. To compete for jobs, even many low-skill jobs, creativity skills also will be required. If many residents of distressed communities were failing to receive the left-brain skills of the last era, how can community economic developers intervene to broker the right-brain skills of a new era?

The emergence of a creativity economy has two important implications for community development corporations. First, if economic success will be largely determined by the ability to create new products, reimagine old ideas, see unlikely connections, and develop novel solutions to complex problems, the corporations must focus on finding and catalyzing these skills in the communities they serve. Community development organizations are well positioned for the job, with their history of social activism, service delivery, and community diagnosis and capacity building. Second, they must embrace creativity in how they work. In 1986, MDC called on community-based development organizations to serve as public entrepreneurs. Their role is to bring new vitality to languishing areas. Community development corporations responded with a model of physical development that arguably was not always innovative and often failed to reach scale. Today, clarion calls for public entrepreneurship must be renewed by a chorus of voices, and the response must capture the spirit of an emerging class of social entrepreneurs.

CONCLUSION: COMMUNITY DEVELOPMENT CORPORATIONS AND UPPING THE CREATIVITY MOJO OF DISTRESSED COMMUNITIES

Other regions across the country and around the world are seeking to develop their creative economies. How will the South compete, and how will it support its low-income communities seeking to grow their versions of the next Apple, GE, or Proctor and Gamble, just three of the many companies betting their future on creativity?

People will pay more for a haircut that is offered in a novel way or environment, will frequent eating establishments that offer unique experiences, and will retain the care assistant who offers boutique services. For some of the population served, community development corporations have the opportunity to support the development of such creative enterprises. For other

> For communities to be competitive in today's economy, they must develop a workforce capable of thinking and working creatively.

populations, the corporations may need to focus on ensuring that creativity pays dividends at the lower end of an increasingly bifurcated job market while connecting residents to the higher skills they will need for high-paying jobs in professional and creative fields. To do so, these community development corporations will need to form new partnerships with universities, community colleges, art groups, and companies like online retailer Zappos, which is moving its service workers through an internal career ladder from entry ranks to managers. While the fastest-growing jobs are found in a low-paying service sector, these workers are a potential source of innovation, and building a support base for developing their creativity is essential for the communities in which they live and for the regional economy as a whole.

It is no secret that creativity flourishes in special interactive environments. These environments contain numerous factors that together provide fertile soil for the generation of new ideas and their execution in the form of products, services, processes, and new paradigms. Community development corporations across the South will need to focus on four areas if creativity is to transform distressed communities.

- Foster connectivity to encourage the exchange of ideas, increase efficiency, and build important partnerships. They will need to create physical and virtual spaces where community residents can come together to exchange ideas as well as bridges that make it easier for community residents to access existing educational and entrepreneurial support resources.

- Enhance education to infuse creative practices into core curricula as well as offer greater opportunities for cross-disciplinary collaboration. Community development corporations are not educators, although many offer summer and after-school programs to youth and skill development to dislocated workers. More broadly, the corporations will need to help parents and community leaders understand the importance of offering opportunities to develop creativity in schools and beyond.

- Transfer ideas to market through an established process designed to transform creative ideas into marketable products, processes, or services. There is no question that residents in distressed communities have entrepreneurial skills. Social Enterprises UK, a body set up to promote social ventures, recently announced that of the 62,000 new businesses operating in Britain, many are in the most distressed communities. The same scale could be achieved in the South.

- Cultivate creative assets and gain broad-based public awareness and support of creative culture to promote and sustain positive economic and community development in both urban and rural areas of the state. Abandoned buildings and the creative skills of some dislocated workers offer unending opportunities for new cultural enterprises.

By doing these things well, community development corporations can take significant steps forward in efforts to catalyze creativity. In times of scarce resources and with the increasing premium being placed on creativity, innovative, sustainable business models will need to be used to drive large-scale social change in distressed communities. Much has been made recently of social entrepreneurship, a still largely undefined concept that nevertheless has increasingly recognized potential for lasting, transformational benefit to society.

Social entrepreneurs use innovation to deliver direct, large-scale change. A profitable or high-performing business model is important for rewarding innovation, ensuring sustainable financing, and in turn promoting large-scale adoption and social impact. Community development corporations will face increasing pressure to prove that they are creating something that did not exist before by exploiting innovations of new products, processes, services, organizations, markets, or skills. Polls consistently indicate that members of the public would contribute more to antipoverty efforts if they believed that the problems could be meaningfully addressed. Community development corporations are a unique vehicle for redress, and the creativity economy might offer just the emphasis on skill and scale needed to transform distressed communities.

REFERENCES

Institute for Emerging Issues. *New Thinking, New Jobs.* Raleigh: North Carolina State University, 2010.

MDC. *The State of the South 2002: Shadows in the Sunbelt Revisited.* Chapel Hill: MDC, 2002.

Strategic Philanthropy *and the* State of the South

DAVID DODSON

INTRODUCTION

As the South looks forward to the next quarter century, few regional goals are more urgent than closing the gaping structural inequities in education, income, assets, and health that have long defined us relative to the rest of the nation. Our region cannot be competitive, attractive, and secure unless we set in place incentives, systems, and policies that will move substantial numbers of our poor and underachieving neighbors from the margins to the mainstream of economic and civic life. Among the most potent and underutilized assets in this task is institutional philanthropy—investment by independent, family, community, and corporate foundations.

The creative hand of private philanthropy has made historic contributions to the competitive capacity of the South as we know it today. It is impossible to imagine our region without the universities, hospitals, research institutions, community development organizations, and cultural amenities that institutional philanthropy has either seeded or strengthened. Not only has philanthropy helped build the organizational infrastructure required for the South to compete nationally and globally, it has had an immense indirect influence on regional well-being by funding the civic and community organizations that add measurably to quality of life.

And occasionally, if too infrequently, private philanthropy has helped the South shed light on long-neglected issues such as poverty, environmental degradation, and racial inequities, helping reset the regional agenda and spur remedial action to shore up profound threats to our collective well-being.

Yet when regional leaders take up the task of setting long-term economic and community strategy, private philanthropy often is not an active partner. We may call on philanthropy to pay the bills, but history shows us that at its best, private philanthropy is capable of a much more generative and contributory role. To fail to ask institutional philanthropy to join in shaping the South's future is to neglect a powerful ally.

REGIONAL PHILANTHROPY

So why is private philanthropy not more central to forward thinking and strategic implementation in our region? There are several reasons:

The South does not fully understand philanthropy's distinctive past contributions to the region. Former Ford Foundation executive and philanthropy scholar Paul Ylvisaker has called private philanthropy society's "passing gear." Unconstrained by the pressures of the electoral cycle and free of the private market's focus on short-term return on investment, private philanthropy at its best can help society take the long view, sponsor social innovation, and seed and nurture unconventional ideas. The historical record of transformative, passing-gear philanthropic investments in the South is significant: The Peabody Fund (today the Southern Education Foundation) was among America's earliest champions of education for newly emancipated African Americans in the 19th century. The Rosenwald Foundation, created by the chair of the Sears, Roebuck department store chain, funded more than a thousand high-quality public schools for African Americans in the Jim Crow South, deftly overcoming public refusal to invest in decent facilities for black children and helping soften the indignity of segregation. The Rockefeller Foundation's investments in public health and agriculture helped impoverished Southern states eradicate chronic threats such as pellagra and the boll weevil in the 1920s and 1930s. Investments by the Ford, Z. Smith Reynolds, and Mary Reynolds Babcock Foundations enabled Governor Terry Sanford to create the North Carolina Fund, a prototype for the War on Poverty that among other achievements prefigured the federal VISTA volunteer program and the community development movement.

Southern philanthropy generally has not embraced the social venture capital role as vigorously as have its peers in other regions. Historically, most passing-gear investments in the South have come from foundations outside the region rather than from Southern philanthropy itself. Susan Wisely and Elizabeth Lynn have described four "traditions" that have defined American philanthropy since colonial times: charity, which seeks to relieve immediate need; improvement, which seeks to maximize human potential; social reform, which seeks to dismantle the structures that perpetuate problems and address problems "upstream" at their source; and civic engagement, which seeks to build community. Southern philanthropy has tended to favor the risk-averse traditions of charity and improvement (scholarships, social services, health and hospitals, arts and culture) rather than social reform, the tradition most closely aligned with passing-gear social venture investments. By contrast, major national foundations (Gates, Ford, Rockefeller, Pew, Lumina, Casey) and prominent regional foundations in the North and Midwest (McKnight and Northwest Area in Minnesota, Joyce in Illinois, Heinz in Pennsylvania, and Edna McConnell Clark in New York) have embraced the reform tradition. Regional history and culture may have shaped the South's historic philanthropic priorities, but stubborn regional inequities and constrained government resources may soon prompt Southern philanthropy to walk a bolder path.

The size of the South's philanthropic assets is small relative to the scale of our challenges. The South is home to one-third of the nation's poverty, one-quarter of the nation's population, and one-sixth of the nation's philanthropic assets. The total assets of all Southern foundations are less than those held by the three largest national foundations (Gates, Ford, Robert Wood Johnson) alone. Viewed in this context, philanthropy can appear to be an inadequate tool for the task of shaping the South's future, especially if policymakers are conditioned by history to see foundations as sources of charity rather than passing-gear social venture capital.

Private philanthropic resources are inadequately distributed across the region and heavily concentrated in the most populous states. Complicating this regional inequity, the South lacks a cadre of deep-pocketed foundations willing and able to work across state lines to address regional challenges. This spatial mismatch works against vigorous philanthropic problem solving in areas of high need.

HISTORICAL AND EMPIRICAL TRENDS

Recent decades have seen a steady growth in Southern philanthropic assets, providing our region an expanding base for tackling entrenched issues (see tables 12.1–4). How Southern foundations deploy these growing assets across Wisely and Lynn's four traditions will determine

> Not only has philanthropy helped build the organizational infrastructure required for the South to compete nationally and globally, it has had an immense indirect influence on regional well-being by funding the civic and community organizations that add measurably to quality of life.

how potent the foundations can be as a force for change and regional uplift.

Recent years also have witnessed the emergence of two other important trends: a revived appetite among some foundations to tackle big problems and support big ideas, and a concern for "measurable impact." The first trend is welcome and plays to philanthropy's role in risk capital. If philanthropy provides society's risk capital, it should embrace, not flee, tough issues. The second trend merits caution and requires philanthropy's ability to provide "patient" capital. Impact matters greatly, but this preoccupation may ironically lead some foundations to pursue only short-term goals that are safely in reach. To address structural inequity in the South is to assume a generational task. Disciplined but bold patience is required of the philanthropic investor.

RETROSPECTIVE AND PROSPECTIVE ANALYSIS: BACK 25 YEARS, FORWARD 25 YEARS

Looking back 25 years, we can see some encouraging examples of bold philanthropic leadership by Southern foundations and resulting transformational impact. At the civic level, private philanthropy has been the catalyst for the renewal of Chattanooga, Tennessee (Lyndhurst Foundation); downtown Greenville, South Carolina (Peace Family Foundation joined by the Daniel-Mickel, Symmes, and other family foundations); and Greensboro, North Carolina (Bryan and Weaver Foundations and the Community Foundation of Greater Greensboro). Pioneering investment by the Z. Smith Reynolds Foundation, reinforced by subsequent support from state government and private financial institutions, has enabled North Carolina to develop the South's most sophisticated network of community development corporations, responsible for developing thousands of units of low-income housing and countless neighborhood stabilization projects. Across the region, a new infrastructure of community development finance institutions has blossomed through philanthropic seed capital: the $19.9 million (as of 2009) Southern Development Banc Corporation in Arkansas (Winthrop Rockefeller Foundation with subsequent support from the Walton Foundation and national investors), the $22.8 million (as of 2009) Self-Help in North Carolina (Babcock and Reynolds with subsequent support from national foundations, corporations, and religious institutions), and vigorous community development finance institutions such as the Mountain Association for Community Economic Development in Kentucky and the Lowcountry Conservation Loan Fund in South Carolina (beneficiaries of the Babcock Foundation's organizational

development and program-related investment programs). Large foundations in rural Louisiana and Southside Virginia, born from the sale of rural hospitals, are now actively working at the pivotal intersection of economic security and community health, while one of the South's oldest and most distinguished foundations, the Duke Endowment, has partnered with the federally funded Social Innovation Fund and the Edna McConnell Clark Foundation to bring the pathbreaking nurse–family practitioner program to low-income expectant mothers in the Carolinas, a powerful strategy to address intergenerational poverty and health outcomes.

Looking forward, as philanthropic wealth grows in the region, so could foundation capability to engage in deeper and larger-scale passing-gear activities. It is possible to identify several areas where private philanthropy could build on past experience to spur progress, enhance competitiveness, and reduce the inequities and disparities that threaten the South's collective well-being:

Educational Attainment
Southern philanthropy could help bring research-validated K–12 and postsecondary reform strategies into states and substate regions that have not previously benefited. Southern philanthropy could partner aggressively with national foundations and state governments to bring reform-focused demonstration projects across the region to close the postsecondary credentials gap so fundamental to regional competitiveness and individual economic advancement. Achieving the Dream and the "early college" high school movement are models to emulate.

Poverty Reduction
Poverty and economic inequity lie at the heart of many of the South's deepest challenges, including educational attainment and health inequities. Poverty reduction

requires long-term attention and a multidisciplinary approach that play to the characteristics and pluralism of the foundation sector. A deep partnership among philanthropy, government, and the private sector focused on building strong pathways to move people out of poverty would be an important "grand challenge" for the region and its leaders.

Institutional Infrastructure

Philanthropy excels at building institutions. Over the past quarter century, it has created a community development infrastructure of lending institutions and neighborhood housing developers, helped land trusts and environmental advocacy organizations proliferate, and sustained community health centers. As the South becomes more metropolitan and more racially pluralistic, more integrated with the global economy, more like than unlike the rest of the nation, how might philanthropy help the region give birth to institutions that can enhance community, civility, cooperation, and shared well-being?

IMPLICATIONS FOR POLICY

What would it take to activate private philanthropy's potential as a full partner in advancing the South?

Philanthropic leaders can:

- Communicate goals, strategies, results, and lessons. Policymakers and regional leaders are hungry for ideas to address society's stubborn problems. What social returns on investment is Southern philanthropy generating? How can public policy help sustain what philanthropic investment has begun? Where have foundation programs fallen short of expectations, and how can this experience help us learn what not to do?

- Cross the sectoral divide. Initiate dialogue with policymakers to address the trepidation many foundations have about getting entangled with policy and politics. Learn from foundation peers who have successfully engaged in public problem solving.

- Create structures to facilitate collaboration. Ensure that strong intermediary structures exist to manage large-scale, multi-sectoral approaches to critical issues. Big ideas need strong institutions that can implement complex strategies and be accountable to multiple constituencies from the boardroom to

the neighborhood. Philanthropy can lead by making sure states or multistate regions have these intermediary institutions.

Policymakers can:

- Ask private philanthropy to play an increased social venture capital role to seed innovation in areas where it has expertise. Look to philanthropy to seed, not sustain, ideas that do not fit the time frame or risk tolerance of the public sector.

- Co-invest with philanthropy to create vehicles that can take promising innovations to scale. State or regional social innovation funds, modeled on the federal effort, could be created through public-private partnerships.

Private philanthropy has a remarkable power to enrich society through the wise deployment of its financial, intellectual, and reputational capital. The South needs to ask more of its foundations, and foundations need to use their passing-gear power more deliberately and more often to lift our region to its potential.

REFERENCES

Foundation Center. *FC Stats.* http://foundationcenter.org/.

Lynn, Elizabeth, and Susan Wisely. "Four Traditions of Philanthropy." In *The Civically Engaged Reader: A Diverse Collection of Short Provocative Readings on Civic Activity*, ed. A. Davis and E. Lynn. Chicago: Great Books Foundation, 2006.

MDC. *The State of the South 2007—Philanthropy as the South's "Passing Gear."* Chapel Hill: MDC, 2007.

TABLES AND FIGURES

table 12.1 TOTAL FOUNDATION ASSETS, 1975 TO 2009

	SOUTH		SOUTH, NOT INCLUDING TEXAS		UNITED STATES
	AMOUNT (IN $ BILLIONS)	AS % OF UNITED STATES	AMOUNT (IN $ BILLIONS)	AS % OF UNITED STATES	AMOUNT (IN $ BILLIONS)
1975	n/a*	n/a*	$2.20	7.3	$30.13
1995	n/a*	n/a*	$25.29	11.2	$226.74
1998	$65.7	17.1	$45.5	11.8	$385.1
2009	$99.8	16.9	$67.2	11.4	$590.2

*data not available publicly prior to 1997
Note: Due to rounding, percentages may not be exact.
Source: Foundation Center; MDC, State of the South 2007.

table 12.2 TOTAL FOUNDATION GIVING, 1998 AND 2009

	INTO THE SOUTH*		INTO THE SOUTH, NOT INCLUDING TEXAS*		UNITED STATES
	AMOUNT (IN $ BILLIONS)	AS % OF UNITED STATES	AMOUNT (IN $ BILLIONS)	AS % OF UNITED STATES	AMOUNT (IN $ BILLIONS)
1998	$1.8	19.5	$1.3	14.1	$9.3
2009	$3.96	19.7	$2.97	14.8	$20.1

*by Southern and external foundations
Note: Due to rounding, percentages may not be exact.
Source: Foundation Center.

table 12.3 50 LARGEST U.S. FOUNDATIONS BY SIZE OF ASSETS: NUMBER BASED IN SOUTH, 2002 AND 2009

	2002	2009
In South	9	6
In South, not including Texas	5	4

Source: Foundation Center.

table 12.4 GROWTH IN ASSETS BY FOUNDATION TYPE, 1998 TO 2009

	INDEPENDENT			CORPORATE			COMMUNITY		
	1998*	2009*	% CHANGE	1998*	2009*	% CHANGE	1998*	2009*	% CHANGE
In South	$55.9	$80.0	43.0	$2.42	$4.20	73.3	$3.74	$9.38	150.6
In South, Not Including Texas	$38.9	$53.5	37.5	$1.57	$3.39	115.9	$2.86	$7.29	155.0
United States	$327	$483	47.7	$13.1	$19.3	47.2	$23.0	$49.5	115.6

* in $ Billions
Note: Due to rounding, percentages may not appear to be exact.
Source: Foundation Center.

GLOBALIZATION AND URBANIZATION:
The Changing Context *of* Competition

TED ABERNATHY

INTRODUCTION

The 1986 Commission on the Future of the South took a critical look at the current conditions in the South "to mobilize support for those public policies and public-private partnerships which will increase per capita income, reduce poverty, and reduce unemployment for Southerners by 1992." Maybe the challenges that we face do not change over time as much as we think, or maybe the Southern Growth Policies Board's *Halfway Home and a Long Way to Go* was uncannily insightful, but 25 years later, many of the regional objectives presented there remain part of the policy debate.

By establishing objectives that included a competitive education for all students, a globally competitive workforce, a role for economic development in higher education, technology, entrepreneurship, and globally aware leadership, *Halfway Home* laid the foundation for future state and regional strategies. It is hard to believe that just 25 years ago, most economic development programs did not include an entrepreneurial component, nor did they focus on leadership or promote educational partnerships. Today, every state in the South, every major region, and most local economic development organizations recognize the competitive interdependence of the quality of the workforce, the important role of businesses of all sizes, and the need to engage leaders in strategic plans and resource allocations.

While many issues and goals remain the same in 2011 as they were in 1986, the context in which we face those challenges looks very different. Simply stated, the world in which the South must compete has changed. In addition to demographic shifts that have changed the face of the South and migration patterns that have brought unprecedented growth, two major contextual changes, each identified in the report a quarter of a century ago, stand out: the internationalization of the Southern economy, and the urban-rural disparities in economic progress.

In 1986, most policy analysts assumed that we would be competing and trading with European countries whose economies were similar to ours and with a few lower-cost countries where low-wage manufacturing was beginning to migrate. The fall of the Soviet Union in December 1991 and the opening of Eastern Europe in 1989, the market reforms in India in 1991, and most significantly the economic transformation of China precipitated by Deng Xiaoping's free-market reforms beginning in 1978 have dramatically changed the number and types of free-market workers with whom Southern workers must compete. The scale was unimaginable in 1986.

NEW GLOBAL SOUTH

Over the past 25 years, global trade has exploded. China leads the list of countries whose participation was negligible in 1986 but that today are central to all economic global planning. According to the U.S. Census Bureau, U.S. trade with China in 1986 totaled $4.7 billion in imports and $3.1 billion in exports. By 2010, those figures had reached $364.9 billion and $91.9 billion, respectively. In North Carolina, China is now the second-highest country for exports, behind only Canada.

Globalization has affected the South with jobs and traditional industries such as textiles and apparel lost to new competitors. Public policies such as the North American Free Trade Agreement accelerated some of that change. However, globalization has also brought insourced jobs with increased foreign direct investment by multinational companies and new markets for manufactured and agricultural goods for export. The balance of the impact remains hotly debated, but the states of the South now operate in a very different world than was imagined in 1986.

States have opened economic development offices all over the world to sell Southern goods and aggressively recruit foreign firms. New, growing industry clusters in the South such as automotive, aerospace, energy, and life sciences count foreign firms as major contributors, and Southern higher education institutions have collaborated globally for innovations and students.

Place competition for prosperity has heightened. The effects of accelerated globalization have exacerbated the gap between the places that are prospering and those that are not. *Halfway Home*'s recognition that the "sunshine on the Sunbelt has proved to be a narrow beam of light, brightening futures along the Atlantic Seaboard, and in large cities, but skipping over many small towns and rural areas," has unfortunately changed little in 25 years. While many cities and regions in the South have enjoyed economic success, growth has been too slow or even negative in others.

Low-cost manufacturing, the traditional backbone of small-town economies across the South, has continued to migrate to lower-cost labor abroad. The persistent brain drain from rural communities combined with the more intensive focus by corporations on educated workers to drive innovation has reduced rural communities' ability to compete for emerging new-economy jobs. Dense

> Supply chains, workforce, and investments are determined less by state or country boundaries and more by market opportunity and competitive advantage. With the ubiquity of digital data and the reduced costs of logistics, the borderless economy can be expected to accelerate.

populations offer greater worker choices for employers, and job opportunities have fueled the migration of educated workers. The new infrastructure favored or even required by businesses—air service, broadband, and access to higher education resources—has favored cities.

Some rural areas and small towns, especially those within commuting distance of fast-growing metropolitan areas, have prospered as housing, retail, and jobs have moved out. So, too, have places that enjoy beaches, national parks, mountains, or some other tourism attribute. Gaming or other entertainment developments have transformed some places, but debate about the actual benefits remains ongoing. More recently, rising commodity prices and alternative energy sources have funneled wealth into rural areas.

Looking forward over the next 25 years, globalization and urbanization will continue to influence the South in more profound ways. Today, small and midsized businesses are following the trail blazed by multinational companies. Supply chains, workforce, and investments are determined

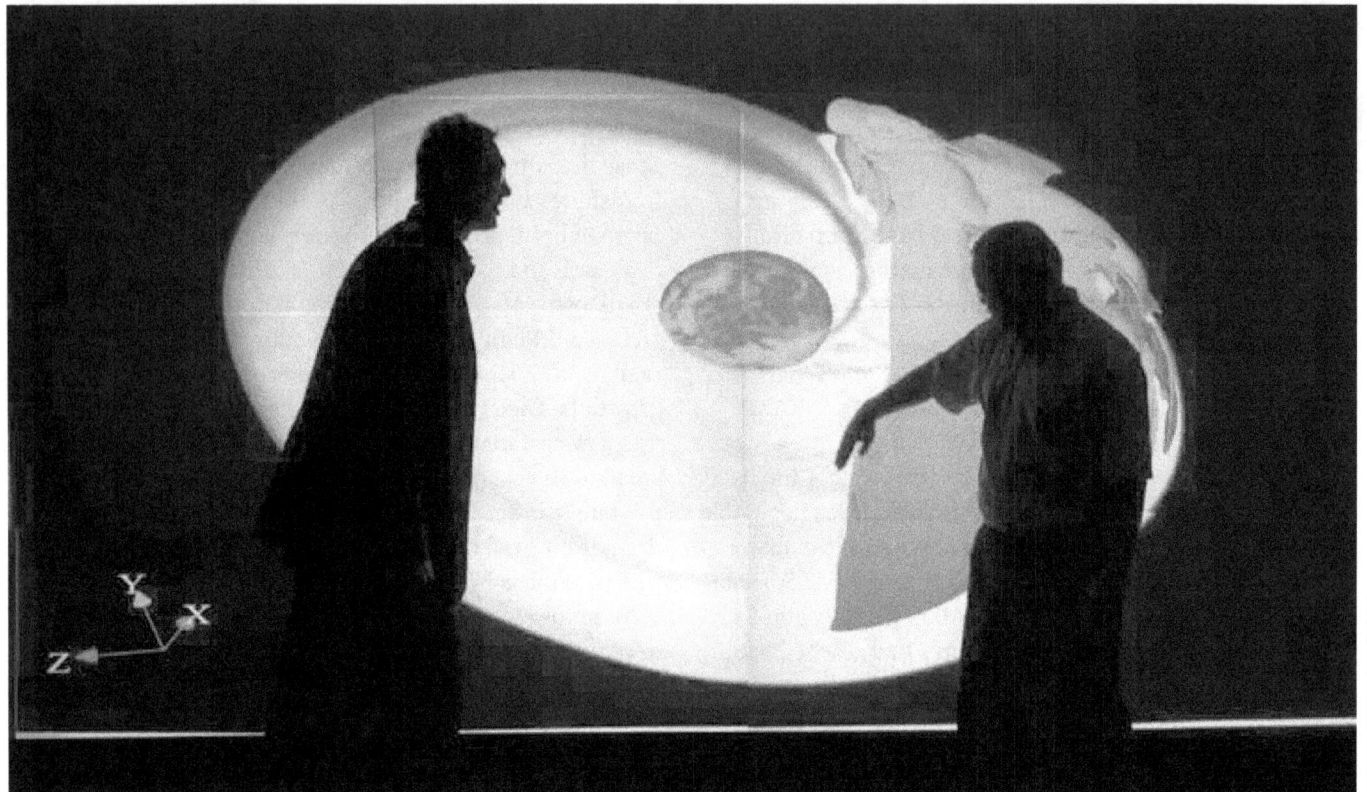

less by state or country boundaries and more by market opportunity and competitive advantage. With the ubiquity of digital data and the reduced costs of logistics, the borderless economy can be expected to accelerate.

Young educated people will continue to cluster in urban areas that offer the combination of amenities and career opportunities they seek. Whether it is author Richard Florida's vision of the "creative class" looking for amenities in center cities or author Joel Kotkin's ideas about the inherent advantages and attraction of a more suburban lifestyle, both visions point to metropolitan regions continuing to prosper.

Since 1986, *Area Development* magazine has been conducting a poll that asks about factors for relocation decisions. Every year, four quality-of-life factors score the highest: safety, health care, schools, and housing. Smaller communities can compete effectively on those factors but remain disadvantaged because they have fewer choices and because job growth remains the key to attracting talent.

Unlike the recent past, when the South struggled to assimilate talent from other countries into the region's culture, during the next few decades, we will have to work hard to keep our homegrown talent from migrating to opportunities abroad. Our Southern metropolitan regions will be in fierce competition for talent with global cities, which in many cases are bigger, growing faster, and offering incentives.

CONCLUSIONS

Here are three recommendations for the future:

First, the emerging regional clusters in the South, the engines for future job growth, are not contained in one state. The support networks, sources of innovative ideas, and supply chains are scattered across the South. New collaborations must be created to deemphasize state-to-state competition and work across state lines to improve regulations, workforce development, logistics, and capital that support the regional success. Many of our metropolitan regions already are multistate and can offer a road map for this type of collaboration.

Second, the global talent bar will continue to rise. Workers will need new skills in ever-shortening cycles. Companies will reward those places that can quickly train and retrain workers. One of the traditional Southern strengths has been our community colleges and worker training programs. Technology, budget cuts, and demographics are all influencing the traditional worker-training model. In these times of high unemployment, we must reimagine the role of community colleges and other skills-training programs. Training must be offered more quickly, more flexibly, and less expensively. After evaluating current efforts across the South, best practices must be shared and broadly adopted.

> For Southern policymakers, somewhere between anecdote and ideology we must find ways to collaborate and compete.

Finally, we must build on the collaborative nature of the South and the collaborative capacity we have created to reposition the Southern brand. As we compete globally, we can improve our competitive position if we work together and present a unified product. Last year, the Southern Governors' Association began an effort to present the American South as a great place for Chinese foreign direct investment. Representatives of a dozen states, led by their secretaries of commerce, traveled together to highlight our combined strengths. The states represented by the association include 40 percent of the U.S. population and have a gross domestic product approximately the same size as China. Collaboration has created efficiencies and advantages on which we can build. This effort should be expanded and used as model for economic development cooperation.

For Southern policymakers, somewhere between anecdote and ideology we must find ways to collaborate and compete. The Southern Growth Policies Board continues to help policymakers anticipate future trends and offers policy options. In 1986, the format was a multiyear public process with formalized expert input and a detailed analytical and prescriptive report as the product. The board reflects the changes in the world and today provides information in many forms: web pages, webinars, blogs, tweets, short white papers, and citizen gatherings. We need to hear from you.

REFERENCES

Florida, Richard L. *The Rise of the Creative Class and How It's Transforming Work, Leisure, Community, and Everyday Life.* New York: Basic Books, 2004.

Kotkin, Joel. *The Next Hundred Million: America in 2050.* New York: Penguin, 2010.

CONCLUSION

A WAY FORWARD: BUILDING A GLOBALLY COMPETITIVE SOUTH

The Future of the South *and*
A Way Forward

DANIEL P. GITTERMAN AND PETER A. COCLANIS

In an effort to draw out a single sweeping conclusion from a diverse collection of essays, we, in typical 21st-century fashion, googled a phrase for a little inspiration: "Plus ça change, plus c'est la même chose [The more things change, the more they stay the same]." Indeed, 25 years after the 1986 Commission on the Future of the South proclaimed that the region was "halfway home with a long way to go," much has changed, but many of the same problems and challenges remain. On topics that range from education and a globally competitive workforce to economic development and entrepreneurship, each contributor, from policy practitioner to university chancellor, offers visions of a path toward economic prosperity for all North Carolinians and Southerners.

Terry Sanford apparently came up with the idea for the Southern Growth Policies Board while driving through the desolate unplanned sprawl that was northern New Jersey in the late 1960s. A regional organization, he hoped, would help his rapidly growing home avoid "northern mistakes in southern settings." Since the Garden State was in Sanford's mind at one of the beginning points of our story,

New Jersey—or, more precisely, the lyrics to New Jersey rocker Bon Jovi's song "The More Things Change"—seems apropos as we end:

The more things change the more they stay the same

Ah, is it just me or does anybody see

The new improved tomorrow isn't what it used to be

Yesterday keeps comin' 'round, it's just reality

It's the same damn song with a different melody

The market keeps on crashin'

Tattered jeans are back in fashion

'Stead of records, now it's MP3s

I tell you one more time with feeling

Even though this world is reeling

You're still you and I'm still me

I didn't mean to cause a scene

But I guess it's time to roll up our sleeves

"It's time to roll up our sleeves" is a good way of summing up the most compelling conclusion our contributors have reached. The public and private sectors must come together to create a pro-growth economic agenda and to support policies and programs that help all people acquire the knowledge and skills needed to earn a living, whether by means of entrepreneurial self-employment or by working for someone else in the formal sector of the economy. Our state and our region must have adaptable workforces with a mixture of skills and a supportive economic environment to enable each of us to add value to the free flow of capital, information, and technology in a new global economy.

By moving beyond the cheap labor strategies of the 1960s and 1970s, the South made significant progress in closing the income and wealth gaps between it and the rest of the nation. In an increasingly competitive global economy, many of the low-skill jobs on which the South once relied have either been rendered obsolete by new technology or moved to countries and regions where labor was even cheaper. The current challenge is not so much to retain jobs by shying away from new technology or resisting global market forces but to keep current workers fully employed, moving them within or between firms at ever-higher skill levels. As former Alabama governor Bob Riley noted in the Southern Growth Policies Board's *Globally Competitive South (Under Construction)*, "We have a choice of learning to work smarter or being willing to work cheaper. Since the second option is unacceptable, we must make sure that our workforce is always globally competitive." Learning to work smarter is the only solution.

Perhaps the North Carolina Board of Education sets the right new goal: "Our guiding mission is that every public school student will graduate from high school, globally competitive for work and postsecondary education and prepared for life in the 21st Century." We must invest in

learning opportunities, from preschools to universities to job training programs. The federal government; the public, private, and nonprofit sectors; and philanthropy all have a role in securing this future. If our leaders, Republicans and Democrats alike, work together to build a shared agenda conducive to economic growth, if they continue to invest in avenues for building human capital, and if our fellow citizens remain flexible in their skill sets and willing to secure new skills and make adjustments when necessary, North Carolina and the American South can prepare the adaptable, globally ready students and workers who will be in demand tomorrow. We might not agree on every step, but we must continue to find a way forward.

REFERENCES

Bon Jovi. "The More Things Change." http://www.elyrics.net/read/b/bon-jovi-lyrics/the-more-things-change-lyrics.html.

Clinton, Jim. *The Globally Competitive South (Under Construction): 2004 Report on the Future of the South.* Research Triangle Park, N.C.: Southern Growth Policies Board, 2004.

North Carolina State Board of Education. *Future Ready Students for the 21st Century.* Goals approved by the North Carolina State Board of Education, September 7, 2006. http://www.dpi.state.nc.us/stateboard/about/goals.

ABOUT THE AUTHORS

Ted Abernathy has been the executive director of the Southern Growth Policies Board since 2008. He previously spent 30 years as an economic developer, most recently serving as the executive vice president of the Research Triangle Regional Partnership.

Maureen Berner is a professor in the School of Government at the University of North Carolina at Chapel Hill.

Leslie Boney is associate vice president for international, community, and economic engagement at the University of North Carolina System Office, University of North Carolina General Administration. He works with campuses, businesses, and economic development groups to deepen relationships between public universities and the private sector, to promote improved application of research, and to enhance community and international engagement.

Andy Brack is president and chair of the Center for a Better South, a pragmatic regional think tank based in Charleston, South Carolina. The center seeks to develop and push practical ideas for thinking leaders who want to make a difference in the American South.

Anita Brown-Graham serves as director of the Institute for Emerging Issues at North Carolina State University. She directs its programs on education, health, the economy, and environment. She has written extensively on developing economically distressed communities.

David L. Carlton is associate professor of history at Vanderbilt University. He is the author of *Mill and Town in South Carolina* (1982) and is coauthor with Peter A. Coclanis of *The South, the Nation, and the World* (2003).

Peter A. Coclanis is Albert R. Newsome Distinguished Professor of History at the University of North Carolina at Chapel Hill and is director of the Global Research Institute.

Patrick J. Conway holds the Bowman and Gordon Gray Distinguished Term Professorship in Economics at the University of North Carolina at Chapel Hill.

Patrick Cronin is assistant director for policy and programs at the Institute for Emerging Issues at North Carolina State University. A recovering academic, he spent ten years on the faculty at the Thunderbird School of Global Management in Glendale, Arizona.

David Dodson is president of MDC Since joining MDC in 1987, he has directed major projects to increase student success in public schools and community colleges, address regional economic decline, strengthen community philanthropy, and build multiracial leadership across the South and the nation.

Maryann Feldman is the S. K. Heninger Distinguished Professor of Public Policy at the University of North Carolina at Chapel Hill. Her research and teaching focus on the areas of innovation, the commercialization of academic research, and the factors that promote technological change and economic growth.

Lacy Ford is a professor of history and vice provost at the University of South Carolina. He is the author of a number of books and articles on the history of the South Carolina and has twice been a National Endowment for the Humanities Research Fellow.

Joe Freddoso is president and CEO of MCNC, an independent, nonprofit organization that employs advanced networking technologies and systems to improve learning and collaboration throughout North Carolina's K–20 education community. The company was initially funded by the North Carolina state government in 1980 as a catalyst for technology-based economic development.

Lance D. Fusarelli is a professor in the Department of Leadership, Policy, and Adult and Higher Education at North Carolina State University. His recent publications include "School Reform in a Vacuum: Demographic Change, Social Policy, and the Future of Children," published in the *Peabody Journal of Education* (2011).

Hannah Gill is assistant director of the Institute for the Study of the Americas and research associate at the Center for Global Initiatives at the University of North Carolina at Chapel Hill.

Daniel P. Gitterman is an associate professor of public policy and a senior fellow at the Global Research Institute at the University of North Carolina at Chapel Hill. He has served as a senior policy adviser to North Carolina governor Beverly Perdue and is the author of *Boosting Paychecks: The Politics of Supporting America's Working Poor*.

Buck Goldstein is university entrepreneur in residence at the University of North Carolina at Chapel Hill.

Ferrel Guillory teaches in the School of Journalism and Mass Communication at the University of North Carolina at Chapel Hill, where he is also director of the UNC Program on Public Life. He is a senior fellow at MDC, a nonprofit research firm in Chapel Hill, and served as a principal coauthor of MDC's seven *State of the South* reports published since 1996. In February 1989, the Southern Growth Policies Board published his essay, "Challenges for an Urbanizing South."

John Hardin is the executive director of the North Carolina Board of Science and Technology and an adjunct assistant professor of public policy at the University of North Carolina at Chapel Hill. His research and teaching focus on American politics and public policy, particularly how policymaking institutions simultaneously shape and respond to changing issue agendas.

Annie Jenkins is an MSW Candidate in the School of Social Work at the University of North Carolina at Chapel Hill. She received her BA in Psychology from the University of Virginia. Her interests include empowerment programs for girls and teen pregnancy prevention.

James H. Johnson Jr. is the William R. Kenan Jr. Distinguished Professor of Entrepreneurship at the University of North Carolina at Chapel Hill and director of the Urban Investment Strategies Center in the Frank Hawkins Kenan Institute of Private Enterprise.

Arne L. Kalleberg is Kenan Distinguished Professor of Sociology at the University of North Carolina at Chapel Hill. His most recent book is *Good Jobs, Bad Jobs: The Rise of Polarized and Precarious Employment Systems in the United States, 1970s–2000s* (2011). He served as president of the American Sociological Association in 2007–8.

Thomas Kemeny is research assistant professor of public policy at the University of North Carolina at Chapel Hill and a special sworn status researcher at the U.S. Census Bureau's Center for Economic Studies. He studies comparative urban and regional economic development and economic geography.

Louis Kyriakoudes is associate professor of history and director of the Center for Oral History and Cultural Heritage at the University of Southern Mississippi.

Nichola Lowe is associate professor of city and regional planning at the University of North Carolina at Chapel Hill. Her research interests include regional economic and labor market adjustment, industrial upgrading, and workforce development.

Mac McCorkle was an aide to Terry Sanford and a member of his Raleigh law firm who went on to become a Democratic political consultant. He teaches the politics of public policy at Duke's Sanford School of Public Policy.

Charles Nelms is chancellor at North Carolina Central University, where he has worked to increase student retention, graduation, and outreach.

Gene Nichol Boyd Tinsley Distinguished Professor of Law at the University of North Carolina at Chapel Hill School of Law and is director of UNC's Center on Poverty, Work, and Opportunity. He is president emeritus of the College of William and Mary.

Sharon Paynter is an assistant professor of political science at East Carolina University.

Scott Ralls serves as the president of the North Carolina Community College System. He holds a bachelor's degree with highest distinction from the University of North Carolina at Chapel Hill and master's and doctoral degrees in industrial and organizational psychology from the University of Maryland.

Brittany L. Reid is an undergraduate double major in public policy and English at University of North Carolina at Chapel Hill

Stuart Rosenfeld, principal and founder of Regional Technology Strategies in Carrboro, North Carolina, has more than 30 years of work experience in public policy research and analysis, with emphasis on education and training, rural development, and technology policy. Rosenfeld holds a doctorate in educational planning and social policy from Harvard and a bachelor's in chemical engineering from the University of Wisconsin at Madison.

Jay Schalin is the director of state policy for the J. W. Pope Center for Higher Education Policy. He holds a master's degree in economics from the University of Delaware and a bachelor's degree in computer science from Richard Stockton College and he previously worked as a software engineer and freelance journalist.

John C. Scott is an assistant professor in the Department of Public Policy at the University of North Carolina at Chapel Hill and a research scientist at the UNC Institute on Aging. His research covers work and aging, tax policy, and the policymaking process.

Amanda Sheely is an Assistant Professor in the School of Social Work at the University of North Carolina at Chapel Hill. Her research focuses on evaluating the effectiveness of the U.S. social safety net in serving economically disadvantaged families.

Trip Stallings is a senior research associate at the Friday Institute for Educational Innovation at North Carolina State University. His recent work includes participation in the development of North Carolina's successful Race to the Top proposal and comanagement of the evaluation of the state's use of those funds.

Jennifer E. Swanberg is an associate professor of social work at the University of Kentucky with joint appointments in the colleges of public health, medicine, and business. She also is the founder and executive director of the Institute for Workplace Innovation at the University of Kentucky.

Holden Thorp is chancellor of the University of North Carolina at Chapel Hill.

Michael L. Walden has been at North Carolina State University since 1978, where he has teaching, research, and extension responsibilities. He has written eight books, and his work focuses on the North Carolina economy and related public policy issues. As part of his outreach work, he does daily radio programs and a monthly radio call-in program, writes a biweekly newspaper column, and develops the monthly North Carolina State University Index of Leading North Carolina Economic Indicators. In 2010, he was awarded the University of North Carolina Board of Governors Award for Excellence in Public Service.

Deborah Weissman is the Reef Ivey II Distinguished Professor of Law and serves as an executive committee member for the Consortium in Latin American Studies at the University of North Carolina at Chapel Hill and Duke University. She is also a member of the advisory board of UNC's Institute for the Study of the Americas.

Jerry Weitz is associate professor and director of the Urban and Regional Planning Program at East Carolina University. He holds a bachelor's degree from Emory University, a master's degree in city planning from the Georgia Institute of Technology, and a doctorate in urban studies from Portland State University.

Jesse L. White Jr. is an adjunct professor in the University of North Carolina at Chapel Hill School of Government and recently retired as director of the Office of Economic and Business Development. He was executive director of the Southern Growth Policies Board from 1982 to 1990 and directed the work on *Halfway Home and a Long Way to Go*.

Randy Woodson is North Carolina State University's 14th chancellor. He has extensive experience as a member of university faculty and administration with a reputation for consensus building and strategic visioning. He holds bachelor's, master's, and doctoral degrees in horticulture from the University of Arkansas and Cornell University.

Gavin Wright is the William Robertson Coe Professor of American Economic History at Stanford University. His current project is a book on the economics of the civil rights revolution in the South.

www.ingramcontent.com/pod-product-compliance
Lightning Source LLC
Chambersburg PA
CBHW060313240426
43661CB00059B/2749